Plain Enemies

Best True Stories of the Frontier West

Plain Enemies

Best True Stories of the Frontier West

Bob Scott

Cover design by
Teresa Sales

The CAXTON PRINTERS, Ltd.
Caldwell, Idaho
1995

Scott, Robert, 1938–
    Plain enemies : best true stories of the frontier West /
Bob Scott.
        p.   cm.
    Includes bibliographical references and index.
    ISBN 0–87004–364–1 (pbk.)
    1. West (U.S.)--History--To 1848. 2. West (U.S.)--History--
1848–1860. 3. West (U.S.)--History--1860–1890.
    I. Title.
    F592.S38 1995
    978' .02--dc20   95–4103
                                                                          CIP

Lithographed and bound in the United States of America by
The CAXTON PRINTERS, Ltd.
Caldwell, Idaho 83605
159055

To
Ona Scott,
my mother, who taught me to love learning;
and

Bernice Wagle,
my seventh grade social studies teacher,
who taught me to love history.

Contents

It is our manifest destiny to overspread the continent allotted by Providence for the free development of our yearly multiplying millions.

John L. O'Sullivan

Our great mission is to occupy this vast domain!

US Senator John C. Calhoun,
South Carolina

Preface

WHEN THE BRITISH CLAIMS to North America were successfully crushed in the American Revolutionary War, the young United States republic began to feel invincible. Not only could America do anything she wanted, but her strength was skyrocketing; an exciting new global reputation began to bring floods of emigrants from throughout the world flocking to the east-coast shores.

America's founding fathers viewed this influx of humanity as a great opportunity, almost a godly edict to expand as rapidly as possible. For the next hundred years it was the official policy of the United States government to encourage immigration and expansion. White settlers pushed ever westward; it was a patriotic responsibility to civilize the great untamed wilderness that stretched from the Ohio Valley to the Pacific Ocean.

This duty of patriots eventually came to be known as "manifest destiny"—the obligation of white Americans to go west and occupy the land in the name of the United States. Never mind that the West was already occupied; those who were there, after all, were not real people—they were only Indians. The Native Americans were viewed as pests, in much the same manner as ants that inevitably harass picnickers: although bothersome (but not to be taken seriously), they cannot effectively compete for what is "rightfully" the property of the invaders.

The Indians didn't fully understand what was happening, at least not at first. They never felt a need to formally claim land anywhere and were hard-pressed to understand the white man's insistence that all the land must belong to someone. On the other hand, the Indians knew that their hunting grounds were quickly being destroyed by this invasion of whites. Because the Indian lived by hunting—the vast majority of his food was buffalo or dog meat—he began to resent and then to resist the white invasion. At first the resistance was mild and scattered, but as the white man kept on coming in ever increasing numbers the Indian resistance became stronger and more organized.

For more than four decades, stretching from roughly 1830 to 1876, Native Americans fought back with increasing vigor. The Great Plains Indian Wars of this era claimed thousands of lives, and probably included more women and children as victims than any other war ever fought. It was war unmatched in its ferocity and brutality; victims on both sides were tortured, mutilated, and killed without apparent emotion—and often without provocation, save only one's physical location.

Indians routinely beat and raped captured white women, then passed the women from warrior to warrior and tribe to tribe. Kidnapped white children were deliberately slashed with knives—either as a prelude to murder, or as part of a training routine to accustom

Some key locations in the
GREAT PLAINS INDIAN WAR

Montana

Little Big Horn •

Rosebud •

Fetterman disaster •
Ft. Phil Kearney •

Wyoming

Ft. Robinson • Nebraska

Ft. Laramie •

• Ft. McPherson

Ft. Cottonwood
• (Ft. Kearney)

Beecher Island •

• Ft. Wallace

• Ft. Hayes
Ft. Riley •

Fort
Leavenworth

Colorado

Kansas
• Ft. Larned

Sand Creek•
Ft. Lyon •

• Ft. Dodge

• Ft. Union

• Camp Supply

Adobe Walls

Oklahoma

• Washita

• Ft. Sill

New Mexico

•
Palo Duro Canyon

T e x a s

them to the rigors of life in their "adopted" tribe. Scalps were collected, frequently without the technicality of making certain the victim was already dead. The torsos of enemies were slashed open and their entrails dragged across the prairie; in at least one case captured white men were beheaded and the victorious Indians played a sort of primitive kick-ball with the heads of their victims.

Whites treated their victims no better. Soldiers scalped Indians as often as Indians scalped soldiers. There are numerous documented cases in which the leg of a captured warrior was held over a campfire and roasted to encourage the brave to supply information to the whites. Captured Indian warriors were frequently hanged; Indian women in captured Indian villages often complained of having been raped by numerous white soldiers. There is little reason to doubt the accuracy of those claims. No quarter was given by either side.

It was a dirty war.

This book is not an effort to criticize nor to defend either the Indians or the white men; historians and social reformers have spent decades doing that in hundreds of books. This is merely a collection of "true" and fascinating stories from the violent frontier; stories of incredible bravery, awful viciousness, and sometimes surprising results. Please note that the word true is in quotes—because in some cases details cannot be verified. In all instances, these are white men's accounts of history, since the Indian kept no written records from which to reconstruct incidents. Besides, to fairly and accurately represent the Indian point of view would require a thorough and complete understanding of the Indian psyche, the life style, the history, the emotion, and the culture. For a white author to write from an Indian point of view would be hypocrisy.

But these stories are told without trying to make any particular statement. There is no ax to grind, no finger to point, no accusation to make. They are told because they are interesting, intense, and a basic part of our national legacy. They tell of incredible bravery, frightening inhumanity, amazing strength, sheer stupidity, unbelievable insensitivity, great love, and impassioned hatred.

I hope you enjoy these stories from America's heritage.

Bob Scott

Illustrations

Plain Enemies
Best True Stories of the Frontier West

The war brought indescribable terror and affliction upon the infant settlements. It is impossible to understand, and much less to describe, in any adequate manner, the misfortunes which the merciless warfare visited upon the feeble settlers of the wilderness. The confederated savages, in the secret conclaves of the forests, under the inspiration of their powerful and relentless chiefs, had organized the bloody design to utterly extinguish the settlements...There were few families or individuals who had not lost some near relative in this savage strife.

Captain William F. Goodwin,
US Army

-ONE-

The Sacking of Julesburg

SATURDAY MORNING, JANUARY 7, 1865, 5:30 A.M. The tiny community of Julesburg, Colorado—situated at the spot at which the Oregon Trail intersects with the main road leading to Denver—was just beginning to awaken. Not that there were all that many people to rouse: on one side of the town's only street was the Overland Stage Coach building, a boarding house, a blacksmith shop, a granary, a storehouse, the stables and a corral. On the other side of the street stood the general store, the saloon, a bank, the Pacific Telegraph office, the barber shop, and the sheriff's office. Several small houses were at either end of the street.

Three miles east of town the morning Overland stagecoach lumbered into view, heading toward the village. Besides the driver and guard, there were two passengers aboard. One was a traveling salesman heading to Denver; the other was the military paymaster, bringing two locked strongboxes of cash to meet the regular monthly payroll at Fort Segwick.

1

The fort, located at the far edge of Julesburg (the west side), was still under construction. The perimeter walls were completed, but building inside the compound had just begun; the troops still slept on the ground. A guard positioned on top of the outer wall watched disinterestedly as the stage coach crawled along the dusty road, eventually vanishing from sight as it dropped into a small river valley a half mile away.

The appearance of this stagecoach rolling across the countryside conjures up an idyllic image of peacefulness. But its approach this particular morning represented a major and unexpected crisis. Hundreds of Indian warriors were hidden in trees and bushes along the banks of the Platte River—the same valley into which the stage coach had just disappeared from the guard's view.

The main problem was that the Indians did not want to be discovered—at least not yet. Discovery could wreck their carefully laid plans. The warriors were still working their way into position for an attack on both the town and the fort, and premature discovery could spoil the whole thing.

The Indians tried to devise an alternate plan, but already it was too late. The stage coach topped a hill and plunged down into the river valley—into the very midst of the Indian warriors. The startled driver knew at once that something was terribly wrong. He lashed the horses, which lunged forward against their traces. As the animals raced forward in sudden panic, hundreds of arrows filled the air. One struck the driver and several more thudded into the side of the stage coach. Two horses were hit by the missiles, but both managed to continue running in spite of their injuries. The driver frantically whipped the animals, hoping that he could out-race the Indians into town and simultaneously arouse villagers to come out and fight the assembled braves.

The unexpected arrival of the Overland stage coach startled the Indians as much as their presence alarmed the occupants of the coach. The arrival of the coach forced the Indians to make an instantaneous decision they were ill prepared to make. After several seconds of hesitation, Chief Big Crow and ten of his warriors recovered from their initial surprise, kicked their ponies forward, and tore out of the river bottom at full gallop—screaming and waving their weapons above their heads as they raced toward Fort Segwick.

But already, all opportunity for surprise was gone. The braves drove directly toward the open front gates of Fort Segwick, giving every appearance of planning a frontal assault on the little army outpost. At the very least, they appeared hopeful of arriving before the soldiers inside comprehended what was happening, and closed the gates against attack.

Chief Big Crow, leading this race toward the fort, was the head of the Cheyennes' Crooked Lance society, comparable in ferocity to the greatly feared Dog Soldiers. The men he trained were among the best soldiers of his people. They were smart, brave, and strong—and they were outstanding in battle.

Startled sentinels at Fort Segwick could hardly believe their eyes as the small band of Indians thundered over the ridge and dashed toward the enclave. As the soldiers hastened to slam the gates, the little knot of warriors raced almost to the wall itself. When they finally came nearly within touching distance of the fort, the braves brazenly fired their rifles toward the guards atop the wall.

This was an offense that no soldier could tolerate. Just as the Indians obviously hoped would happen, the army responded immediately to their challenge. The gates of the fort swung open again and out poured a troop of soldiers. Captain Nicholas James O'Brien and about sixty soldiers from Company F, Seventh Iowa Cavalry, thundered through the gates directly toward the little knot of eleven yelling Indians.[1] O'Brien was a decorated Civil War hero, and not at all afraid of battle action. Certainly, he was not frightened by this small group of Indians. As O'Brien and his men rode from the fort, the braves spun their ponies around and headed back toward the river at full speed. O'Brien spurred his horse onward, closing the gap on the fleeing band of Indians.

A veteran combat soldier such as O'Brien should have suspected a trap, but he clearly did not. Caught up in the adrenaline rush of the chase, O'Brien was driven to either kill or capture these brazen warriors who had symbolically thumbed their noses at the United States Army.

As if missing the first indication of a trap wasn't bad enough, O'Brien compounded the error twice more. He had a second opportunity to smell a rat, and certainly should have become suspicious of the rapidity with which he closed the gap on the warriors. There was even a third warning, had O'Brien been alert. Mental alarms should have clanged loudly when the braves rode directly into a narrow, conveniently-located arroyo. However, if O'Brien gave these clues any thought, there certainly was no indication of such in either his actions of the moment or in his official report.

The oversight was most unfortunate for the white men. Lying concealed in the bushes and trees lining either side of the arroyo lay Charles Bent and several hundred other eager Cheyenne and Arapaho warriors.

All of them were anxious to draw blood—and Charles Bent was more zealous than most of the others.

Bent was the youngest son of white fur trader William Bent, a Colorado patriarch. But father and son were as different as day and night. The elder Bent was known throughout the country as a loyal friend of the Union and a solid supporter of the US Government.

William Bent, nonetheless, was also respected by the Indians. Until she was killed a short time earlier, Bent was married to a Cheyenne woman and bore five children by her. This put him in a unique position to know both the white man and the Indian, and situated him to serve frequently as a trusted go-between in matters involving the two races.

Nevertheless, the Bent family was sharply divided in terms of its loyalties. William and his two oldest children, Robert and Mary, thought of themselves as white. Although trusted by the Indians, these three clearly represented the mind set of the typical frontiersman. They were supporters of Abraham Lincoln, enemies of the Confederacy, and leading citizens of the new Western civilization.

William Bent's wife, Owl Woman, was pure-blooded Cheyenne, and never forgot her heritage. Her three youngest children, George, Charles, and Julia (in striking contrast to the two oldest children) considered themselves not only to be Indian, but enemies of all white people. On at least one occasion, this animosity was directed toward their husband and father, William Bent. Charles tried to murder his father a few months after the attack on Julesburg. The two younger boys, Charles and George, were both veterans of the Confederate Army. George saw action at both Pea Ridge, Arkansas, and Corinth, Mississippi—wounded and captured at the latter. Both he and Charles were eventually

released from the Confederate military: George upon
swearing allegiance to the Union when he was captured
and taken to a US POW camp in Missouri, and Charles
when the Confederates found out that he was only sixteen years old.

This youngest Bent boy, at about seventeen years of
age, became one of the most brazen of the young Dog
Soldiers, passionately hating all white men. This youthful Cheyenne was known as one of the cruelest and most
audacious warriors on the Great Plains. In the words of
one author, Charles had already, "gained a reputation as
the worst desperado of the West, by using his white
appearance and western know-how to trick, deceive, and
murder."[2]

Charles Bent's hatred of frontier people was not
merely because they claimed this region as Union territory. Charles' mother, Owl Woman, was killed and his
brother George wounded by Colonel John Chivington's
Third Colorado Volunteers, during an attack on Black
Kettle's village just six weeks before the Julesburg
attack. The assault on Julesburg was almost certainly
launched in retaliation for the Sand Creek Massacre
(the popular name for the earlier Colorado battle).

At a crucial moment, luck came to the rescue of the
blundering soldiers, who were rushing into the jaws of a
Cheyenne trap: for Charles Bent made one of his rare
mistakes as a warrior. Apparently overly eager to take
revenge on the white men, Bent and a number of other
young warriors leaped to their feet and exposed their
positions prematurely—well before the entire army unit
could be trapped in the canyon. As the frantic soldiers
tried to stop their horses, hundreds of Indians poured off
the hillsides and sped toward the surprised troops.

Although he had no way of knowing it at the time,
Captain O'Brien's group of sixty soldiers was facing

Courtesy Colorado Historical Society
Sitting Bull
One of the best Indian "generals" ever, Sioux Chief Sitting Bull preferred peace but was willing to fight overwhelming odds to stop the encroachment of the white man. Sitting Bull participated in the attack on Julesburg and Fort Segwick. At the Battle of Little Big Horn, he led the several thousand Sioux and Cheyenne warriors who overwhelmed and wiped out General George Armstrong Custer's command.

1,200 Cheyenne Dog Soldiers and other angry warriors. Among this staggering array were Cheyenne, Arapaho, and Sioux warriors, including Sioux Chiefs Spotted Tail, Pawnee Killer, and a young Oglala warrior named Sitting Bull. The Cheyenne contingent included the well-known "peace chief" Black Kettle, and (according to most historical accounts) Dog Soldier Chief Roman Nose.

Confronted by this sudden appearance of hundreds of warriors, Captain O'Brien ordered a hasty retreat. As the soldiers whirled around to head back toward Fort Segwick, they found the path already blocked by braves. Although the soldiers managed to breach the warriors' line of defense, it was the soldiers who were then in full flight, and the Indians who were in hot pursuit.

When the soldiers first realized they had blundered into a trap, Captain O'Brien signaled his bugler to sound retreat. But according to Cheyenne warrior Charles Bent, the bugler was the first man killed by the Indians—shot from his saddle before he could blow a single note. As several of the soldiers' horses were hit by gunfire or by arrows, O'Brien shouted at his men to dismount and fight on foot. (The Indians' first target in this and most other battles was the horses: thus placing the enemy at a disadvantage by making the soldiers' retreat more difficult.)

Fighting was at point-blank range, and sometimes hand-to-hand. As the soldiers' horses were hit by arrows or rifle fire, the men crouched behind them, using the animals' bodies as barriers between themselves and the Indians.

The warriors soon encircled the soldiers, firing arrows and rifles into their midst. Many of the white men were hit, and the battle field became a scene of great, noisy confusion. Western writer Ruth Dunn wrote, "dirt and sand were churned into the air by the stomping hoofs [of the Indian ponies], and mixed with the pungent odor of gun smoke until it was hard to breathe."[3]

As the battle soared toward its climax, an incredulous Captain O'Brien spotted a lone warrior standing on a high bluff overlooking the battlefield. The warrior was signaling to the hundreds of Sioux, Arapaho, and Cheyenne braves below, using a mirror to reflect sunlight. From time to time, another warrior waved buffalo robes in a way that clearly sent specific information, or orders, to the warriors. The Indians on the battlefield responded with a series of maneuvers that were obviously the same tactics and strategies as were taught in the United States and Confederate Armies.

Captain O'Brien's account about warriors employing such coordinated and complex military operations was the first of many similar reports that followed shortly thereafter. Presumably, these white man's military maneuvers were learned from Confederate agitators, who had been working for three years or more to turn Indians against settlers on the western frontier. Granted, both Charles and George Bent were former Confederate soldiers, but it is improbable that they were able to teach so many Indians as were using such signals over the next few months. It was more likely the work of Confederate infiltrators, who actively recruited Indians to fight for the Confederacy right up to the end of the Civil War.[4]

While the battle at Julesburg raged on, Captain O'Brien slowly led his embattled troops back toward the fort, desperately fighting off swarms of attackers on all sides. Each soldier fought his individual battles with specific braves, as well as contributing to the overall fight.

As the grim struggle inched back toward Fort Segwick, the group of soldiers inside the battle ring grew smaller and smaller. About half of the soldiers died in the battle's opening minutes, most of them falling lifeless on the battlefield within a hundred yards of the fort's front gates.

Private George Barnett, who just that morning had been formally recommended for promotion to corporal, was the second to be killed (after the bugler). Barnett was struck in the forehead by an arrow and fell heavily backward at the feet of Captain O'Brien.

Four noncommissioned officers died as heroes moments later, standing shoulder to shoulder and fighting courageously to protect their companions. Sergeant Alanson Hatchett, Corporal William Gray, Corporal Anthony Koons, and Corporal Walter Talcott were cut down after simultaneously volunteering to stand atop a small knoll and hold the enemy at bay as long as possible. They made this courageous stand to allow the other men more time to reach the safety of the fort. But their bravery hardly seemed worthwhile: all four were dead within about sixty seconds.

A civilian who accompanied the soldiers into battle, John Pierce, was shot to death after rising to his feet, calmly emptying his rifle at the attacking horde, then tossing the weapon aside and emptying his Colt revolver at the enemy.

Pierce was a young man who had a particular hatred for the Indian people. His entire family was killed in an attack on a wagon train a decade earlier. Then only ten years old, Pierce was captured by the attackers and adopted into a Sioux tribe. Over the ensuing years, John forgot how to speak English and forgot many of the white man's ways: but he never forgot watching his father, mother, and two sisters killed, scalped, and mutilated.

Early in December of 1864, about a month before the Julesburg attack, Pierce finally managed to slip away from his captors. He showed up a few days later at Fort Segwick. Pierce made it understood that he wanted to join the white man's army and fight Indians. The men at the fort took an instant liking to the youth, but army rules required that he be able to speak English before they could accept him as a soldier. Over the past few weeks, Captain O'Brien and several others had been tutoring the lad. Although he progressed quickly and was nearly ready to become a soldier, he had not yet taken the oath. John Pierce died as his family had died: a civilian, battling Indians on the open prairie.

Among the last of the soldiers to be killed outside the fort was a nineteen-year-old Irishman named John Murphy. He was a New Yorker who spoke with a thick Irish brogue. When the soldiers finally had backed up literally against the gate of Fort Segwick, Murphy was firing as fast as he could. He was trying desperately to protect several of his wounded buddies as they were being dragged back inside the walls. Then as Murphy sought to follow the others through the gate, he was shot in the chest and dropped dead.

The oldest white soldier on the battlefield that day was Private Jim Cannon, age thirty-eight. When his rifle jammed, Cannon swung the weapon like a club, knocking a startled brave from his horse just as the Indian tried to run a lance through another soldier. Cannon was shot in the stomach a few seconds later, but managed to crawl back inside the fort. Although critically wounded, he survived the battle.

A former Oregon lumberjack, Corporal Thomas Forbush, was shot several times as he stumbled back inside the walls of Fort Segwick. Bleeding heavily from wounds in the back, chest, shoulder, and neck, he was not expected to survive—but fooled everyone by doing so. Nevertheless, Forbush's wounds were so multiple and severe that he was not released from the base hospital for sixty days, and never fully recovered from the injuries.

Ruth Dunn wrote of a highly unusual injury to one of the defenders:

> One young soldier was hit by the finely-sharpened handle of a frying pan, secured to the end of a large arrow. It struck him in the hip and buried itself in the pelvic bone. Luckily, he was near the stockade and [was] protected until he could enter the gate. One of the men used a pair of blacksmith pincers, turning the boy face down, with feet planted firmly on each side of his body as he pulled the arrowhead out. Despite his agony, the young man recovered under the care of Dr. Joel Wisely in the hospital at the fort.[5]

Inside the fort, Lieutenant John Brener had been left behind to keep an eye on things when the original pursuit of Indians began. When gunfire erupted seconds later, he ran to the top of the wall and watched helplessly as his friends battled desperately for their lives. He saw many of his companions fall to the Indian assault, but his chance was coming.

Brener waited until the soldiers had battled their way almost back to the gates of the fort before he opened fire with a howitzer. He deliberately fired far short of the attackers, hoping to lure them closer to the walls. He wanted the warriors to believe the howitzer could not reach them any further away. The ruse worked, and the

Indians began riding quite close to the walls of Fort Segwick. Finally, Brener raised the barrel of his weapon and fired directly into the midst of the assailants. Witnesses said that many of the Indians were killed in the several volleys Brener was able to fire.

Only a relative handful of the sixty soldiers who rode out of the fort were able to return to it a few moments later. Although most accounts of the battle list eighteen men as fighting their way back inside the walls, at least half of these were wounded—some mortally. They and the few who had remained inside the fort could now do nothing more than try to keep the Indians from overrunning the stockade.

But of course, only half of the battle was taking place at or near the fort.

When the panicky stage coach thundered through Julesburg toward the fort in the early moments of fighting, local citizens were alerted that an Indian attack was underway. Several townspeople observed that the stagecoach driver had been hit by at least one arrow, and saw other arrows protruding from the coach and the horses. To these experienced frontiersmen, it was obvious what was happening. As it turned out, the driver was only slightly injured. Wearing a heavy buffalo-robe coat because of the cold January weather, the arrow barely scratched his skin!

Most of the civilians of Julesburg fled to the fort for protection as the attack began. But several others ran the opposite direction, seeking shelter in the bushes or along the river bed outside of town. From these hiding places, they watched the Indians drive the soldiers back to the fort.

Now that the soldiers had been decimated and the few survivors were penned up inside the fort, the troops no longer posed any threat to the attackers. A handful of warriors continued to circle the fort, taking occasional shots at it just to make certain the soldiers stayed put. The remaining Indians turned their attention to the village itself.

The warriors systematically entered and looted every building in town. They burned several sacks of mail and took bolts of brightly-colored cloth from the general store. One made a sash from the end of a bolt of bright red material, then raced his pony across the prairie, trailing a long banner of the fabric behind him.

Another warrior smashed the latch on a strongbox, recovered from the disabled stagecoach outside the fort. Disappointed to find nothing but green paper inside, he began tossing handfuls of the white man's money into the air. Charles Bent reacted differently than his less civilized brother; he stuffed all the money he could carry into every available container, which he then lashed to his pony. The following day, troops were sent out to try to find the money that blew away. About half of it was eventually recovered.

One group of Indians went to the edge of town, tossed ropes over the talking wires (telegraph lines), and pulled them down to keep the survivors from reporting the attack. Telegraph agent Philo Holcomb worked until mid-morning the following day making emergency repairs, in order to report the attack to the rest of the world.

The Indians probably would have hunted down the civilians who had not fled to the fort, but Providence intervened on behalf of the whites. One group of warriors was looting the town's general store, and found several bottles of what they presumed to be whiskey. Opening the bottles, they were disappointed to find that the substance had a strong odor and was clearly unfit for drinking. In disgust, they smashed the bottles on the floor.

As they continued looting the store, liquid from the smashed bottles began soaking into their moccasins. Suddenly, one and then another let out cries of pain and went jumping and yelling into the street. Other Indians entered the store to find out what was wrong, only to fall victim to the same sudden, unexplained, excruciating pain.

By the time a half dozen warriors were yelping across the prairie, hopping on one foot and rubbing the other, the Indians decided that the gods must not want them to attack the village. The warriors quickly vacated the store and the rest of Julesburg, never bothering to search for the civilians who were hiding nearby.

The bottles smashed by the looters contained highly caustic nitric acid, commonly used on the frontier to make explosives. When it soaked into the moccasins and began burning the feet of the warriors, it no doubt saved the lives of a considerable number of civilians.

There was one other highly unusual scene in the town. In the general store, the Indians found a shipment of cowboy boots. The warriors loved the pretty colors and intricate designs in the leather, but hated to wear anything more substantial than moccasins on their feet. The braves neatly solved the problem by cutting off the bottom part of the boots, then slipping the top part onto their legs and wearing them as leggings.

The wild celebration in the village contrasted sharply with a grim scene being played out a short distance away. While the looting was underway in town, wounded soldiers left behind on the battlefield were suffering an awful fate. Warriors who were responsible for making certain healthy soldiers could not leave the fort, now occupied their time by rounding up the still-living but wounded white survivors from the battlefield. These hapless soldier-victims were dragged within sight of the fort and then staked spread-eagle to the ground. There the Indians proceeded to torture and horribly mutilate them .

When the grim scene began to play out near the fort's wall, some of the soldiers inside began shooting at their wounded comrades, trying to kill them before the Indians could inflict their prolonged torture. The braves soon figured out what was happening and dragged the survivors out of rifle range, then continued their torture.

Most of these soldiers met horrible deaths in the hours that followed. They were slowly tortured; many had their tongues cut out. The Indians frequently cut off the penis of a helpless soldier and jammed it into the victim's mouth. A fire was built near the extended hand of a captive, who screamed in pain as his fingers blistered and blackened. When that hand was completely fried, a fire was built beside the other hand, then beside one foot, and then the other. With all the extremities thoroughly roasted, a fire was then built on the victim's chest, finally ending his hours of extreme torment. Several of the soldiers were scalped while still alive. Many were slashed open and their entrails dragged out onto the prairie.

None of these wounded and captured men died an easy death. The agonized onlookers were relieved when the last of these men eventually succumbed. When the final screams at last faded away, only the chants of the Indians could still be heard. People in the fort stood in stunned, drained, helpless silence—or cried bitter tears of rage.

It was about mid-afternoon when the last of the soldiers perished and the Indians had their fill of the awful ceremony. As the final soldier died, the warriors suddenly vanished from the battlefield; one moment they were there, and in the next moment the killing grounds held only the gruesome remains of the deceased victims.

Captain O'Brien, Lieutenant John Brener, and Private Charles Pickens—the only men at Fort Segwick who had not been either killed or wounded—cautiously emerged from behind the walls to survey the grisly scene. They found the bodies of fifty-six braves—most of them Cheyenne or Sioux—lying close to the main gates of the fort. These warriors had fallen so close to the fort that their bodies could not be carried away by their departing comrades. The actual death toll among the Indians will never be known.[6]

But the Indians were not the only ones who suffered heavy losses; O'Brien's small command was decimated by the battle. The dead included Sergeant Alanson Hatchett, four corporals, and at least eleven enlisted men. Additionally, four civilians attached to the base died in the fighting, as did about a dozen civilians from the community. Five other soldiers, Lieutenant Thomas Ware, First Sergeant Tom Patten, Corporal Thomas Forbush, and two enlisted men, were so badly wounded they were never able to return to duty. About two dozen other soldiers and four or five civilians suffered lesser wounds and survived.[7]

When it was clear that the Indians had really gone from the Julesburg area, the people at the fort emerged and spent the remainder of the day burying their dead.

The following morning, spliced-together telegraph wires conveyed word of the attack to the rest of the world. Captain O'Brien reported to military headquarters at Omaha, Nebraska, that he had been in "a desperate fight," had lost two-thirds of his men, and that many of the survivors were badly wounded. His message said he needed immediate medical help. The wire also said that his military strength was so decimated by the battle that he could no longer effectively defend the fort, the community, or the Oregon Trail.

Notes

1. There is considerable confusion as to the number of men at Fort Segwick at the time the raid began, and as to the number of men who rode out to challenge the Indians. Various historical accounts list anywhere from a total of only about 30 men at the fort to more than 100 in the band that pursued the Indians. The figure used in our story is given in at least three accounts, including military documents and in Donald J. Berthrong's *The Southern Cheyennes* (Norman: University of Okla-homa Press, 1963), 228. To be consistent with figures used elsewhere in the story this book uses the sixty-man figure found in most official references to the battle at Fort Segwick. In addition, known casualty figures amount to about forty soldiers, and Captain O'Brien's wire to Omaha reported that he had lost two thirds of his command.

2. Samuel Arnold, *Trappers of the Far West* (Lincoln/London: University of Nebraska Press, 1934), 239.

3. Ruth Dunn, unpublished notes of "Indian Vengeance at Julesburg" (Lincoln, Nebraska public library, Heritage Collection), 7.

4. Bob Scott, *Blood at Sand Creek* (Caldwell, Idaho: The Caxton Printers, Inc., 1994) gives complete details on this Southern strategy.

5. "Indian Vengeance at Julesburg," 10.

6. Indians routinely carried their dead away from the scene of battle, both to permit proper burial and tribal ceremonies, and to keep the enemy from knowing how successful he had been in battle. Generally speaking, the only bodies left behind by departing Indians

were those which could not be successfully retrieved because they were too close to enemy lines.

7. This account of the sacking of Julesburg includes general information from the brief manuscript written by Ruth Dunn, the account given in *The Southern Cheyennes*, 225–228, official US government records, and several other sources. While each account varies slightly in detail, they are in general agreement as to the material presented here, excepting (as already noted) the number of men on duty at Fort Segwick.

A common practice at the time was for Indian Agents in the field—often in collusion with their superiors in the Indian Office and with politicians to whom they owed their appointment—to withhold annuities from Indians, trading the provisions and goods, instead, to other tribes for hides or robes, or selling the annuities secretly at low prices to traders. In either case, the agents kept the proceeds for themselves and others who were participants in the theft. The schemes defrauded not only the Indians but the Federal Government. President Lincoln was aware of the rampant corruption in the Indian system, but while the Civil War raged he could give little attention to it. He told Minnesota's Episcopal Bishop Henry Whipple, "If we get through this war and I live, this Indian system shall be reformed."

Donald Berthrong,
THE SOUTHERN CHEYENNES

-TWO-

Unendurable Confinement

ATURDAY EVENING, AUGUST 16, 1862. Four dejected teenage Indian boys trudged along the dusty road near Acton, Minnesota. The boys were returning to the Sioux reservation following an unsuccessful deer hunt. They were bitterly disappointed at their failure to kill a deer, but not simply because of wounded pride. In truth, their families were near starvation and desperate for the meat a successful hunt would have supplied. The boys and their families were depending on the venison to feed the dozens of people in their households.

In one of the worst (and most consistent) tragedies in the history of white relations with Native Americans, Indians forced to live on reservations were subject to squalid poverty and near starvation. By the early 1860s, the Sioux living on the Minnesota reservation were a microcosm of the entire United States reservation system; they were mistreated, angry, and increasingly desperate for food. Although corruption was widespread throughout the Bureau of Indian Affairs, it was probably worse in Minnesota than any other place in the country. For years, Minnesota reservation officials had conspired with unscrupulous white traders to cheat the Indians out of their promised annuities, and then forced the Indians to buy the food intended for them in the first place, at greatly inflated prices.[1]

As the four boys walked past a farmhouse on this particular afternoon, one of them spotted a chicken nest containing several eggs. Over the objection of his companions, the young brave reached through the fence and helped himself to several eggs. Unfortunately for the boys, the farmer had been watching through a kitchen window, and now raced outside to confront the teenagers.

History records several different versions of what happened next. Most accounts say that shooting erupted within seconds—but some reports say that after an initial confrontation everyone seemed to calm down and began chatting in a friendly manner. According to this latter version of the incident, the Indian lads eventually challenged the farmer and his son-in-law to a target-shooting contest with the eggs as the prize. In the middle of the ensuing contest, the Indian boys suddenly turned their weapons on the white men.

Whichever version of the story is accurate, virtually all accounts agree that there was a bloody confrontation that night at the Acton farmhouse. When the shooting stopped, three men and two women lay dead in the farm yard. Because of the remoteness of the area, the bodies of the victims would not be found for another week.

Following the shootings, the four boys fled from the farm to their own nearby reservation. Once there they apparently reported exactly what had happened. Tribal elders hastily called a council to discuss what should be done.

Tensions between whites and Indians were already high on the reservation, mostly because the Indians were near starvation. Although game was plentiful in most of Minnesota, the Indians were severely restricted as to where they could hunt. They were also limited as to what they could do to solve the problem because the white man's rules seemed senseless and insensitive to Indian needs.

Confronted by this new and most serious crisis, the murder of five whites by the Indian boys, the tribal elders were in a quandary. They agreed that if the boys were turned over to white authorities, not only the teenagers but everyone on the reservation would suffer. The elders agreed that confessing would only bring more problems to their people, and that nothing would improve. They would still be starving and, because of the white man's rules, they felt unable to cope with the crisis. It was a classic "no win" situation.

Several weeks earlier, reservation Sioux and local whites clashed sharply over the increasingly desperate condition of the tribe. There was an infestation of insects during the summer of 1861, virtually destroying the Indians' crops. White traders controlling the reservation took advantage of the resulting food shortage to charge outrageous prices for poor-quality food supplied through the agency; the meat was spoiled and the flour wormy. The desperate Indians wanted the supplies anyway, and traded almost anything of value to get food for their families.

The Sioux felt that if they could simply hold out until their annual annuity payment, things would be all right. And so it might have been, had not even that normal payment been delayed by bureaucracy. The United States Government, caught up in the Civil War, couldn't decide whether the cash portion of the annuity should be paid in gold (as it had been in the past), or in the new paper money being issued as a matter of wartime necessity. The dilemma over this question resulted in typical governmental gridlock, so that in the end, nothing was done at all. In the meantime, the Indian people continued to starve.

On Monday, August 4, two weeks before the shooting, food supplies intended for the Indians were delivered to the Minnesota reservation. However, local authorities locked the desperately needed food in a warehouse, refusing to distribute it until the cash annuity question was resolved in Washington. The Indians were fully aware that the food was in the warehouse, tantalizingly close to their hungry families. By nightfall of August 4, they were tired of waiting; a group of Indians broke into one of the storehouses.

Army guards dashed to the warehouse and confronted the Indians "stealing" the food that already belonged to them, threatening to shoot the Indians as thieves. Following a noisy argument, the Indians were allowed to keep food they had taken before the arrival of the troops, but the soldiers resealed the warehouse and stood guard to prevent any additional "thefts."

Over the next two days, Indian leaders met repeatedly with white officials to plead for release of the food, but the answer was always the same: no food could be released until Washington instructed otherwise. The Indians proposed an alternative solution. They asked the government to arrange credit for them to buy food at local stores. The debt would be paid out of the annuities, as soon as the federal government settled the issue over the type of payment to be made to the Indians.

The operators of several stores agreed to meet with the Indians to discuss such a plan, and a council was set for the afternoon of August 6. In the course of the meeting, several local businessmen said they would go along with whatever decision was made by community leader Andrew J. Myrick, owner of the largest store in the area and one of the most politically influential people in Minnesota. Generally hated by the Sioux, Myrick had avoided trouble with them in the past because of his marriage to a Sioux woman.

During the meeting Chief Little Crow pleaded for Myrick's help. In his closing remarks, Little Crow made a statement that some of the whites felt to be a direct threat: "When men are hungry, they help themselves." Whether Little Crow was really threatening to break into the warehouses, or merely warning that trouble was likely unless the desperate Indians were fed, remains a matter of conjecture.

Myrick, however, heard the statement as a blatant threat against whites, and wasn't about to tolerate such insubordination from "mere Indians." He leaped to his feet and shouted, "So far as I am concerned, if they are hungry, let them eat grass!" Myrick stormed out of the meeting, followed by all the other white store owners. Dejected Indians also left to return to their starving families.

Two days later, on Friday, August 8, army Captain John Marsh found himself desperately trying to mediate between the two angry groups. Marsh and a relative handful of soldiers were assigned to keep the peace on the reservation. The captain called another meeting for Saturday morning, but noted in his official Friday report that he found the Indians "considerably more angry" than they had been in the past.

Captain Marsh was also angry, and tended to side with the Indians. He demanded that agency officials immediately distribute food to the starving Indians. Marsh warned that unless the agency did so voluntarily, he would order his troops to break into the warehouse and permit the Indians to take what they needed.

In the face of Captain Marsh's threat, agency officials reluctantly permitted distribution of some of the warehoused food. Unfortunately, the food was handed out only to the upper tribes—those living at the northwest end of the Minnesota River. Those Indians living in the lower agency, who were just as desperate for food, were not fed at all. Unaware that the forced distribution had not solved the problem, Captain Marsh took his troops and left the area.

Monday, August 11. Reservation supervisor Thomas Galbraith finally decided to distribute food from the lower warehouse. But upon arriving there, Galbraith found that local Indians had just begun harvesting their summer crops. Galbraith reached the incredible conclusion that with the harvest underway, the Indians no longer needed the food in the warehouse; distribution could be delayed until a more convenient time. Galbraith returned to the main agency offices without taking action.

All during the following week, Sioux leaders fumed over the white man's insensitivity to their needs in refusing to distribute available food to their starving people. By the time those four Indian boys went deer hunting the following Saturday, discontent was reaching the boiling point.[2]

The council following the shootings lasted several hours, as leaders agonized over their course of action. One of the chiefs said that the time had come at last to fight the white man and his system that had brought such tragedy to the Sioux people. Chief Little Crow was among the most outspoken in favor of going to war.

Some historians say that Little Crow was initially opposed to the hostilities, warning that they were too few and too poorly armed to fight the white man. Under severe criticism from other leaders, however, he eventually gave in. Although there is no documentation to support this portion of the story, Little Crow apparently believed the Indians could not win a showdown with the whites. He told other chiefs, "You are little children. You are fools. You will die like rabbits when the hungry wolves hunt them in the hard moon. ...[But] Little Wolf is not a coward; he will die with you."3

After a lengthy debate the other chiefs agreed that armed confrontation was now the only alternative. They voted unanimously to wage a war on the white man. That decision was reached on Saturday, August 23—six days after the killings. Amazingly, the victims at Acton still had not been discovered, and other whites were blissfully ignorant of the disaster sweeping toward them.

The following morning Chief Little Crow attended the white man's church nearest his lodge, just as he had done every Sunday for months. Following the service, Little Crow shook hands with many of his white "friends," then left to help organize the war party. Later, some of the people who were in church that day would say they detected sadness in Little Crow's farewells. That may well be, for Little Crow knew what the congregation did not: the war had already begun.

Not surprisingly, the Indians chose as their first target the store owner, Andrew Myrick. There are indications that warriors broke into Myrick's two-story home sometime before dawn. Myrick apparently spotted the intruders; he crawled out an upper story window and was trying to shinny down a drain pipe when struck by several arrows. The Indians dragged his body to the middle of the yard, and crammed his mouth full of grass.

Monday, August 18, 8:00 a.m. In the little community of New Ulm a rally was held to recruit volunteers for the Union Army. After several stirring, patriotic speeches, five wagon loads of townsmen set off for another village to continue recruiting efforts. A short distance out of town, however, the lead wagon suddenly stopped. Lying in a ditch beside the roadway was the body of a white man. The army recruiters leaped from their wagon and raced to the victim, whom they discovered had been shot—and scalped.

While they were still trying to figure out what this meant, a dozen or so warriors suddenly leaped from behind bushes and began shooting. Several of the recruiters were killed, but many others managed to escape. One of them ran to a nearby farm, took a horse, and raced back to New Ulm to sound the alarm.

The sheriff believed the attackers were most likely "some drunken Indians," still under the influence of a Saturday night binge. The lawman hurriedly rounded up a thirty-man posse. As a precaution, however, he also alerted a number of people around town to be prepared in case the attack represented something more than he suspected.

It did, of course. The sheriff hurried back into town a short time later, reporting that white bodies were everywhere. He ordered the town to throw up street barricades and prepare to defend itself from the inevitable attack.

Within twenty-four hours, the entire west–central section of Minnesota was aflame with terror. Two hundred whites were killed on Monday alone; dozens of women were kidnapped and raped. Before the uprising was over, a staggering 1,400 whites would be killed. Some 269 white women would be kidnapped and brutalized before eventually being rescued.[4]

At about the time the sheriff was discovering "bodies everywhere," Captain John Marsh and a detachment of forty-six soldiers were riding out of Fort Ridgely on routine patrol. They had no idea that a war had started. The men were stopped by several Indians, who were standing in the road ahead of them. They told Marsh that there was "some trouble" at the reservation, and asked if the captain would come and speak to those causing the problem so that peace could be restored. While the Indians were talking to Captain Marsh, other warriors were quietly surrounding the army patrol.

All at once the Indians opened fire. The first volley of shots killed twenty-three of the soldiers and wounded several others. The survivors leaped from their horses and stood in a circle, firing back at their attackers. Unfortunately, the soldiers had not been prepared for battle, and soon ran critically low on ammunition.

Because the fighting was literally on the bank of the Minnesota River, Marsh shouted at his men to try to swim to the far side; he saw it as their only hope of surviving the attack. For Captain Marsh, though, it was already too late. Hit by gunfire as he leaped into the water, the captain went under and was swept away by the current.

Sergeant John F. Bishop and twenty-two other survivors managed to reach the opposite shore, although five of the soldiers were badly wounded. Bishop ordered the men to head at once to Fort Ridgely. Unfortunately, the men were now on foot and the journey would be a difficult one. Fortunately for the soldiers, their attackers did not pursue them across the river, and the survivors finally staggered into Fort Ridgely about nine o'clock that night. At that moment, the fort was manned only by Lieutenant Thomas Gere and twenty-two enlisted men.

Lieutenant Gere asked for a volunteer to ride for help, and when all the men at the fort stepped forward, Gere selected Private William J. Sturgis. The private left within minutes, and in a feat possibly never matched, rode the 125 miles to Fort Snelling in just over eighteen hours.

Along the way, Sturgis happened to meet agency supervisor Thomas Galbraith, who was escorting fifty Indians to the state capitol. There they were to be inducted into the Union Army as the Renville Rangers. Before that chance meeting Galbraith was unaware of the reservation uprising. Learning now of the attack at Fort Ridgely, Galbraith and his fifty recruits turned around and headed as quickly as they could toward the fort, while Sturgis continued on toward Fort Snelling.

At Fort Ridgely, meanwhile, Lieutenant Gere found himself ill-prepared to defend against any major Indian assault. Not only was he short of manpower, but of those men at the base fully one-fifth were sick with an epidemic of mumps. Gere himself was so sick he could barely walk or talk, and eventually had to surrender his command to Sergeant John Jones.

Defending the fort was made all the more difficult by the fact that Fort Ridgely was not really a fort at all; it was merely a collection of broken-down old buildings and had no stockade. Fortunately, what it lacked in form it made up in firepower. Ridgely had two twelve-pound mountain howitzers, a six-pound field gun and one huge twenty-four-pound howitzer. The men at the base hurried to ready the weapons, for the attack they were certain was coming.

By midnight, the fort had even more trouble: Sergeant Jones was overrun with civilians seeking refuge. A constant stream of settlers flowed into the compound, and by morning more than 200 people had sought shelter there. A vast majority were women and children from nearby farms and villages.

When it got light enough to see, lookouts at the fort found their worst fears had become reality: dozens of warriors were gathered on the flat prairie just to the west of the fort. The soldiers began bracing for attack. The anticipated assault, however, did not materialize. After a tense hour, the Indians disappeared, apparently believing that the nearby town of New Ulm would be an easier target than the fort.

About the time the Indians disappeared from sight, Lieutenant Timothy Sheehan and fifty men of Company C, Fifth Minnesota Volunteers, arrived at Fort Ridgely. Sheehan had been on routine patrol the previous evening, when he encountered Private Sturgis. When he learned what was going on, Sheehan force-marched his men forty-two miles in just over nine hours, to come to the aid of the beleaguered fort. The fort's situation eased even more about noon, when Captain Galbraith and his fifty recruits also arrived to join in the defense.

Tuesday, August 19, 3:00 p.m. The citizens of New Ulm had been preparing for an attack for a full day, and were ready when it finally materialized. Women and children who had remained in town were crowded into several buildings at the center of the community, while male volunteers manned road blocks on all approaches to the town.

The assault came in the form of a frontal attack. Hundreds of whooping and shouting Sioux warriors raced toward one of the roadblocks, showering the defenders with arrows and rifle fire. Several of the warriors lobbed flaming arrows into town and managed to set fire to various buildings—all of which, fortunately, had already been evacuated.

As the battle raged at the edge of town, fifteen more white men rode into the community from the opposite side and quickly joined the defenders on the front line. After about an hour of fierce combat, a severe thunderstorm swept through the community. During the storm the Indians broke off the attack and disappeared.

When it stopped raining and became apparent that the Indians were gone, defenders recovered the bodies of eleven people just outside the city. The eleven had apparently been overtaken and killed as they tried to head into New Ulm—probably having ridden squarely into the midst of the warriors who were leaving town. In addition to those eleven dead on the road, six defenders of the town were killed, and several others wounded during the battle.

All during the afternoon, more settlers poured into the community as word spread across the countryside that an Indian uprising was underway. By sundown, 116 more white men had entered New Ulm, and by Wednesday morning, more than 300 men were defending the little community.

Wednesday, August 20. Four hundred Sioux warriors attacked Fort Ridgely about 11 a.m., sweeping out of the woods to hit all four sides of the fort simultaneously. Within minutes troops had been driven back from the northeast corner of the compound, and the Indians managed to enter and occupy several buildings there. They eventually were driven out again, but during the time they occupied the buildings the braves managed to take all of the army's horses and mules from a nearby corral.

The battle at the fort raged for several hours, although the battle was one-sided. By early afternoon the fort's cannons were exacting a heavy toll on the Sioux, and most of the shooting was being done from long range. The braves were at a distinct disadvantage in this duel, and when it began to get dark the warriors withdrew.

On the reservation itself, the four Sioux tribes of the Santee Nation were bitterly divided over this war against the white man. Two of the tribes—the Sissetons and Wahpetons—officially refused to join the uprising, although 350 of their younger warriors did so as individuals.

By Wednesday night, more than 1,000 Sioux were on the warpath. Minnesota's governor sent panicked telegrams to the White House, appealing for aid. President Lincoln wired back that, because of the Civil War, no troops were available for the defense of Minnesota. However, the president authorized Minnesota to delay in sending to Washington those troops it had earlier been ordered to recruit for the Civil War; they could be used instead, he said, to defend the region from Indians.

Thursday, August 21. It was cold and overcast, and a chilly rain fell most of the day. The Indians staged no new attacks, and substantial numbers of additional whites managed to reach both Fort Ridgely and New Ulm.

Friday, August 22, 6:45 a.m. It was barely light enough to see when an estimated 500 Indians swooped out of the woods and attacked Fort Ridgely. Chief Little Crow personally supervised the battle from the seat of a black buggy, which had been taken from a nearby farm. He parked the buggy atop a nearby hill and from there had an excellent view of the entire panorama of battle.

The attack had the potential to cause real damage, since during the night many Indians had crawled close to the fort without being discovered. However, fortunately for the fort and unfortunately for him, a white man picked that moment to try to ride to the fort—and rode directly into the midst of the hidden Indians. They shot him, and in so doing gave away their position.

A vicious battle erupted and raged for several hours. Soldiers lowered the barrels and fired their cannons at point-blank range, sometimes blasting into buildings at the edge of the fort to drive out occupying Indians. Several buildings were set afire, as was the dry grass surrounding the fort.

At the height of the battle Chief Little Crow was severely injured—struck in the head by a chunk of rock kicked up by a cannon ball.[5] A few seconds later (for the first time in the contest) the army blasted its huge 24–pounder into the midst of the Indians. The cannon shot undoubtedly startled and amazed the warriors, and apparently inflicted heavy casualties. The Indians broke off the attack at once and withdrew from the area.

The Sioux later claimed that only six warriors were killed and seventeen wounded in this battle, but nearly all historical accounts estimate a much greater toll. The army officially estimated that at least 100 warriors were killed or injured, and military records say the bodies of twenty warriors were recovered from the battlefield after the shooting ended.

Saturday, August 23, 7:15 a.m. Several hundred Sioux attacked the northeast corner of New Ulm. Defenders broke and ran when the attack was launched, permitting the warriors to seize a number of buildings at the edge of the community.

As the defenders pulled back into the heart of the city they set fire to a number of buildings between themselves and the attackers. They hoped the fire would create an open space between the opposing combatants. The Indians also set fire to several buildings, and within minutes six to eight square blocks were in flames.

Gunfire broke out everywhere, and the two sides fought a pitched battle lasting for several hours. Finally, the Indians set fire to grass on the southeast side of town—knowing that a stiff afternoon breeze would blow smoke into the city, making it hard for the white defenders to see. About sixty warriors raced into town through this cloud of smoke, but ran squarely into the concentrated gunfire from scores of defenders.

The fighting continued far into the night, but began to taper off about two o'clock a.m. When the sun rose the next morning, the Indians suddenly broke off the engagement and withdrew. The whites counted 36 dead and 23 wounded in the community; Indian losses could not be accurately estimated. One hundred ninety-six buildings were consumed by fire.

At about mid-morning, 150 civilians rode into New Ulm from the town of Mankato, thirty miles to the southeast. The newcomers were a rescue party. They helped evacuate New Ulm, loading women, children, and the elderly into 153 wagons, then escorted the entire group back to Mankato.

Monday morning, August 25. Several thousand whites fled from villages in South Dakota after learning of the atrocities in Minnesota. Warriors then entered several of those communities. The town of Sioux Falls and several smaller settlements were looted and burned.

The governors of Nebraska, Iowa, and South
Dakota individually telegraphed the White House,
demanding that President Lincoln send help to defend
them from "50,000 attacking hostiles."[6] There was no
immediate response from Washington, which was fully
occupied with the Civil War.

Monday, 9 a.m. The first sizable relief column finally
rode into Fort Ridgely. Henry Hastings Sibley[7] brought
with him some 1,400 soldiers, most of them raw recruits.
Three hundred of the men were ordered to escort an
equal number of civilians and wounded soldiers to
Mankato, while the remainder went on the offensive.

On the same morning, Indians attacked the communities of Acton, Forest City, and Hutchinson,
Minnesota. The villages were mostly empty except for a
handful of male defenders; even so, the better-armed
white men eventually drove the Indians away with min-
imal losses.

Monday, 11:00 a.m. General Sibley ordered a seventy-
man military burial party to search the area around
New Ulm and bury all the dead they could locate. The
burial party toiled throughout the day to execute their
grim task. When night fell, the unit was fifteen miles
from the fort, on the banks of the Minnesota River.
Realizing it was too late to return to the fort while it was
still daylight, the commander decided the men would be
safer to camp right where they were. During the night,
an estimated 200 Indian warriors quietly surrounded
the burial detail.

Tuesday, August 26, 4:00 a.m. A guard fired at what
he thought was a wolf or some other wild animal, sneak-
ing up on army horses at the edge of the burial party's

camp. The "animal" turned out to be a Sioux brave trying to steal or frighten away the horses. The shot triggered a full-scale Indian attack on the camp.

Many of the soldiers were felled by gunfire before they could either find shelter or fire their weapons in self defense. Eventually, however, the soldiers got organized and put up a spirited defense; the resulting battle raged for more than two hours. As it began to get light the Indians withdrew. When the shooting stopped the soldiers counted nineteen dead and sixteen wounded from their party.

Fortunately for the soldiers, the night had been unusually calm—so the sounds of the fierce riverside battle carried all the way to Fort Ridgely. General Sibley knew at once what was happening and immediately sent 240 men to rescue the burial detail.

As the rescuers came within three miles of the burial party's camp, the rescue party, itself, was attacked by about 400 warriors. The soldiers dismounted and formed a defensive circle from which they battled back.

Meanwhile, as the sounds of the new battle carried back to the fort, General Sibley rounded up all his remaining troops and raced to their rescue. Even so, it was late afternoon before they reached the battlefield. There they quickly overwhelmed the Indian force. The Sioux broke off the attack and fled. Sibley and his enlarged troop drove on to the burial detail's camp, and rescued them, as well.

Although technically the soldiers had defeated the Indians in each confrontation, the battles severely crippled the army's ability to respond to the war. By the time Sibley's main body had rescued all of the soldiers, only twenty-five army horses remained to serve his entire detachment of 1,100 men. All of the other horses had been stolen or killed by Indian warriors.

Wednesday, August 27, 11:15 a.m. Several hundred Sioux attacked Fort Abercrombie, just inside South Dakota. One hundred fifty soldiers inside the fort successfully held off the attackers for three days; the Indians eventually withdrew. The army suffered two dead and three wounded in the seventy-two-hour battle.

Friday morning, August 29. General Sibley, learning that Little Crow had been injured a few days earlier, believed the chief might be growing weary of the battle. Sibley wrote a note to the chief, and nailed it to a shattered tree stump near where the burial party had been attacked. The note offered to negotiate with the Indians.

Several hours later, an army patrol found an answering note from Little Crow. It listed more than twenty Indian grievances against the white man—including the withholding of food supplies from starving women and children—and demanded that the issues be resolved before the war could stop. Little Crow claimed that his Sioux warriors were holding "many" white women and children as their prisoners (an obvious threat of harm if the Indian demands were not met).

General Sibley immediately sent back a second note. This one said, "Little Crow: Return me the prisoners under a flag of truce and I will talk with you then, like a man."[8]

Saturday morning, August 30. President Lincoln telegraphed the governor of Minnesota, ordering the creation of the Military Department of the Northwest. It would encompass North and South Dakota, Nebraska, Wisconsin, Iowa, and Minnesota. General John Pope, recently relieved of his Civil War command (after losing the Second Battle of Bull Run) was placed in charge of this new military department. He was given orders to quickly put down the Minnesota Indian rebellion.

Tuesday evening, September 4. Chief Little Crow and several hundred of his warriors attempted to make a camp in the upper reservation near the South Dakota border. They were confronted by several hundred other Sioux warriors, who wanted no part of Little Crow's war with the whites.

The peaceful Sioux demanded that the hostile Indians get out of the upper reservation. When Little Crow hesitated, the "peace" Indians fired several shots in the general direction of the hostile warriors. Little Crow got the message and agreed to leave. During that confrontation, however, the peace Indians managed to free more than fifty of the white women and children prisoners, and began caring for them until they could be handed over to soldiers.

Friday, September 7. Chief Little Crow sent another note to General Sibley. This time the Sioux chief claimed to be holding 155 white prisoners, and asked Sibley under what conditions he could make peace.

At about the same time that Sibley received Little Crow's latest letter, he also received word from friendly Indians that a plot was underway against Little Crow. The plot involved the capture of Little Crow and other leaders of the hostile warriors, and setting loose all the white prisoners. Sibley did not answer the chief's note, but sent a letter to the friendly Indians. In it he said he would be leaving Fort Ridgely and moving northwest along the river. He said friendly Indians should put the white prisoners in a conspicuous place, under a conspicuous white flag, where they could be easily found by soldiers. And he promised that the peace Indians would not be harmed if they cooperated.

Saturday, September 8. Two hundred seventy battle-hardened Civil War veterans of the Third Minnesota Infantry rode into Fort Ridgely to reinforce Sibley. The men had all been captured while fighting Confederates in Tennessee, and were released after promising they would not again take up arms against the South until formally "exchanged" (on paper) for Confederate prisoners. They were perfect for Sibley's needs and he put them immediately on the front lines of the Indian war.

Tuesday, September 11. General Pope arrived in Minnesota and met with General Sibley. Pope told Sibley that between them they easily had enough men and arms for "exterminating or ruining" the Indians.

Monday, September 13. General Sibley and more than 1100 soldiers began moving slowly northward along the Minnesota River. The movement could hardly have been hidden from Little Crow and his warriors, and the Indians began preparing for battle. By this time, nearly all white prisoners originally seized by hostile Indians were under the control of peace Indians, and many of the captives had already been set free.

On the evening of the thirteenth, Sibley made camp near Wood Lake, Minnesota. The hostile war Indians of Chief Little Crow were gathered less than a mile away, hiding in ravines and trees, waiting for an opportunity to attack the soldiers. After some discussion, the Indians decided to sneak as close as possible to the soldiers during the night, and launch an all-out attack at the first light of dawn.

Tuesday, September 14. Several early-rising soldiers decided to try to find fresh potatoes growing on nearby farms. Without authorization from their officers, the men took two wagons and headed cross-country toward a nearby potato field. They rode directly into the middle of a ring of warriors. When the Indians opened fire on the soldiers a major battle erupted.

For two hours, the battle raged—at times involving hand-to-hand combat. In the thick of the fight, Little Crow's lieutenant, Chief Mankato, was struck in the back by a cannon ball and killed out-right.

At about 9:00 a.m., the Indians broke off the battle and fled back into the woods. They left twenty-five dead and about an equal number of badly wounded survivors on the battlefield. General Sibley's official report later listed seven whites killed and thirty-four wounded. The "Battle of Wood Lake" is seen by most historians as the official end of the Minnesota uprising, although battles with the Indians who rebelled there would actually go on for more than a year thereafter.

Following the Battle of Wood Lake, General Sibley was shocked to find that several of his soldiers had scalped the bodies of three Indian warriors they found on the battlefield. Sibley was furious, and ordered that the soldiers be arrested. He also issued an order that would later become an issue in the hue and cry against Colonel John Chivington following the Sand Creek Massacre in Colorado.[9] Sibley's order said, "The bodies of the dead—even of a savage enemy—shall not be subjected to indignities by civilized and Christian men!"[10]

Thursday, September 20. General Sibley's troops crested a small hill and found a Sioux village of 250 tepees below. Every tepee was flying a large white flag. There were also white flags on nearby trees, and even white flags fluttering from the necks and tails of Indian ponies tethered nearby. Sibley rode into the village of peace Indians and released more than 200 white and mixed-blood prisoners.

Over the next two weeks, soldiers rounded up more than 2,000 warriors who were accused of participating in the attacks. Sibley appointed a five-man military commission to try these Indians—to determine which ones were the ringleaders and which ones had committed documented atrocities against whites.

Eventually, three hundred ninety-two of the Indian men were ordered to stand trial for war crimes. Three hundred seven of them were eventually convicted of murder and/or rape. All of the 307 were sentenced to be hanged. Sixteen others were given lengthy prison sentences.

The Episcopal bishop of Minnesota, Henry B. Whipple, thought that the trial had been highly biased, and that the sentences were far too harsh. Whipple hastened to Washington to make a personal appeal to President Lincoln, asking the president to intervene on the Indians' behalf. Eventually Lincoln did commute all but thirty-nine of the death sentences to life in prison.

Friday, December 26, 1862. On the morning after Christmas, the thirty-nine Indians (whose death penalties were upheld) were hanged simultaneously from a single scaffolding. Three of the executed were later found to be innocent of any crime, the apparent result of mistaken identities.[11]

As to the other Indians who were captured, 1,700 were held for the remainder of the winter at Fort Snelling, which was ill prepared to deal with them. The Indians were kept out of doors most of the time, even in the worst winter weather. Warm clothing was scarce or non-existent, and food was in short supply. Dozens of the Indians died of exposure, hunger, and disease before the arrival of spring.

Many of the hostile Indians who were not captured fled into Canada. Most of them were subsequently rounded up by Canadian authorities and forced to live on reservations not much better than the one in Minnesota.

Two of the leading Sioux war chiefs—Shakopee and Medicine Bottle—were tracked to Canada by angry white Americans. The Americans disregarded the international border, entered Canada (possibly with the cooperation of Canadian officials), and took the two chiefs prisoner. The Indians were drugged, bound, and gagged, then returned to the United States. Both were imprisoned in Minnesota early in 1863, and both were hanged in 1865.

Friday, July 3, 1863. Two white men were riding through the woods a few miles from New Ulm when they surprised two Indian men—one middle-aged and the other a teenager—picking raspberries. The white men asked no questions, but immediately opened fire. The older Indian was killed and the younger fled.

The white men scalped the body of the dead Indian, then took the remains into the town of Hutchinson. After the body was displayed on the town's square, it was dumped on a pile of steer entrails at a local slaughterhouse.

The following day, the younger Indian was captured. He quickly admitted to being the son of Little Crow. He said that the old Indian, shot in the woods the previous day, was his famous fugitive father. Town officials at Hutchinson retrieved the chief's scalp, which was later displayed by the Minnesota Historical Society.

Although most of the world now turned its attention to other matters, the army was not yet through trying to capture the ring leaders of the Minnesota uprising. General Sibley was regularly given new information on where the largest band of these Indians were, and set out in early spring to try to catch them. He would not get close, however, until summer was half over.

Friday, July 24, 1863. General Sibley was leading several hundred soldiers through North Dakota, not far from Bismark. As he neared a mountain known as "Big Mound" his troops spotted a large Sioux village. Sibley was uncertain whether these were the Sioux he was chasing, but approached the village and asked for a conference with the chief. The Indian with whom Sibley spoke asked him to wait a few moments and the chief would come out to meet him.

As Sibley waited, his soldiers chatted amiably with several Indian braves who wandered out to meet them. Apparently a number of other braves were simultaneously encircling the troops. Suddenly there was a shot from somewhere near the tepees; a bullet struck and killed a doctor accompanying the troops.

Immediately, gunfire erupted all over the camp. The troops were well armed, however, and reacted swiftly. After a brief fire fight the Indians fled, leaving "numerous" of their dead on the battlefield. General Sibley ordered his troops to pursue the Indians, and the foes fought many running battles over the next several days. Eventually the Indians crossed into Canada and went to Fort Garvey to seek help; the British arrested the Indians and confined them on a nearby reservation.

Sunday, July 26, 1863. Another detachment of Sibley's command battled a small group of Sioux warriors near

Dead Buffalo Lake, North Dakota. The battle was indecisive and the Indians fled after only a few minutes. On Tuesday, July 28, the same two groups clashed again at Stony Lake, North Dakota. Again, the Indians vanished after a brief skirmish.

This time the troops continued in hot pursuit, however, and literally chased the fleeing Indians to the edge of the Missouri River. When they came to the water, some Indians set up a defensive line, firing at the troops to hold them at bay while other Indians hastily constructed rafts. When night fell a short time later, the Indians managed to evacuate most of their women and children.

On the following morning, many other women, old men, and warriors were still on the near side of the river when the army attacked at first light. The frightened Indians began leaping into the water, trying to swim to the opposite shore. Soldiers scurried to the edge of the water, firing their rifles at them. Many of the Sioux were killed in the river, struck by gunfire, and several others apparently drowned in their panic.[12]

After the confrontation, Sibley's troops burned 150 wagon loads of Indian supplies abandoned by the Sioux.

The Missouri River battle was the final one fought by General Sibley, who returned to Minnesota to enter politics. However, he handed his command to General Alfred Sully, and Sully continued to pursue the Indians involved in the Minnesota uprising. Sully was under specific orders to "punish" the Sioux so that they would never again stage a bloody uprising such as the one in Minnesota.

Friday, September 3, 1863. General Sully's advance guard of about 300 soldiers, working a mile or so ahead of the main body of troops, stumbled onto a huge Sioux camp containing possibly as many as 5,000 Sioux men, women, and children. As the soldiers approached the camp, Indians came out to meet them and asked to speak to the officer in charge.

Several of Sully's junior officers stepped forward to talk with the Sioux warriors in what they said was a "friendly manner." The troops apparently did not notice that hundreds of other warriors were also coming out of the village. Soon, warriors began to appear on ridges and hills on either side of the troops, and then on the road behind them. The soldiers eventually figured out what was happening, but it was too late to make an issue of the situation without triggering hostilities. One soldier did manage to slip away and ride for more help.

While the Indians continued chatting with the troops, the soldiers noticed that all those not involved directly in the conversation were putting on war paint, and Indian women and children were quietly leaving the area. The soldiers fully expected to be attacked at any moment.

Just then, General Sully arrived on scene with the main body of his troops. As they rode into sight, Indians opened fire. The fighting was fierce, but the fire power of the soldiers quickly overwhelmed the braves.

When the Sioux fled a short time later, Sully reported twenty-two soldiers killed and thirty-eight wounded. Sully said that about 200 dead Indian braves were found on the battlefield and another 150 were captured—many of whom were wounded.

Sully ordered his troops to destroy the Sioux village. The soldiers set fire to the tepees and burned everything therein, including what the army estimated to be 400,000 pounds of buffalo meat.

The general forced the 150 captured warriors to walk all the way back to the reservation in Minnesota, a distance of more than 200 miles. Although most of the Indians apparently survived the march, it was extremely tough and the Sioux thereafter always referred to it as the "death march."

The final battle in the Minnesota uprising was fought nearly eighteen months after most of the ring leaders were hanged in Minnesota. The stage for the final showdown was set on Tuesday, June 28, 1864, when three Indian warriors attacked and killed a US Army engineer, Captain John Fielner. Other soldiers were nearby and promptly killed the three assailants. General Sully, infuriated by the brazen and "unprovoked" attack on the engineer, ordered that the Indians' heads be chopped off and impaled on poles "set high on a hill" as a warning to other Sioux.

The beheading violated Indian taboos as well as their sensibilities; it infuriated the Sioux. They apparently began planning their revenge at once.

A few days later, General Sully was ordered to escort a large, slow moving ox-drawn wagon train of 200 travelers heading for new gold fields in Idaho. At first, Sully considered the assignment a great irritation. But apparently his attitude changed after being told that a huge group of Sioux who were "eager to fight" were waiting for the wagon train in western South Dakota.

Sully lectured the civilians on the train regarding their behavior, and promised he would do his best to protect them. Then the general gathered 2,400 soldiers and set out across the prairie.

Sunday, July 24, 1864. Sully's scouts reported fresh signs of Indians all along the trail. Sully ordered 300 of the soldiers to remain with the wagon train, then raced ahead with 2,100 others in an effort to catch up with the Indians.

Thursday, July 28. Sully's scouts found a large Sioux village, containing an estimated 1,600 tepees and perhaps as many as 6,000 Sioux. (The army report said 6,000 warriors were in the village, but that report appears to have been greatly exaggerated.)

Sully guessed that the Indians knew he was coming and that they were most likely just as prepared as he was. To attack the Indians while protecting himself from an Indian surprise raid from behind, Sully devised an ingenious scheme. He ordered his soldiers to form a giant square—possibly as large as one half mile long on each side—with troops forming the four walls. Inside the square he placed his wagons and horses, and they moved together as the square advanced toward the Indian community.

Within minutes, Indians were circling the soldiers, probing for a weak place in this moving square, but could find none. As the square of troops crossed a ridge, they saw an Indian battle line blocking the road just ahead. The troops ground to a halt.

One Indian (some reports say a "very elderly" warrior) rode out from the Indian battle line and began taunting the soldiers. At least one report says he fired a shot at the troops, although that report appears highly questionable. A soldier eventually shot the warrior, and heavy fighting erupted at once.

Over the course of the next ninety minutes the Indians were driven slowly backward—back through their village and up the slope of a mountain just beyond. The troops shelled the Indian positions with several mountain howitzers, but were unable to dislodge them from the slopes. The Indians fled after dark.

The following morning, Sully ordered the Indian village burned to the ground. The resulting fire destroyed 1,600 tepees and perhaps a half million pounds of buffalo meat, plus thousands of pounds of other Indian belongings.

The Indians subsequently claimed to have lost only thirty-one warriors in the battle, while General Sully's official report says his troops located and buried 150 Indian warriors on the battlefield. Sully lost 5 dead and 10 wounded in the confrontation.

The final shots had not yet been fired in the Minnesota–related battles when all American Indians began paying a high price for the uprising. President Lincoln, who had earlier expressed dismay about crooks at the Bureau of Indian Affairs, now took a hard line approach to the Indian problem. In his State of the Union message in 1863, the President said one of the highest priorities for the nation over the next twelve months was to "make the West secure for whites", and for a concentrated national effort to develop the West's vast mineral resources. The President added that the ability to control the Indians and bring the gold and silver out of the West was vital to achieving victory in the Civil War.

Lincoln's new commissioner of Indian Affairs, William Dole, said it was important that all western Indians be rounded up and placed on reservations where they would be "out of the way of whites."

Notes

1. There are many accounts of the horrible mistreatment of Minnesota's Sioux Indians and the white men who were involved in such nefarious activities. For an outstanding discussion of the Minnesota situation and the Sioux uprising it triggered, see Alvin M. Josephy, Jr.'s *The Civil War in the American West* (New York:

Alfred A. Knopf, 1991, 95–156, and Benjamin Capps, The Indians (New York: Time–Life Books, 1973).

2. This summary of events preceding the Acton shootings is based on numerous published accounts of the Minnesota uprising.

3. *The Civil War in the American West,* 111. Little Crow frequently referred to himself as "Little Wolf" when talking with fellow Indians.

4. Paul Wellman, *Death on the Prairie* (Lincoln/London: University of Nebraska Press, 1962), 8, quotes the Historical Society of Minnesota as listing 644 civilians and 757 soldiers killed in the uprising, and supplies the figure of 269 as the number of white women kidnapped and sexually assaulted.

5. Some accounts of this battle claim Little Crow struck his head on a rock while diving out of the wagon to avoid cannon fire. There is some uncertainty as to which version is accurate.

6. The actual exact number of Indian participants in this uprising is unknown, but even liberal figures usually put the numbers no higher than 10,000. Many historians believe the number was more like 3,000 to 5,000.

7. No kin to Henry Hopkins Sibley, the Confederate general who led the invasion of New Mexico earlier this same year.

8. *The Civil War in the American West,* 133.

9. Bob Scott, *Blood at Sand Creek* (Caldwell, Idaho: The Caxton Printers, Ltd., 1994).

10. *Death on the Prairie,* 22.

11. *The Civil War in the American West,* 232.

12. The exact number of casualties is unknown.

My convictions upon this subject have been confirmed. That those tribes cannot exist surrounded by our settlements and in continual contact with our citizens is certain. They have neither the intelligence, the industry, the moral habits, nor the desire of improvement which are essential to any favorable change in their conditions. Established in the midst of another and a superior race and without appreciating the causes of their inferiority or seeking to control them, they must necessarily yield to the force of circumstances and ere long disappear. Such has been their fate heretofore, and if it is to be averted it can only be done by a general removal beyond our boundary and by the reorganization of their political system upon principles adapted to the new relations in which they will be placed.

President Andrew Jackson

I have heard that you intend to settle us on a reservation near the mountains. When we settle down, we grow pale and die. A long time ago this land belonged to our fathers, but when I go up the river I see camps of soldiers on its banks. These soldiers cut down my timber. They kill my buffalo, and when I see that, my heart feels like bursting. I feel sorry. I have spoken.

Kiowa Chief Satanta

–THREE–

The Meeker Massacre

T HE EARLIEST WHITE MEN IN COLORADO flocked to the region because of its great climate—warm, pleasant days and cool nights. It was weather for farming and ranching: especially ideal was the abundance of natural grasslands stretching 200 miles from the western Kansas border all the way to the Rockies. Colorado's high country was pretty, but it offered virtually nothing of real interest to these newcomers. They concentrated on building their homes on Colorado's eastern plains.

The Utes, who were among the earliest Indians in Colorado, were not at first particularly alarmed by the influx of whites to the plains country. The Utes preferred the high ground anyway. They avoided the lower land even more when Cheyennes and Arapahos, natural enemies to the Utes, began pouring into Colorado. Because of the influx of white settlers, the newly–arrived Cheyennes and Arapahos concentrated on fighting them, and ignored the Utes. This seemed like a perfect solution to the problem of intertribal warfare.

But that perspective began to change in 1858, with the discovery of gold in Colorado. Within months, tens of thousands of gold miners began flocking to the Colorado hills. Still thousands more came a few years later, when silver was discovered in the mountains.

Still, the Utes seemed to tolerate the white men better than did other Native Americans. There rarely was any serious trouble between Utes and the white newcomers. Thus, when the gold and silver booms began to fade and white men began leaving the mountains, there was no reason to suspect that major trouble lay just ahead.

By 1878, most of the Great Plains Indians had either been driven into the last of the "wild West" (Arizona, primarily) or they had been confined to reservations in Oklahoma or the Dakotas. The Utes who had not already fled to the desert southwest went quietly to live on a large mountain reservation in the northwestern corner of Colorado. They were living there serenely and apparently without much difficulty.

Early in 1878, one of Colorado's most respected pioneers, N.C. Meeker, asked the governor to appoint him as the new agent, or supervisor, for the Ute reservation. Meeker was the founder of Greeley, Colorado, which he had named after his friend, newspaperman Horace Greeley. As the patriarch of that village, Meeker gained a reputation not only as a thoroughly honest and hard working man, but one who had no sense of humor and very little tolerance for anyone who disagreed with him. Meeker believed that virtually any problem could be solved by harder work and additional Bible reading, and he drilled his philosophy into everyone with whom he had contact.

Courtesy Colorado Historical Society
Nathan Meeker
A no-nonsense Colorado Pioneer, Nathan Meeker would not tolerate dishonesty, liquor, or idleness. Although he had no apparent interest in affairs of Native Americans, he got himself appointed supervisor of the Ute Indian Reservation—and promptly made himself the most hated man in the region. His harsh demands triggered a bloody uprising.

It's not exactly clear why Meeker asked for the appointment as supervisor of the Ute reservation, but his timing was perfect. The government needed a new supervisor, and Meeker seemed to be the ideal candidate. The happy marriage of man and job, however, soon began to experience serious problems.

Meeker's sullen moodiness and demanding nature quickly became an issue on the reservation. Even the Utes, who were normally quiet and compliant, were beginning to complain about Meeker. Sometime later, one of the Ute leaders said of Meeker's no-nonsense attitude, "He was always mad. I think he was sick in the head. We never knew what to do; he was mad all the time."[1]

In a short time, Meeker had drawn the ire of nearly all the Indians on the reservation. In his first official act as Indian agent, Meeker ordered the agency's government buildings moved from their original location. The new site was in the very center of a peaceful valley, fifteen miles away. The new location chosen by Meeker (apparently without consulting anyone else) lay squarely in the middle of prime Ute deer hunting territory. The Utes strongly protested, but Meeker brushed off their criticisms and ordered the construction to continue.

About two miles from these new agency offices, the insensitive Meeker ordered that an Indian schoolhouse be constructed. Again, he chose a terrible spot for the building; the construction site was in the middle of a horse track, built two years earlier by the Utes. The Indians loved horse racing and spent a considerable portion of their free time at the track. Furious because Meeker destroyed their race track with the schoolhouse project, they sent a delegation to file a formal protest with the supervisor.

Meeker's response to the complaints was fairly typical. He decided that the Indians simply had too much idle time on their hands: the devil was making work for idle hands, and so forth. To stop their complaining, Meeker ordered that all the braves would have to get involved in "full work days," primarily as farmers. Any Indian who refused to work at his assigned task would simply no longer be fed.

Outwardly, the Utes seemed resigned to tolerate these ongoing problems with Meeker, but their simmering anger was beginning to build. Only the seemingly endless patience of the number one Ute chief, Ouray, prevented an open outbreak of hostilities. Time after time, Chief Ouray soothed the warriors, cooled their tempers, and prevented serious trouble.

Monday, September 16, 1878. Meeker sent for all the chiefs of the Ute tribes on the reservation. At the time, Chief Ouray and several lesser chiefs were away from the reservation on a perfectly legal, extended deer hunting trip. However, three other chiefs, Colorow, Douglas, and Matogoras, who were on the grounds responded to Meeker's summons.

Meeker told the chiefs that it was time for them to send their children—and all the other Ute children on the reservation—to the new school house for the beginning of the fall term. The chiefs were dismayed at the news. They responded that the weather was still too hot for school; children could not concentrate during such warm weather. They said the children would come to the white man's classes when the weather turned cooler, in about another month—just as they had always done in years past.

Meeker was infuriated by their resistance to his instructions. He raged that the Utes clearly did not

Courtesy Colorado Historical Society
Ouray
A Ute Chief, Ouray considered himself a statesman and a friend of
the white man—but even he could not stop the bloody uprising that
killed Nathan Meeker and several other settlers. Ouray's untimely
death also left three white women as abused captives of
the angry Ute tribe.

understand the calendar. It was September, and therefore time for school! Meeker demanded that the children
come to classes at once. If the children did not show up
for classes the following day, he threatened to send for
soldiers to enforce his order.

In the heat of the argument, Meeker somehow concluded that the Indians had capitulated and agreed to
send the children—although the Indians said they never
agreed to anything. Obviously there was a serious communications gap. Eventually the chiefs left Meeker's
office amid great confusion; each side believed the other
understood, when in fact, no one understood.

Several days passed. When the children still did not
show up for classes, Meeker made good on his threat. He
sent to Fort Steele, Wyoming (about thirty miles to the
north) for soldiers to come and enforce his order that
reservation children must report to the schools. A handful of soldiers rode half-heartedly to the agency one day
later, confronted the three old chiefs and scolded them
for their disobedience. Satisfied that they had done all
that was required of them, the soldiers turned around
and rode back to Fort Steele.

Wednesday, September 25, 1878. The Indian children
still had not shown up for school, and Meeker was debating what to do about it. At the same time, the agent
issued a seemingly unrelated order. He instructed that,
for the first time ever, the floor of the valley (containing
the new reservation offices) be plowed in preparation for
planting crops the following spring.

The plowing order was probably of no great significance to Meeker, but once again the Indians were
furious. They did not want to be farmers, and did not
want the beautiful valley destroyed by turning it into a
farm. They protested to Meeker that some of the land

had special religious significance to them, and to plow it would anger their gods. As usual, the insensitive Meeker brushed off their complaints and ordered the plowing to commence.

Later that afternoon, several white employees of the reservation began the plowing, just as Meeker had ordered. Almost as soon as the horses and blades showed up, however, so did a sizable contingent of highly agitated Indians. There was an angry shouting match between several warriors and Meeker's staff. At the height of the argument, someone fired a shot. (As always, each side blamed the other for the gunfire.)

No one was hurt in the shooting incident, but the plowing came to an immediate halt. The Indians returned to their lodges, and Meeker sent a messenger racing back to Fort Steele. Meeker's message to the army was that a possible Indian uprising was underway; he pleaded for troops.

Major Thomas T. Thornburgh responded quickly, leaving the fort at dawn the following morning with 150 soldiers. He had barely crossed out of Wyoming into Colorado when five Indian chiefs appeared on the trail and stopped the troops. The chiefs asked Major Thornburgh to ride no further, warning that if the troops insisted on continuing toward the agency, it would mean certain war.

The confrontation surprised Major Thornburgh. He told the chiefs that although he did not want a war, it was his obligation to protect the whites at the reservation. He also said that his troops must be free to go wherever they wanted. Thornburgh promised the chiefs that he would merely ride to the vicinity of the agency buildings and set up a camp "to prevent trouble."

Apparently Major Thornburgh thought his mid-road conference with the Indians had settled the matter peacefully. Once again, though, there was a communications failure. The Indians had drawn a line in the Colorado mountain dust, and were determined that no soldier would cross it. They left the brief confrontation determined that the soldiers would progress no further toward the agency.

Forty-five minutes later Major Thornburgh led his troops into a narrow, deep mountain gulch called Red Canyon. By this time his troops were fairly spread out along the trail. Captain Philip Payne and about fifty men of the Fifth Cavalry were in the lead, followed closely by Captain Donald Lawson and another fifty men. Their wagon loads of supplies and the final fifty men, under the command of a Lieutenant Paddock, were now nearly a half mile behind the main body of soldiers.

Shortly after the leading troops entered the canyon, someone spotted an Indian standing on top of a ridge ahead of the troops. Major Thornburgh halted his soldiers, sending Lieutenant Cherry and ten enlisted men forward to investigate.

All at once, Ute warriors filled the valley. They were behind every tree, every bush, every rock. Dozens of arrows and numerous gunshots filled the air. Lieutenant Cherry and his men hastily retreated to the main body of troops, but these soldiers, too, were now under heavy attack.

Major Thornburgh stood up in his stirrups and shouted for his men to pull back. The order was cut off in mid-sentence, as the major was shot in the chest; he tumbled from the saddle, apparently killed outright. The remaining soldiers began a hasty retreat toward the wagons, which were now also under heavy fire. Fortunately, Lieutenant Paddock had seen the initial outbreak of trouble in front of him and managed to get his wagons into a defense circle near the banks of a small stream.

Paddock could hardly have picked a worse spot to defend from an all-out attack. The wagons were at the lowest point in the valley, with high hills on three sides and the stream on the fourth. Indians occupied all the high ground, and poured a constant barrage of gunfire and arrows into the circle of wagons. Even so, the troops were relieved to reach the wagons, taking shelter inside the circle.

A breeze was blowing up the floor of the valley toward the wagons. After several minutes, the Indians set fire to the dry grass and underbrush below the soldiers' position. As the flames swept toward the soldiers, warriors followed close behind—hidden by the smoke, but firing through it in the general direction of the wagons. Fortunately for the soldiers, the wagons were on barren and sandy ground, and the flames died out twenty-five feet from the nearest wagon.

For three hours the Indians kept up a constant barrage of gunfire and arrows, but were unable to penetrate the army's defense. At dark the shooting tapered off and eventually stopped altogether, but the soldiers knew the warriors were still there. They knew, as well, that the warriors would still be there with the first light of morning.

Captain Payne, who with the death of Major Thornburgh was now the senior officer of the detachment, called for a volunteer to ride for help. Many of the men responded. Payne selected Private Sean Murphy for the task.

Wrapping his horse's hoofs in rags to muffle the sound, Murphy then sneaked out of the circle. Walking and leading his horse, he expected to be gunned down at any moment. Finally, amazed that he had safely covered a mile of trail, Murphy leaped into the saddle and raced away toward Fort Steele.

TWENTY-FIVE MILES TO THE SOUTH, N.C. Meeker had no idea that there was any violence on his reservation. At the moment the soldiers were first being attacked, Meeker was returning to his office following a brief inspection of the lodges nearest the agency buildings. Since everything appeared calm, he concluded that (in spite of the earlier threats and the distressing gunshot incident) the Indians were once again completely serene. He would not need help from the soldiers after all.

Meeker tried to telegraph Fort Steele to say that everything was now all right (his note was later found by the telegraph key), but the line was dead. A non-working telegraph line in the Colorado Rockies was not unusual; the rudimentary line, strung only a few months earlier, was subject to frequent breaks. Meeker went to his desk and jotted a brief letter to Major Thornburgh, advising him that the trouble was over and that no help was needed at the reservation.

About the middle of the afternoon, Meeker sent an aide, Wilmer Eskridge, to hand-deliver the letter to Fort Steele. He also summoned Ebenezer and Antelope (two Indians who frequently assisted at the agency offices) asking them to ride along with Eskridge on the thirty mile ride to the army base.

Eskridge and his two companions mounted their horses and rode in the direction of Fort Steele. They had gone just over a mile, and were out of both sight and hearing of the office, when the Indians turned on Eskridge. He was dragged from his horse and stabbed to death. After rolling Eskridge's body under nearby bushes, the two returned quietly to their tepees and told their chiefs what had happened.

By that time, every Indian on the reservation knew that a battle was underway at Red Canyon. The only people who did not know about the fighting were the white men (and women) at the agency offices. Meeker and his family spent the remainder of the quiet afternoon in routine fashion. After dinner, Meeker went to the agency warehouse to take inventory, assisted by a man named Bill Post. Mrs. Meeker and her daughter, Josie, washed the dishes in their home.

Mrs. Shadduck Price was doing laundry at the rear of the agency office. Mr. Price and a teenage boy named Frank Dresser were in the bed of a wagon, throwing an insulating layer of dirt onto the roof of a newly constructed building. Another white employee of the agency, Art Thompson, was on top of the roof, spreading the dirt. About a dozen other white men were also on the reservation, although their whereabouts and activities are unknown.

Suddenly, about twenty warriors burst out of the bushes and ran toward the agency's main offices, firing rifles as they came. Shadduck Price and Art Thompson were hit by the first volley of gunfire. Shadduck fell dead in the bed of the wagon, and Thompson tumbled from the roof, fatally wounded. The teenager, Fred Dresser, was hit in the leg, but managed to grab a rifle, leap from the wagon, and run for the house occupied by Mrs. Meeker.[2]

When the shooting began, Mrs. Meeker and Josie heard the noise and raced to a window, joined there by Mrs. Price. The women saw Dresser running toward their house, dragging his injured leg. Ironically, the women panicked and the wounded boy was the only one

calm enough to think things through and devise a plan
of action.

Dresser warned the women that the Indians would
soon set fire to the house. Their only hope, he said, was
to make a break for the milk house, a small sod building
about twenty-five yards away. Although bleeding profusely and barely able to put weight on his leg, Dresser
led the dash toward the adobe building.

As the three women and Dresser dived into the milk
house they heard gunfire from all sides. They assumed
that some of the other whites on the reservation were
under attack and might be offering resistance. Whether
that was the case has been forever lost to history.

Within seconds, the agency's wooden buildings were
all on fire. Thick clouds of smoke filled the little milk
house, choking the four terrified occupants and making
it impossible for them to remain inside. Dresser decided
that they stood a chance of escape if they could reach a
heavily-timbered hillside another twenty yards or so
beyond the building.

The four terrified souls crouched at the door for several seconds, waiting for a letup in rifle fire. Finally,
Dresser gave the signal and everyone started running.
The boy, still clutching the rifle, brought up the rear. He
made it only a few steps from the milk house before
being cut down by gunfire, and was probably killed outright. Another bullet struck Mrs. Meeker in the arm,
and she decided to surrender and throw herself at the
mercy of the Indians.

The death of Dresser and surrender of Mrs. Meeker
seemed to take the fight out of the other two women.
They also surrendered. Mrs. Price began sobbing and
pleading for her life, and one of the Indians promised
the women they would not be killed. It would be worse
than death, he said, for the women were to be kept alive

and shared by all the braves on the reservation. A crowd of warriors surrounding the women began arguing loudly about who had first rights to which of the captives. As was the fate of other white women captives throughout the frontier, the three were eventually passed around and ravaged by dozens of warriors.

At Red Canyon, a full moon rose and eradicated the pitch black that had permitted Murphy's escape; the encircled wagons were bathed in eerie brightness. Wounded soldiers inside the circle were begging for water, and several other soldiers volunteered to try to reach the stream and fill canteens. The water was only a dozen yards away, but as soon as the soldiers showed themselves beyond the wagons they came under withering gunfire from the Indians.

Determining that this could be their only chance to get water, the desperate soldiers devised another plan. When the volunteers were ready to dash to the river, dozens of other soldiers opened fire simultaneously at the Indians on the opposite bank. Under this covering fire, the volunteers raced to the river, filled the canteens, and then scrambled back safely.

When daylight came the following morning, a barrage of gunfire and arrows were close behind. The Indians, well concealed in the heavy underbrush, were nearly invisible to the soldiers. The troops could determine where a shot was fired only from the puff of smoke that rose into the air. By the time the soldiers saw the smoke and fired in its direction, the Indian who had fired the shot had already moved to some new location.

Captain Payne knew that his only hope was if Private Murphy had survived his wild dash for help. If more troops were not on the way, all the soldiers trapped at Red Canyon were clearly doomed. Payne's most immediate concern was that his men had only limited ammunition with them; they had not expected to be engaged in a war. Payne ordered the soldiers to conserve their ammunition as much as possible, firing only when they had a certain target.

By noon time, all of the army's horses had been shot by the Indians. Several more of the soldiers had also been hit by gunfire or arrows. About mid-morning, Lieutenant Paddock was shot in the head and died instantly. The surgeon accompanying the troops, Dr. Grimes, scurried to Paddock's side and was also shot to death.

By nightfall, the soldiers' situation had become really desperate. Thirteen men were dead, forty-three others wounded; it appeared as if most of the wounded were in critical condition and would soon die without help. Because of the death of Dr. Grimes, the wounded men received only rudimentary first aid. Captain Payne personally crawled from man to man, trying to encourage them to hang on. He repeatedly assured the men that help was on the way, although he privately feared that his statements might not be true. The night dragged by slowly, punctuated by an occasional gunshot, or the cries of pain, or the meaningless ranting of a wounded man who had become delirious from thirst or the loss of blood.

Wednesday, October 2. At the first hint of daylight the Indians resumed their all-out assault on the beleaguered troops. Then, over the roar of the firing, the soldiers could suddenly hear a different sound—an almost unbelievable one! Yet, there it was again. There was no mistaking the clear notes of a bugle sounding "Boots and Saddles," the army's call to action. Suddenly there were dozens of soldiers thundering over the hill behind the trapped men.

The first men to charge over that ridge were a troop of the Ninth Cavalry, led by Captain Thomas Dodge. The rescuers galloped down the trail in the best John Wayne tradition, firing toward the surprised Indians. As the troops inside the circle of wagons cheered lustily, Dodge and his men reached the trapped soldiers. The Utes seemed to recover quickly from their initial surprise, and now turned their full attention to the newly arrived soldiers. Dodge had only forty men with him, but he had two other things the beleaguered soldiers needed desperately: plenty of ammunition, and news that considerably more help was on the way!

When the newly-arrived soldiers were inside the circled wagons, the Indians concentrated on killing the horses of these new defenders. Within minutes they were entirely successful; every single horse was shot to death. But the arrival of the troops and the news that more help was on the way was enough for the men behind the wagons. They rallied and began pouring a deadly and constant barrage at the Ute enemy. The Indians had to pull back on three sides of the wagons, and were unable to advance throughout the remainder of the day.

While the battle continued, help was coming as fast as possible from several different locations across southern Wyoming. General Wesley Merritt raced out of Fort Russell with 200 cavalry and about fifty infantry troops, riding in wagons. At Rawlins, he was joined by 200 more infantrymen in wagons. These 450 troops pushed on throughout the night.[3]

Thursday, October 3. As the sun began to brighten the sky in the east, General Merritt's lead elements were within five miles of Red Canyon. On the trail these troops discovered the remains of a small wagon train destroyed by Indians, apparently within the past few hours. The nine men with the wagons had been killed and scalped, the wagons looted and burned, and the horses taken away by the attackers. There was no sign of the women who presumably also accompanied the wagons.

Merritt pushed on harder. Within forty-five minutes, his 450 soldiers thundered over the ridge behind the encircled wagons, and headed toward the trapped soldiers.

At first, the Utes seemed unimpressed by these newest arrivals. Instead of running, they stayed to fight. One warrior shouted that there were now simply more horses to kill and more white men to shoot.

Instead of racing directly into the poorly positioned circle of wagons, General Merritt halted his troops in a small depression a short distance away. He instructed the men to take a fifteen-minute break before joining the battle. Although exhausted from the night-long dash to Red Canyon, the soldiers were eager to join the fight. Rechecking their weapons, they prepared to assault the Indian lines. The behavior of the troops seemed to catch the attention of the Utes, and all firing came to a halt.

During the brief lull that followed, the Utes apparently began to feel differently. A white flag appeared on the ridge to one side of the wagons, then another, and another.

After several minutes, a white man and one Indian emerged from the bushes and walked down the trail toward General Merritt. The white man was a fur trader named Joseph Brady, a friend of Chief Ouray. He carried a message for the general—a letter signed by Ouray.

The Chief said that although he was far away on a deer hunt, he had learned of the battle being fought at Red Canyon. He had sent word to those Utes involved in the fighting to stop at once, and said the white soldiers were free to go whenever and wherever they wished.[4]

When Brady had delivered the message, General Merritt cautiously sent several scouts out to check the area. The scouts returned within minutes, reporting that there were now no signs of the Utes; the warriors had completely vanished from the area.

The soldiers suffered no new casualties after the first day, so the final military casualty toll at Red Canyon was thirteen dead and forty-three wounded; seven of the wounded later died. The Indian toll is unknown. Indians claimed only six of their warriors died in the fight, although that figure almost certainly was inaccurate. Whites believed at least thirty-seven warriors were killed, and claimed to find the bodies of "more than" thirty warriors around the battle site.

With the trail now open, General Merritt ordered his troops to proceed "with extreme haste" to the reservation offices. Along the way the soldiers found considerable evidence of the bloody uprising. They found the body of teamster Carl Goldstein, sprawled on the trail about six miles above the agency. Nearby, they discovered the body of another teamster—Julius Moore—tied to a tree, hacked, and mutilated.

Two miles further down the road the troops found the body of Henry Dresser (apparently the father of the teenager killed at the milk shed). The elder Dresser apparently bled to death after being shot in the stomach with an arrow.

Just one mile from the agency buildings, the troops spotted the mutilated and scalped body of messenger Eskridge.

The body of Agent N.C. Meeker had been dragged to the edge of the complex, and his skull was caved in. A later examination indicated the head injuries were probably inflicted after Meeker was already dead from gunshot wounds. A barrel stave had been jammed into Meeker's mouth, ripping open both cheeks. A logging chain was looped around his neck, and the body showed evidence of having been dragged a great distance.

Fred Dresser's body—shot in the leg and the chest—was lying at the edge of the trees forty-five yards from what had been the main agency building. George Eaton's body was nearby, partially eaten by wolves but clearly showing a bullet wound to the face.

There was no sign of the three women, and it was not immediately clear whether they had died in the fires and shooting or had been captured and taken away by the Indians.

General Merritt set up headquarters near the still-smoldering remains of the agency offices and began trying to establish control of the entire reservation. He learned within the first hour that at least three women were being held somewhere on the reservation. Merritt sent two scouts to look for the women or someone with whom to negotiate for their release. The scouts were shot and killed. Indians claimed they killed the soldiers in self defense; the troops, they said, fired first.

Although everyone on both sides was jittery, the killings of the two soldiers did not trigger a renewal of the general war. Merritt sent larger patrols out to look for someone who was willing to negotiate for the release of the women.

He soon found Utes who were willing to talk, but none who was eager (or had the ability) to order the women's release. The Indians told Merritt that the women could not be released unless all Indians on the reservation were granted total amnesty for participating in the uprising. Merritt said he had no authority to make such a promise. The negotiations were deadlocked.

For the next several days—every morning and every evening—Merritt met again with the Indian negotiators, trying to progress toward freeing the captured white women. He was unwilling to go any further in the talks until they released the captives. The Indians, in turn, were unwilling to consider releasing the women until their other demands were met. Each of the negotiating sessions ended after only a few minutes when it became clear that neither side was willing to budge.

More than two weeks dragged by, and there was no end in sight to the stalled talks. Then Merritt got help from a totally unexpected source: Chief Ouray's sister Susan, the wife of one of the lesser chiefs of the tribe. Ten years earlier, Susan was kidnapped by Cheyenne warriors, and some white men rescued her. From that time forward she considered white men to be her friends. Now she sought to repay them for saving her. Susan began talking with the lesser chiefs of the tribe, begging them to release the three captured white women and to harm them no more.

Wednesday morning, October 23. Indian negotiators finally told General Merritt that they would release the captives later that day. They asked again for amnesty and renewed their long list of demands, but Merritt stood firm: no further talks until the women were free. The morning session ended with an air of expectation.

The remainder of the morning dragged by. Merritt paced back and forth, waiting for a development. Then, shortly after noon, the Ute woman—Susan—appeared on the trail below Merritt's tent. She led three haggard looking women, who stumbled as they walked toward the soldiers. The Meeker Massacre was over!

Immediately following the release of the three women, both the army and the Bureau of Indian Affairs began an investigation of the "Meeker Massacre." Testimony was taken for nine days, but the hearings suddenly collapsed when Chief Ouray unexpectedly dropped dead, apparently the result of a heart attack.

The chief's death brought an end to the formal Meeker investigation. The white council met in private for several hours, and then announced that six Indian ringleaders would be punished. The six—Persune, Douglas, Johnson, Ahu-u-tupu-wit, Matagoras and Colorow—were sentenced to the federal prison at Leavenworth, Kansas. They all were released two years later, but during that time Matagoras had lost his mind: he was shot to death by other Utes a short time later because they feared he was going to harm someone.

Within a few months after the uprising, the BIA announced that it was closing the reservation for good. The Northern Utes were taken to a new reservation in Utah, the Southern Utes were sent to a reservation in extreme southwestern Colorado.[5]

Notes

1. Paul Wellman, *Death on the Prairie* (Lincoln/London: University of Nebraska Press, 1962), 251.
2. As was always the case in these confrontations, there is a dispute about who fired the first shot in this battle. The three white women all insisted that the shooting started as described here. Indians later claimed that the white men had somehow figured out that something was wrong, and came looking for the

Indians with weapons. The Indians claim it was the whites who fired the first shots.

3. Wayne C. Lee and Howard C. Raynesford, *Trails of the Smoky Hill* (Caldwell, Idaho: The Caxton Printers, Ltd., 1980) 197–8.

4. Other Indians later claimed that the warrior who was with Brady was Chief Ouray himself, and say he had ridden all night to personally command his warriors to stop the attack. White soldiers at Red Canyon were just as insistent that the Indian was not Ouray. Logic indicates it was not Ouray at the battle site; if he was really there one presumes he would speak for himself and not deliver a handwritten note.

5. The Meeker uprising is well documented. Except as otherwise noted, the information in this report is generally accepted as accurate and most of it is contained in *The Indians, World Book Encyclopedia, The Denver Post,* and several other publications.

*Some of the whites had been captured alive
and had undergone the most awful torture, such
as cutting out of tongues and other parts of their
persons, then burning them alive...*
HARPER'S WEEKLY, 1866

*Brothers. I have listened to a great many
talks from our Great White Father —but they
always begin and end in this: "Get a little farther; you are too near me." I have spoken.*
Creek Chief Speckled Snake, 1829

-FOUR-

The World Aflame

IGHTEEN SIXTY-FOUR was the bloodiest year of the Great Plains Indian war—but only marginally worse than 1865. The new year started with the bloody raid on Julesburg and Fort Segwick (See Chapter 1). Attacks lessened for a time after the Julesburg battle, but only because Indians rarely waged war in the winter time. When spring arrived the war resumed with vigor.

Within days after the first warm weather bathed eastern Colorado, waves of Indians were carrying out attacks against whites wherever they could find them—in towns or on isolated ranches, in covered wagons or on army bases. Unlike earlier years when the Indians occasionally managed to have up to 200 warriors in a major attack, there were now frequently between 500 and 1,000 braves—and sometimes even more—in a single raiding party.

Wednesday, July 26, 1865. Friendly Indians in central Wyoming warned the army that a large raiding party was planning to attack wagon trains and settlers moving westward along the Oregon Trail. In response to the threat the army ordered military escorts increased for all wagon trains and other travelers using the trail.

At the time the warning was issued, a large army supply train happened to already be on the trail, traveling to a remote outpost. An escort of twenty-four soldiers, led by Sergeant F.W. Custard, guarded the train. After receiving the warning, the army felt that the mere handful of soldiers assigned to the task were insufficient to assure the safety of the train.

The army was already worried that the wagon train was a prime target for Indian attackers; it was filled with food, clothing, ammunition, and other items the Indians coveted. Lieutenant Caspar Collins (the son of Colonel William Collins) and twenty-five cavalrymen of the Eleventh Ohio were dispatched to intercept the wagon train and double its protection from attack.

The morning of July 26 was extremely quiet—so quiet that it was almost eerie. Birds were not singing, and not a breath of wind stirred the prairie grass. Veteran frontiersmen who were riding with the wagon train were uneasy over the stillness; it was an ominous sign.

Shortly after 8:00 a.m., the wagon train came to a place at which the road dropped off a high ridge and plunged down into a deep valley. As it traversed the valley the road passed through a heavily wooded area. Lieutenant Collins stopped the train and surveyed the valley below. He was clearly nervous about the possibility of trouble in the valley. After contemplating the situation for some time, Collins sent Corporal James

Shrader and four other soldiers to scout ahead of the wagons and make certain the valley was safe.

The scouting party had ridden only a half mile when Indians attacked. Shrader and one enlisted man were shot to death; the other three whirled their horses around and dashed back to the wagon train.

After watching the attack below him, Lieutenant Collins ordered the wagons to circle at the top of the hill. The horses were brought inside the circle to prevent them being run off by the attackers, and the men prepared for battle.

They were not, as it turns out, prepared for the battle they got. Suddenly, Indians were approaching the wagons from virtually every direction. It was the largest raiding party recorded anywhere in the country up to that time. About 600 Cheyenne warriors and possibly as many as 1,800 Sioux—a total of 2,400 braves—began circling the wagons, firing at the soldiers with guns and arrows.

The chief directing the attack was an unusually large man. His size and bearing left no doubt in the minds of the soldiers as to who he was—it was the infamous Cheyenne Dog Soldier chief, Roman Nose.

Lieutenant Collins was among the last men still outside the protective circle of wagons. He remained exposed to danger, directing traffic and watching the three returning scouts trying desperately to reach safety. In the chaos of the attack something startled Lieutenant Collins' horse. The animal bolted out of control, and ran directly into the ranks of the attackers.

The soldiers crouching inside the circle of wagons watched in helpless horror as Collins vanished amongst the warriors. But there was no time to worry about their commander; the attack was gigantic and threatened to overrun the troops at any second.

Now under the temporary command of Sergeant F.W. Custard, the soldiers fired their repeating rifles as rapidly as they could shoot—but it was not enough. The battle raged for nearly six hours as the soldiers' ranks grew steadily thinner. The soldiers must have suspected that this was a fight they weren't going to win—or even survive.

At about two in the afternoon, several hundred warriors launched a sudden attack against one side of the wagon train. Most of the defenders raced to that side of the circle to ward off the assault.

At precisely the same moment, scores of additional braves were crawling on their bellies toward the opposite side of the circle. Probably none of the soldiers realized what was happening until the moment the warriors leaped to their feet, vaulted across the tongues of the wagons, and were virtually on top of the defenders.

No one will ever know how many Indians were killed or wounded in the battle. One supposes their casualty toll was heavy. For the soldiers, the losses were total; not a single man survived. About sixty soldiers and teamsters were killed: the lucky ones received a bullet to the head in the heat of battle.

The few who survived the last of the fighting were immediately captured and slowly tortured to death. Their bodies were later discovered, staked out and mutilated. The Indians looted and burned the wagons and drove off about 250 of the army's horses and mules.

When Lieutenant Collins' wagon train had not shown up twenty-four hours later, the army feared the worst. The Platte Bridge station dispatched a detachment of 150 men to search for them. It wasn't long before the soldiers found the battle site and the bodies of most of the men. Among the charred remains they also found unmistakable signs that many hundreds of warriors participated in the attack.

Lieutenant Collins' body, found a short distance away, was bound by telegraph wire, ". . . his hands and feet cut off, his tongue and his heart cut out."[1] Collins' mouth had also been filled with gunpowder and the powder detonated. His face was unrecognizable, but Collins was identifiable by a ring he wore. (It was never clear whether the gunpowder exploded while Collins was alive or after he was dead.)

Nearby were the bodies of six other soldiers, all lying face down. All six of them had been gored and pinned to the earth by a lance. Each had been stripped of clothing, and the bodies were horribly mutilated. They found a civilian wagon master tied to the feedbox of his wagon (slashed open with his entrails hanging out) and evidence that a fire had been built around his legs. Other wagons had been burned after their axles were pried loose and stacked onto living victims who were burned to death.

For the soldiers in the recovery party, the only silver lining to the dark cloud of the slaughter was that the scalps of the dead were found a few feet away. They knew that when Indians abandoned the scalps of their victims (after going to the trouble to cut off the scalps in the first place) it could only mean that the Indians had suffered more casualties than did the whites. Under those circumstances, the Indians felt that there was nothing to celebrate (even if the enemy was eventually overrun), and they would abandon the scalps of their victims.

A city founded near the battle site a short time later was named in honor of the lieutenant. Since Coloradans had already named a city "Collins" (Fort Collins, in honor of the lieutenant's father), the Wyomingites named their city "Casper." Apparently, no one noticed the spelling error until too late to correct it.[2]

The Wyoming confrontation that killed Caspar Collins seemed to mark the beginning of a new era in the titanic struggle between whites and Indians. From this point onward, the Indians would be better organized and more united in their resistance. Their attacks would involve many more braves than in the past, and would be better organized and executed. By then, however, it was already too late for the Indians to win a military victory. With the Civil War over, tens of thousands of whites were flocking to the West. Many of these newcomers were battle-hardened war veterans, entirely capable of defending themselves. The battles between whites and Indians would continue for another thirteen years or so, but the end was already in sight.

For now, though, the war would go on. Word of the Wyoming disaster had barely reached "civilized" America when the next great confrontation occurred.

A fifty-man railroad survey party, was working its way across South Dakota—territory now occupied by Santees and other Sioux. Many of the warriors in this region had fled Minnesota after the 1862 uprising there, and were especially bitter toward whites. Accompanying the surveying party was Colonel James Sawyer and a military escort of 120 soldiers and Pawnee Indian scouts. They were soon joined by a small pioneer wagon train headed for Denver. The train consisted of eight wagons with thirty-two men, women, and children.

Friday, August 25. One soldier, scouting slightly ahead of the wagon train and work party, failed to return at noon as scheduled. Other soldiers were sent out to locate him, and found his body sprawled on the road a short distance ahead. The dead soldier had twelve arrows sticking from his body; he had also been scalped and mutilated.

Colonel Sawyer put his men on full alert, and sent several soldiers to bury the victim. They had hardly begun the task, however, when hundreds of northern Cheyenne and Sioux attacked. Colonel Sawyers ordered his men to circle the wagons. Inside the ring of wagons were the 120 soldiers, fifty surveyors and thirty-two civilians: 202 persons in total.

Within seconds, an all-out battle was raging with the 200 whites against as many as 600 warriors. As usual, the Indians had mostly single-shot rifles or more primitive weapons: a factor which somewhat negated their numerical superiority.

However, what the Indians lacked in weaponry, they made up for in leadership and cunning. The attackers were under the direction of Cheyenne Chief Dull Knife and Sioux Chief Red Cloud, two of the most respected and shrewd warriors on the plain.

The attack lasted two full days. The Indians rode constantly around, or launched quick hit-run strikes during the daylight hours. At night their snipers harassed the whites, making it nearly impossible to sleep or to take care of the necessities of life.

For thirty-six straight hours, the Indian attack continued unabated—with neither side making headway or retreating. At last it became apparent to the attackers that they could not overwhelm the wagon train and its defenders. Being well supplied with both food and ammunition, the travelers and soldiers appeared ready to fight it out indefinitely. The Indians were clearly suffering far heavier casualties than the whites. Unwilling to simply ride away, yet unable to penetrate the wagon train's defenses, the Indians decided to talk. Shortly

before dark on the second afternoon, the Indians signaled that they wanted to council.

Colonel Sawyer viewed the white flag skeptically,
then cautiously stepped outside the encircled wagons. In
the "neutral" zone a few feet away, he met with two
Indian representatives—Charles and George Bent.
(This was the first time the Bent brothers were known
to be operating so far away from their home base in
southeastern Colorado.) Their presence indicated that
this attack was the work of Southern Cheyennes, who
normally operated in western Kansas and eastern
Colorado.

The Bents said the Indians were willing to stop
attacking the wagon train if given ample supplies of
tobacco, coffee, sugar, flour, and meat. Colonel Sawyer
agreed to the demands, and handed over the supplies.
The Indians quickly disappeared into the gathering
darkness.

The whites breathed a collective sigh of relief: an
assuagement that turned out to be extremely premature. Two mornings later the same group of Indians
reappeared. They once again attacked Sawyer's wagon
train. Once again, the colonel and numerous others
identified George and Charles Bent among the attackers. This latest assault by the Bent brothers came in
spite of their personal promises, just hours earlier, to
leave the wagon train alone.

As before, Sawyer circled the wagons and fought
effectively, and the Indians were again unable to overwhelm the defenders. After eight hours and more heavy
losses, the warriors withdrew for a second time.

The whites posted guards and spent a restless night
in their defensive circle. In the morning, the colonel sent
out scouts who soon reported no sign of the Bent boys or
their warrior companions. The weary travelers resumed

their journey, praying that the trouble was finally over—but this was not to be the case.

Four days later, the same band was back for a third time, striking just as the wagon train reached the Tongue River in the southeastern corner of Montana. Besides the Cheyennes and Sioux, a number of Arapahos were now visible among the attackers. The latter braves were led by Black Bear, one of those chiefs who several weeks earlier had pledged "peace forever" at a meeting with the BIA. And once again, the Bent brothers were recognized among the attackers!

The latest attack lasted for a full day. When the sun began to set, the Indians signaled that they wanted to talk. They were again willing to break off the attack—for a price. This time, however, the terms were different.

The Indians offered to let the wagon train reach its destination safely if, once the trip was completed, Colonel Sawyer would negotiate the return of some horses captured earlier by white soldiers. The Indians readily admitted to being desperately short of horses. Sawyer agreed to the latest terms, and three Arapaho warriors were assigned to ride with the wagon train as sort of volunteer hostages, to assure peace until the end of the trail was reached. This time the wagon train completed its trip with no further problem.

Unfortunately, the talks that followed ended in a stalemate. When no agreement could be reached over the horses, the talks were finally broken off by the Indians, who vowed that the white man would pay dearly for his inability to come to terms.[3]

Monday, September 4, 1865. Possibly as a result of the failure of those horse negotiations in Montana, Indians launched a series of new attacks throughout the Dakotas. Shortly after noon on the fourth, an estimated

600 Cheyenne Dog Soldiers attacked two small army detachments near modern-day Rapid City, South Dakota.

One detachment of soldiers was quickly cut off and overrun by the Indians. Of the twenty-two soldiers in the group, twenty-one were killed, scalped, and mutilated.

Captain E. S. Rowland of the Second Missouri Light Artillery managed to avoid capture by faking a wound, collapsing to the ground, and rolling out of sight under the bushes. He was rescued hours later, after a thirty-six-man military detachment fought off another attack a short distance away, and then raced to see if they could help Rowland's men.

The embattled soldiers picked up Rowland and quickly headed toward their fort—with hundreds of Indians following close behind. On September 5, the Indians struck the soldiers again, but were quickly repulsed for a second time. That night, the survivors reached the safety of the fort and the Indians vanished.

Wednesday, September 6, 1865. One hundred twenty-five soldiers of the Seventh Cavalry out of Fort Dodge, South Dakota, chanced upon a wagon train being attacked by about 150 Indians. The attack had been underway for four long, desperate days when the troops appeared.

The soldiers rapidly drove off the Indians and rescued the wagon train. Two white men were killed in the fight. The Indians managed to grab more than fifty horses before escaping. Apparently, they deliberately shot and killed or wounded many other horses and mules before riding away.

The rescue was a tenuous one, however; both the troops and the wagon train survivors were out of food. In addition, the army's horses had been pushed to the limit of endurance, and there was a serious question as to how much longer the animals could survive. Nonetheless, everyone was safe for the moment, and an air of near jubilation settled upon them.

Soon the wagon train was again moving down the trail toward Denver. Five and a half miles further along, they stumbled onto the charred remains of ten more wagons. Nothing was found of the fifteen men who had been with these wagons; presumably, they were all killed.[4]

Thursday, September 7, Central Nebraska. About 1,000 Sioux and Cheyenne warriors attacked the same beleaguered wagon train and its 125–man military escort for the second time. The wagons were again circled and the soldiers opened fire on the attackers. This time, the Indians were led by Chief Roman Nose, operating further north than he had ever before been seen.

Apparently to display his courage and his invulnerability to the white man, Roman Nose broke from the ranks of the attackers and raced his horse directly toward the soldiers' line. Approaching within fifteen yards of the wagons, Roman Nose turned and galloped completely around the circle. His horse was blasted from under him, but Roman Nose appeared unhurt. Rising to his feet, he strolled casually back to the Indian lines— unscratched!

Other Indians resumed racing around the circled wagons, firing at the whites—and the soldiers inside the circle were beginning to get desperate. Because of the two previous battles with the Indians and the several weeks they had already spent on the trail, they were desperately short of both food and ammunition. Worse yet, their horses had been pushed so hard with so little food and water that the animals were near exhaustion.

That night, the weather also turned against the soldiers when a cold front brought a severe sleet storm. By morning, virtually every white man's horse was dead; weakened by hunger and thirst, they froze to death in the storm. It appeared as if the end might be near for the besieged whites.

The storm finally ended in the pre-dawn hours, and the new day dawned clear and bitterly cold. The soldiers and the pioneers with the wagon train glumly dug in and waited to be overrun by the Indians. Instead, the Indians unexpectedly broke off their attack and fled from the battle field.

As the soldiers rose to their feet, watching from behind various barricades in disbelief, the last of the Indians vanished from site. Presently, General Connor and a 400-man relief column of cavalry rode into view over a nearby hill. Their chance appearance saved the beleaguered travelers and soldiers from certain death.

So it went, day after day, from Colorado to the Dakotas and from Montana to Arizona.

Monday, October 2, 1865. Approximately thirty Indians, believed to be Cheyennes, attacked a Butterfield Overland Dispatch stage coach near Monument Station in extreme western Kansas (262 miles east of Denver). After a brief gun battle, the whites fled on foot while the Indians rifled then burned the stagecoach. During this brief interlude the Indians uncharacteristically lost track of the escaping whites.

Fortunately for the whites, they chose to hide in a ditch rather than run on to Monument Station, which was only a half mile away. After destroying the stage coach, the Indians rode to the station looking for the escaped whites and burned the station to the ground.[5]

From that moment on, the Butterfield route—which passed through the center of the Smoky Hill country so precious to the Indians—was under constant attack.

On November 19, Indian warriors struck the Downers Station. Three whites were killed, a stagecoach burned, and eighteen horses stolen.

On November 22, Indians attacked a Butterfield stagecoach as it was leaving the Chalk Bluffs Station, twelve miles east of Monument, Colorado. The stagecoach had an eight-man military escort, however, and managed to drive off the Indians without losses.

The Great Plains were aflame with this bloody war in which the combatants observed no rules. Only the toughest and fastest survived.

While the lonely frontiersmen struggled to survive the horror, the rest of the world watched in horrified fascination—and the newspapers of the day were quick to cash in on the interest.

As a reporter for *Harper's Weekly* (a sort of nineteenth century supermarket tabloid), Theodore Davis was sent to the front. He soon was writing about making a dangerous stagecoach trip to Denver.

Davis said that his stage was almost constantly harassed by Indians and said that during the trip the bodies of "several" murdered whites were discovered along the trail. And Davis wrote,

> . . . some of [the whites] had been captured alive and had undergone the most awful torture, such as cutting out of tongues and other parts of their persons, then burning them alive.[6]

One afternoon Davis's stagecoach stopped to drive away some coyotes which were devouring two murdered white men. The victims were buried and the trip continued—but a short distance further along they found three more "horribly mutilated" bodies.

Davis wrote, "...former Confederate soldier and now Indian warrior Charles Bent was reported to have participated in many of the worst attacks." On occasion some would survive an attack—and many later swore that Charles led the onslaught and personally committed the most outrageous acts of torture on the captives.

Davis reported on an 1865 event involving Charles Bent in an article for the July 7, 1867, issue of *Harper's Weekly:*

The coach had arrived at Downers Station about two o'clock in the afternoon [with] one passenger, the messenger, and the driver being the occupants. At the station they found two stock-tenders, the carpenters, and a Negro blacksmith.

The mules were unharnessed and turned loose, when a band of mounted Indians charged, whooping among them; the men retreated to the cave, or "adobe" as they designate it. Indians came from all directions and completely surrounded the adobe, the occupants of which were prepared to fight.

An Indian will never fight until he has obtained every possible advantage, then he makes a rush. A half-breed son of Bill Bent [Charles Bent]...was one of the leaders of the Indians; being able to speak English, he managed to call to the occupants of the adobe that he wanted to talk. This was attested to. He came up and inquired whether the treaty [of Fort Wise] had been signed. He was informed that it had been, to which he replied, "All right!"

[The Indians] would have peace if the occupants of the adobe would come out and shake hands, leaving their [weapons] behind them, and the Indians would do likewise. The men came out and a general hand-shaking followed. The Indian is great at this; he will shake your hand all day and at nightfall he will take your scalp. It is simply a way he has of expressing his brotherly sentiments toward the white man.

The Indians still further deceived the party by driving up the mules that had earlier been stampeded by them, telling the messenger that the coach should proceed without molestation. Such evidence of friendship disarmed the party of any suspicion of hostility, though the Indians were in full paint and without squaws.

In a moment, all was changed. The Indians turned upon the party—bows, arrows, and revolvers were produced, and a desperate attack at once inaugurated. The messenger, Fred Merwin, a very gallant young man, was killed instantly; others of the party were wounded, and the two stock-tenders captured. Mr. Perine, the passenger, the driver, carpenters and blacksmith ran for the neighboring bluffs, which they succeeded in reaching. Taking possession of a buffalo wallow, they fought until night-fall, when the Indians withdrew and they made good their escape.

Mr. Perine gives an interesting account of the fight from the wallow; "They formed a circle about us, riding dexterously and rapidly; occasionally one more bold than the rest would come within range of our revolvers, but he was careful to keep his body on the side of the pony away from us. Arrows came from all directions; a rifle or revolver bullet would whistle past us or strike the earth near. It was evidently their purpose to exhaust our ammunition, when they would be able to take us alive. Of this fact we were painfully aware and only fired at them when we were sure of a good shot. This kept them at a distance. The Negro blacksmith was armed with a Ballard rifle, with which he was a capital shot. He bravely exposed himself to obtain a shot, and came near losing his life by doing so. A bullet struck him in the head, when he fell, as we supposed, dead. I took his rifle, rolled the body up to the edge of the wallow to serve as a breastwork to shoot from, and commenced to fire. I had made several shots in this way, and had the rifle across his neck with a dead aim on an Indian when the darky came to and remarked, 'What you doin dar, white man?', thus discovering to us that he was anything other than a [goner]. He had been [temporarily] deprived of speech and motion by the shot, but was fully aware of what was going on around him. He was not disposed to regard the use of his body as a breastwork as altogether a pleasing performance.

"While we were fighting from the wallow, we could plainly see the Indians that still remained about the adobe, at work torturing the stockherders that they had succeeded in capturing alive. One poor fellow they staked to the ground, cut out his tongue, substituting another part of his body in its place. Then they built a fire on his body. The agonized screams of the man were almost unendurable; about him were the Indians dancing and yelling like demons.

"The other stock-herder was shoved up to look at the barbarous scene, the victim of which he was soon to be, but they reserved him until night fall, evidently hoping that we might be added to the number of their victims.

"There could not have been less than 150 Indians in the entire party—that is, those who were about us and those near the adobe. [Charles] Bent had told us that Fast Bear, a Cheyenne Chief, had commanded but Bent is worse than any Indian for he knows better. Had there been a possible chance to rescue the stock-herders, we should have attempted it. When darkness came, the Indians withdrew, and as soon as we were convinced of the fact, we followed their example, going, it is unnecessary to remark, in the other direction."[7]

That night the survivors walked twenty-four miles to the Ruthden relay station to get help. There, a messenger was sent on horseback to summon soldiers. While the messenger was gone the others barricaded themselves in the building, expecting to be attacked at any time.

About forty soldiers arrived the following midnight, and accompanied the survivors back to safety the following day. En route they found that the Chalk Bluffs relay station had been burned to the ground. There was no sign of several whites who should have been at the station when the attack occurred.

The troops rode on and reached Downer's station about mid-afternoon and found nothing left of it; it had been completely burned to the ground. The bodies of all whites killed by the Indians were gone. Curiously, the body of one Indian was found nearby, a Cheyenne arrow protruding from his head.

Notes

1. Donald Berthrong, *The Southern Cheyennes* (Norman: University of Oklahoma Press, 1963), 249.

2. Confirmed by the Casper, Wyoming, Chamber of Commerce, in a telephone conversation with the author on September 13, 1993.

3. Based on the account in: Maurice Matloff, ed., *American Military History* (Washington, DC: Office of the Chief of Military History, United States Army, 1969), 300–307.

4. Floyd B. Streeter, *Prairie Trails & Cow Towns* (Greenwich, Connecticut: Devin, 1963), 20–22.

5. Wayne C. Lee and Howard C. Raynesford, *Trails of the Smoky Hill* (Caldwell, ID: The Caxton Printers, Ltd., 1980), 75.

6. *Harper's Weekly,* April 21, 1866, 4–5.

7. *Trails of the Smoky Hill*, 80–82.

There were many men of valor among the valorous Cheyennes, including such leaders of exalted rank as Little Wolf and White Antelope. But none, surely, was more famous at the time to the ordinary public—both Cheyenne and American—than a hook-nosed, six-foot, three-inch warrior named Bat; the Americans called him Roman Nose. Roman Nose was famous because he was invulnerable in battle. He had a magic headdress made for him by Ice, the medicine man, and while he wore it bullets and arrows could not touch him. He proved this time after time, riding at a leisurely lope up and down in front of the enemy while all the enemy shot at him and missed.

THE AMERICAN HERITAGE BOOK OF INDIANS

Tall Bull was the first leader of the Dog Soldiers—but Roman Nose was the best known and bloodiest leader.

Donald Berthrong,
DEATH ON THE PRAIRIE

–FIVE–

The Battle of Beecher Island

N O WHITE MAN CAME WEST without hearing of a giant Cheyenne warrior called "Roman Nose." According to legend, he was the bravest of all Cheyenne warriors—and the toughest! He had a great reputation among his own people who considered him the champion of Indian rights. He was the one man the Cheyennes could count on to never submit to white authority.

Roman Nose was more than simply another Cheyenne chief. He was the leader of the Dog Soldiers, the most aggressive of the Great Plains Indians. Roman Nose hated whites, and used his cunning, skill, and leadership capabilities to become the most feared Indian on the frontier.

From the earliest days, Roman Nose stood out among the Indians. He was bigger, faster, and stronger than any of the other children. At twelve years of age, he had overwhelmed all the other boys of his tribe in hand-to-hand combat (part of the rite of passage to maturity).

He didn't just defeat the other boys: he battered them senseless, and emerged as the undisputed leader of the younger generation. He carried the same strength into manhood.

As a grown warrior Roman Nose was an imposing sight. In an era when most men were between 5'8" and 5'11", he towered well over six feet tall; some descriptions place him at 6'4". He was muscular, and is said to have weighed well over 200 pounds.

White men who had seen him claimed that Roman Nose was always angry, and that no one had ever seen him smile. Even if that description was merely imagination, it added to the chief's reputation as the most fierce warrior of the era.

The first recorded meeting between white leaders and Roman Nose took place on Monday, November 9, 1863. Colorado Governor John Evans had traveled to Fort Lyon, an army base near the Kansas state line, to try to negotiate a new peace treaty with Indians. Roman Nose appeared as one of the many Cheyenne chiefs who attended the conference. Except for his striking physique there was little at first to distinguish him from any of the other leaders.

The peace talks went poorly from the beginning. Governor Evans said he found the Indians to be "surly and uncooperative." After the talks Evans reported that Roman Nose professed personal admiration for whites, but candidly admitted (or threatened) that what he called "other Cheyennes, Sioux, and Kiowas" were preparing to wage a war against the white man. As the veiled threats continued, Governor Evans began to consider this giant warrior a dangerous foe, but one that would have to be reckoned with.

As the talks progressed, Roman Nose's comments became more and more aggressive—and offensive—to

Governor Evans. At last the chief told Evans that he would never personally sign or accept the terms of any settlement. Furthermore, Roman Nose said he would never permit his warriors to live on a reservation, nor would he ever again talk to the white man unless such meetings took place in his tribal village. With that, the big chief mounted his horse and rode away.

In June of 1864, six months after the fruitless Fort Lyon meeting, Indians murdered a ranch family of four near Elizabeth, Colorado. The dead were Ward Hungate, his wife, and two infant daughters. The three females had been horribly tortured before their deaths, and the mother had apparently been repeatedly raped. The word among Plains Indians was that Roman Nose and three of his warriors were responsible for the rape and murders.

Whether Roman Nose actually was a participant in the Hungate killings was never known for certain. However, the mere rumor of his involvement, coupled with Governor Evans' earlier observations, convinced the world of Roman Nose's guilt. From that moment on, Roman Nose was the most feared, most hated, and most wanted Indian in the West.

Later that year, in October of 1864, Roman Nose led a large band of Indians in attacking a wagon train and their 150–soldier escort crossing northern Colorado. By circling their wagons, the travelers were able to hold the Indians at bay, although a fierce battle raged for hours.

In the midst of the stalemate, Roman Nose broke from the ranks of attackers and charged his horse directly toward the encircled wagons. Riding to within fifteen yards of the train, Roman Nose then turned and galloped completely around the circle. Every soldier fired at Roman Nose; they blasted his horse from beneath him, but the warrior was unhurt. Rising to his feet, he strolled casually back to the Indian lines—unscratched! The battle ended when more than 400 additional soldiers chanced upon the battle and drove the Indians away. (A nearly identical incident occurred in central Nebraska; see previous chapter.)

In November of 1864, erroneous reports said Roman Nose was killed when troops of the Third Colorado wiped out a Cheyenne village at Sand Creek. Many newspapers reported his death there, only to retract the story when the chief was positively identified in several subsequent raids.

In mid-June of 1865, Roman Nose had another face to face confrontation with US soldiers in northeastern Colorado. The soldiers, thinking stolen horses were being held in Roman Nose's village, rode out to look for the animals. Roman Nose came to meet the white men, and delayed them while the entire village—men, women, children, and horses—vanished. By the time the soldiers realized what had happened, it was too late.

The furious soldiers threatened to kill Roman Nose. The wily chief said that he had no idea his people were going to leave, and offered to go after them to bring them back for questioning. However, he said, they had taken all the horses and he could not catch them on foot. Incredibly, the soldiers loaned Roman Nose a horse—and never saw the animal or the chief again!

One of the senior army officers who witnessed this confrontation was George Armstrong Custer. He volunteered to go after Roman Nose the following morning. As quickly as the offer was accepted, the dashing young general was in hot pursuit. Custer and his men trailed Roman Nose and the Cheyennes for three days. Along the trail they found numerous burned ranches, cut fences, and evidence that many horses and cattle had been stolen by the retreating Indians.

The second morning of the chase, Custer found the Lookout Relay Station burned to the ground. Bodies of three white men were tied to a corral; all had been horribly burned, then slashed open and their intestines pulled out. Evidence at the scene suggested the mutilations occurred while the men were still alive. General Custer reported that although he could not be certain that Roman Nose and his people carried out the attack, their trail led directly past the station.

June 26. At dawn, while Custer and his men searched the country seventy-five miles away, approximately 300 Cheyenne warriors struck the Pond Creek stagecoach relay station near Fort Wallace. The Indians first tried to steal the horses from the corral, but the animals panicked and bolted. The stampeded horses, thundering past the relay station, alerted the men inside to the attack.

Although Roman Nose was reputedly leading this large group of Indians, the warriors were not able to overwhelm the station. By coincidence, about thirty-five soldiers were inside the main building when the attack began, and they put up a spirited, unexpected defense.

Fortuitously, Company G of the Seventh US Cavalry, under the command of Captain William Barnitz, was less than a half mile away when the battle was joined. As the bugler sounded the charge, another fifty soldiers thundered over the hill toward the melee. The warriors hastily evacuated the area.

The chase was a short one. Reaching the top of a ridge about two miles from the station, the Indian leader (whom the whites say was Roman Nose) signaled for his warriors to turn and meet the army. Captain

Barnitz did not slow down, but led a charge directly into the midst of the warriors. In seconds, the troops and warriors were locked in hand–to–hand combat.

The Indian warrior (whom the whites identified as Roman Nose) knocked a soldier from his horse and prepared to run him through with a spear. At that moment, another soldier placed the muzzle of his rifle against the big Indian's chest and pulled the trigger. The huge warrior was knocked backward from his horse, but incredibly managed to rise again to his feet. Another Indian nearby yanked the big warrior onto a horse and rode away with him. Soldiers who said the man was Roman Nose, also reported that the wound "definitely" was fatal.

Those battlefield reports caused many newspapers to report (for a second time) that Roman Nose had died in battle. Once again, the reports proved to be erroneous. Either the wounded man was not Roman Nose, or Roman Nose made a miraculous recovery.

Eventually, surviving Indians fled from the Pond Creek battle and escaped. Three days later, a band of Indians attacked the supply train that was trying to keep up with General Custer. According to witnesses, Roman Nose led the attack. The troops watched as the Indian leader's horse was shot from under him during the raging battle, but he got up and walked away.

All of these stories about the invincibility of Roman Nose added to the fame of the Cheyenne Dog Soldier Chief. Unquestionably, he was the most famous—and most hated—of the frontier Indians. Roman Nose symbolized everything the white man hated about the Indian; the elimination of this one warrior became the focal point of efforts to bring peace to the Great Plains. It was as if the outcome of a generation of war hinged on killing this one man.

IN DECEMBER OF 1867—at the height of Roman Nose's fame—the military command for the frontier region underwent another shake-up. Such reorganizations were not unusual; the official army history says:

There were frequent modifications of organization, rearrangements of boundaries, and transfers of troops and posts to meet changing conditions. Development of a basic defense system in the trans–Mississippi West had followed the course of the empire; territorial acquisition and exploration succeeded by emigration and settlement brought the whites increasingly into collision with the Indians and progressively raised the need for military posts along the transcontinental trails and in settled areas.[1]

Under the latest realignment, General William Sherman was given command of the Division of the Missouri. His old Civil War friend, Philip Sheridan, became military commander of the increasingly urgent effort to control hostile Indians on the western frontier. Now that the Civil War was over, the army could concentrate its efforts on solving the trouble in the West.

Unfortunately, military reorganization did not necessarily bring seasoned or skillful Indian fighters to the frontier. Most Indian fighters were close to being downright inept. Many were without either the experience or the credentials to effectively lead a campaign against such an enemy: highly mobile, extremely skillful, cunning in battle, and absolutely determined to win. The army history says:

Of the officers who moved to the forefront of the Army in the Indian wars, few had frontier and

Indian experience. At the top levels at the outset,
Ulysses Grant as a captain had had only a taste of
the loneliness of the frontier outpost. Western duty
was unknown to Sherman, and while Sheridan had
served about five years in the Northwest as a junior
officer, neither [of his subordinates] Nelson A. Miles
nor Oliver Otis Howard knew frontier service of any
kind. Wesley Merritt, George Armstrong Custer,
and Ranald S. Mackenzie all graduated from West
Point [straight] into the Civil War, and John Gibbon
had only minor involvement in the Seminole War
and some garrison duty in the West. Alfred Sully,
also a veteran of the Seminole War and an active
campaigner against the Sioux during Civil War
years, fell into obscurity [after the Civil War], while
Philip St. George Cooke was overtaken by age, and
Edward R.S. Canby's experience was lost prematurely through his death at Indian hands. George
Crook almost alone among the Army leaders at the
upper levels of the Indian wars had pre-Civil War
frontier experience, dating from 1852, that he could
bring back to the West in 1866.[2]

Coincidental to Sherman's appointment as the chief
US Indian fighter were the first large-scale deliveries of
the new, seven-shot breech-loading Spencer Repeating
Rifles to the US Army. Possession of these superior
weapons put General Sheridan in a position of enormous fire-power superiority over his Indian foes, some of
whom still fought with lances or bows and arrows. This
tremendous technical advantage came just in time: the
army's personnel were being dramatically reduced in
the wake of the Civil War, and the Indians were becoming better and better at fighting the soldiers. For various
logistical reasons, however, the army was actually

slightly larger now than it had been a year earlier, in spite of the ordered cutbacks. Nonetheless, it was still desperately short of men.

Under the new command alignment, General Sheridan had direct responsibility for conducting the Indian campaign. He also had the politically more important assignment of making certain the railroads pushed through to the West Coast; these were vitally important to the big money interests in the East and Midwest. Because railroad work parties and survey crews passed through the heart of Indian hunting territory, and since the railroads had become a favorite target of hostile Indians, this assignment required about sixty percent of the army's available manpower.

As a result of sending so many troops to railroad duty, General Sheridan had only about 800 men left to fight the Indians—or, as stated in a more positive manner by the military, to protect the settlers. That meant all of the settlers, spread out over thousands of square miles of rugged territory in Kansas, Colorado, Nebraska, and Wyoming had to be protected by 800 soldiers!

General Sheridan thought that under the circumstances the most effective preventive method he could employ was to launch a bold and hard strike against known hostile Indians. Such strikes, he said, would send the Indians a strong statement that no more raids would be tolerated. Furthermore, Sheridan felt the new Spencer repeating rifles were exactly what he needed to make such a strike against the Dog Soldiers and other militant warriors of the Great Plains.

Nevertheless, both Sheridan and Sherman recognized that there were now powerful people in Washington who would oppose such an attack—men like Wisconsin Senator James Doolittle and those at the Bureau of Indian Affairs. (Doolittle was one of the most outspoken men in Washington about what he considered white man's bad treatment of Indians.) As a result of these political   considerations, Sheridan decided it would be best if his planned "punitive campaign" against the Indians was carried out by civilians, rather than by the military.

Thus, in the late spring months of 1868, Sheridan contacted an old friend and fellow Civil War veteran, Major George Forsythe. An excellent commander and an outstanding marksman, Forsythe was already a veteran of the Indian wars. Sheridan could think of no one he would rather have in charge of such an important expedition. To his delight, Major Forsythe readily agreed to organize a semi-secret unit of volunteers. They would be charged with finding—and striking a telling blow against—the most hostile of the Indians: the Dog Soldiers of Chief Roman Nose. The specific orders from General Sherman, passed down through General Sheridan, were to, "employ fifty first-class hardy frontiersmen, to be used as scouts against the hostile Indians, to be commanded by yourself."[3]

Working quietly, Forsythe—who preferred being called major even though he was now breveted to the rank of colonel and then officially placed on leave of absence—began contacting soldiers, army scouts, and reliable frontiersmen. He selected only those men who were excellent riflemen, and who had demonstrated intelligence, bravery, and resourcefulness.

In each case, Forsythe had to ask the soldiers chosen for the unit to resign from the army to accept a special assignment. When the nature of the "special assignment" was quietly explained, not a single man turned him down. That was entirely understandable; all of the soldiers recruited for the special Indian hunting unit had fought the Indians in the past. Furthermore, all had suffered personal losses in those battles. Most of the soldiers had lost family members in Indian attacks. These were men eager for the chance at revenge.

Within a few weeks, Forsythe had gathered fifty of the best shots and toughest men on the frontier. He referred to these recruits as "scouts," although there was little effort to convince the world that these men were really civilians. Each man recruited from the military retained the title of his military rank. Everyone was promised one dollar a day for his services, and an additional thirty-five cents a day for using his own horse.[4]

Every scout was issued one of the new Spencer repeating rifles and 140 rounds of ammunition for it. In addition, each received a Colt revolver and thirty rounds of ammunition for it. Of the seven pack mules that would accompany the scouts, four were carrying nothing but ammunition. Altogether, a total of 40,000 rounds of ammunition were available for the men in the unit; a staggering 800 rounds per man!

The remaining three pack mules carried medical supplies, tents, spare clothing, and other necessary items. Additionally, the men carried seven days worth of cooked rations in their haversacks.[5]

Forsythe named rising young Lieutenant Frederick W. Beecher as his second in command. He appointed Dr. Dewain Moores as his surgeon. One Pawnee Indian was chosen as a guide for the scouts. That brought the total to about fifty—forty soldiers, assorted officers, Pawnee scouts, and a few civilians.

Among the civilians recruited for the scout unit was a young Jewish immigrant named Sigmund Schlesinger. Not quite nineteen, Schlesinger had never been in the army. The young man had occasionally worked for the army as a messenger, delivering letters from Fort Hays, Kansas, to various other nearby forts. He also owned and operated a small distillery where he made beer, which he sold to the soldiers. "Sig" was well known, well liked, and entirely trusted by every soldier he met, among whom was General George Custer. As a friend of "Wild Bill" Hickok, Schlesinger had also become an excellent rifle shot.

Saturday, August 29, 1868. Forsythe, his guides, and his fifty scouts departed Fort Hayes, Kansas, to begin searching for the Cheyenne Dog Soldiers and Chief Roman Nose. The scouts pushed northward to Fort Wallace without encountering the Cheyennes. At Wallace the veteran Indian guide, Sharp Grover, (now sufficiently recovered from being shot in the back by Indians a year earlier) joined the group as chief guide. The troops then resumed their long ride across the prairie.

Tuesday, September 8. After eleven days on the trail without contacting hostile Indians, Forsythe's luck finally changed. A messenger caught up with the scouts early one afternoon, bringing the news they wanted so badly to hear.

The scouts had paused for a midday meal, when a rider galloped into camp. The visitor said that a Mexican wagon train had been attacked by a sizable band of Dog Soldiers on the Santa Fe Trail, near the Colorado–Kansas border. Two teamsters were killed and scalped, the wagons burned, and the mules driven off by the attackers. Evidence at the scene left no doubt that the assailants were Dog Soldiers. The attack site was only twenty-five miles from Forsythe's present location, and the assault had occurred only hours earlier. The scouts set out at once, and arrived on the scene shortly before dinner time the same evening.

The following morning, Forsythe's scouts picked up the raiding party's trail, and set out quickly in pursuit. Pushing their horses to the limit, the scouts covered considerable ground. By early afternoon, they spied a sizable band of warriors in the distance. The watchful Indians, however, spotted Forsythe's band almost as soon as the scouts detected them.

As was their custom when being pursued, the warriors immediately began splitting into smaller groups—hoping to confuse the scouts. Forsythe, a veteran of this tactic, picked one group and stayed on its trail.

Now that they knew they were being followed, the Indians moved more hastily. Because Forsythe's horses were already tired, he could not catch the warriors, but managed to keep close behind them. Frequently he was able to spot his foe only a short distance ahead. When darkness came, the Indians were still safely ahead of the scouts. As the scouts moved out the following morning, the Indians moved simultaneously, maintaining their distance.

For three days the scouts doggedly trailed the raiding party. Their diligence was finally rewarded when several other bands of Indians (those who had earlier split off, and who assumed Forsythe had given up by now) began to rejoin those Forsythe was trailing.

On the afternoon of the third day it appeared that several hundred Indians were again in the main group, about two miles ahead of the scouts. The Indians no longer made any effort to shake off their pursuers or to conceal their movements. Forsythe concluded that they were now simply trying to lead him to a suitable battle-field. Anticipation grew by the hour among the scouts, who were eager for a fight.

At mid-afternoon of the third day, the Indians suddenly began to move faster. Major Forsythe and his scouts were hard pressed to keep pace. The Major wasn't quite sure what the change implied.

Forsythe, although intent on picking a fight with the Dog Soldiers, was in no particular hurry for it to begin. He hoped the warriors were leading him to their main camp, for that would increase the likelihood of Roman Nose participating in the battle.

Eventually, the Indians turned off the main trail (paralleling the Republican River in extreme western Kansas) and began moving toward the southwest along the Arikaree River. Presently, Forsythe's Indian guides expressed alarm because the trail indicated that from 600, to possibly a thousand Indians were just ahead of them. Their observations led them to believe that all of the Indians in the group were warriors.

Forsythe, reminding his men that they had come to fight, said that their main goal was to wipe out the Dog Soldiers. Cautioning the scouts to be ready for ambush, he nonetheless encouraged them to "look forward" to the coming battle. It would be their opportunity, he said, to put an end to Roman Nose's reign of terror.

The scouts pushed onward.

Wednesday, September 16. The Indians began posting lookouts on hills to keep track of Forsythe's company of pursuit. As the lookouts became more numerous the scouts speculated the main Dog Soldier village must be in the near distance. At sundown Wednesday, four days after the chase began, Forsythe ordered his men to pitch camp on the south bank of the Arikaree River. Their campsite was in a small valley, surrounded on three sides by fair-sized hills.

Although the setting appeared peaceful enough, Forsythe knew that a showdown was near. Fearing an attempt by the Indians to stampede their horses,

Forsythe ordered his men to hobble their mounts, then tie the animals to stakes driven into the soft ground: making a stampede difficult, if not impossible.

At this location—just inside Colorado and about seventeen miles south of the modern-day community of Wray—the Arikaree River bed was extremely shallow. The sandy river bottom was about 140 yards wide. The river rarely had much water in it except during the spring months; this time of year most of the stream bed was sandy and dry.

Only in the middle of the river bed did a shallow stream of water continue to run—albeit, sluggishly— even at this time of the year. That little stream surrounded a small island covered by cottonwood trees and underbrush. Forsythe made a mental note that the island might be the most defensible spot around.

September 17, sunrise. Several hundred Indians struck with a fury in the first light of morning. Warriors first tried to stampede Forsythe's horses and leave the white men on foot. Because of the precautions taken the night before, however, the Indians managed to take only two horses and two mules.[6] Scouts aroused from their sleep by the commotion found themselves facing hundreds of Indian warriors—most of them lined up atop the hills in front and on both sides of the island. Some of the Indians were on foot, but most were mounted.

The braves, making no effort to conceal themselves, were plainly visible south, west and north of the troops. It was almost as if they enjoyed flaunting their strength, and were unafraid of the whites.

It was immediately apparent to the men that no Indians were in sight to the east. Because of the size of the enemy force, some of Forsythe's men wanted to retreat in that easterly direction. Forsythe, however, recognized that the absence of Indians in just one direction could only mean a trap; the Dog Soldiers were trying to lure him that way. He believed (and Indians later confirmed) that the Dog Soldiers hoped they would run eastward, leading them into a box canyon. There the scouts could easily have been trapped and slaughtered.

Instead of retreating to the east, Forsythe ordered his men to go out onto the little island in the center of the Arikaree River. From there his men would have a clear view in all directions. The Indians were already within rifle distance, and the scouts expected to come under fire at any second. In their haste to reach the shelter of the island, the soldiers abandoned all of their medical supplies and most of their food. Forsythe did manage to bring along many of their horses and all 40,000 rounds of ammunition.

Even before the scouts had finished scrambling onto the island, however, the Indians opened fire. The attackers' first priority, as usual, was to kill the enemy's horses. In this endeavor the Indian marksmen were most successful. Within a few moments, all of Forsythe's horses were killed or mortally wounded. When the last of the horses had fallen, the Indians turned their attention to the scouts themselves.

From the time the soldiers dashed to the island they had been working feverishly to dig pits in the sand. Now gunfire from an estimated 500 to 700 Cheyenne warriors was concentrated on these men. Within seconds the shooting began taking a toll among the still exposed scouts.

First to die was the young officer who was the mission's second in command, Lieutenant Frederick Beecher. Shot in the chest in the opening volley, Beecher fell to the ground. Surprisingly, he rose quickly and

Courtesy Colorado Historical Society
The Battle of Beecher Island
Noted Western artist, Robert Lindneaux, imagined how scouts trapped on Beecher Island viewed the hundreds of attacking Cheyenne warriors. This scene occurred early in the confrontation, when a few of the soldiers' horses were still alive, and probably depicts the final charge by Roman Nose—the chief with the flowing headdress.

began firing back at the Indians. Then he was hit a second time—in the leg. Although knocked down, he once again stood up and returned the Indians' fire. A third time he was hit, a flesh wound in the side, but he remained on his feet and continued to fire.

Finally, Beecher was struck a fourth time—in the center of the forehead. Slammed backwards to the ground, Beecher did not get up again. As if by unspoken agreement, the men immediately began calling their embattled fortress "Beecher Island."[7]

But Lieutenant Beecher was not the only early casualty of the battle. Major Forsythe (he insisted on being called "major" despite his temporary rank of colonel) was also hit in the early moments of fighting. One bullet shattered the thigh of Forsythe's left leg, and a second broke his right leg about halfway between the knee and ankle. Forsythe fell heavily to the ground, cursing loudly. Then waving off the men who started toward him, Forsythe raised himself to a sitting position and continued to direct the battle. He would spend the next several days propped up in a pit (some sources say against a tree), supervising and orchestrating the defense of Beecher Island.

When Forsythe was first wounded, Dr. Moores tried to crawl to the major's side to render assistance. About halfway to the wounded officer, the physician was struck in the head by a bullet, and collapsed unconscious. He was never really awake after that time, although he opened his eyes from time to time and ranted unintelligibly for several hours. Other soldiers dragged the mortally wounded physician into the underbrush and tried to make him comfortable. The doctor died three days later.

Two other scouts were hit within a few seconds. One man suffered a shoulder wound and the other was hit in the hand. Both were able to continue shooting back at the Indians.

Paul Wellman writes that twenty-three scouts were killed or wounded in the first Indian charge, and this same number is repeated in several other accounts of the battle.[8] The figure apparently is inaccurate, however—at least according to the personal diaries kept by Forsythe and several of his men. Both the unofficial diaries and the official military records of the battle indicate only one man killed and four men wounded in the initial assault.

The first round of the Battle of Beecher Island had clearly favored the Indians! After the opening volleys had taken their toll of scouts—killing Lieutenant Beecher and severely wounding Major Forsythe and Dr. Moores, the Indians broke off the engagement and pulled back out of sight. Forsythe knew that they were not gone—they were simply regrouping in preparation for a major assault. He ordered his men to dig pits as fast as they could, preferably behind the body of a dead horse. In death the animals would continue to serve: their bodies an additional protection from enemy gunfire.

A few minutes later, Indian snipers opened up simultaneously from all sides, raking the scouts with rifle fire. The rain of bullets smashing into trees and bushes, or kicking up sprays of sand, forced the men to crouch in their pits as low as possible, with faces and heads covered. Again Forsythe recognized what was happening. He shouted to his men, warning that as soon as the shooting stopped they were to raise up and be prepared to shoot.

Forsythe, being well acquainted with Indian tactics, knew that the Indians hoped to keep the scouts pinned down with sniper fire while other warriors crawled toward the island. At the appropriate moment the snipers would stop shooting, the other braves would race onto the island, and overwhelm the scouts.

Sure enough, the sniper fire continued at a furious pace for several seconds, then suddenly stopped. As the gunfire lifted, hundreds of mounted Indians raced their ponies down the sides of the hills, sweeping toward the island. Following Forsythe's instructions, however, the scouts raised up and began shooting at the Indians with the massive combined firepower of their repeating rifles.

The effect of the concentrated, rapid fire from the Spencers had a dramatic impact. A number of Indians tumbled from their horses, and the attack appeared to falter. The warriors seemed startled by the massive gunfire pouring from the island where so few men were trapped. As the warriors neared the river bed in the midst of this withering barrage of return fire, they suddenly split into two groups—one passing on the left side of the island, the other on the right. Forsythe's instructions had kept the attackers from overrunning the island.

But the warriors were not the only ones surprised at the firepower of their enemies; Forsythe could hardly believe the force of the Cheyennes. The major was used to fighting Indians who were poorly armed, who still fought mostly with spears or bows and arrows. He was simply astonished at the amount of firepower from these warriors. While they did not possess the new repeating rifle, the braves seemed to have plenty of other modern hunting rifles; only a handful were still armed with bows and arrows. Some of these powerful rifles had been given to the Indians as part of the annual annuities paid by the BIA (Bureau of Indian Affairs), and others were retrieved from soldiers killed in various earlier battles. Evidence uncovered sometime later suggests that Confederates actively armed, trained, and agitated Indians, so it appears possible that the South was also partly responsible for the surprising Cheyenne arsenal.

Several times during the remainder of the morning, the Indians charged toward Beecher Island—and each time they were successfully repulsed by the scouts. The braves would race straight toward the island for several seconds, but after a number of the leading riders had been knocked from their horses, the remaining braves

Courtesy Colorado Historical Society
Beecher Island
This sketch of the Beecher Island battle is by an unknown artist.
Titled "The Defense of Beecher Island", the drawing appeared
in Harper's *New Monthly Magazine* in June of 1895,
illustrating a story called "A Frontier Fight".

would again split into two groups. The riders would then
pass well clear on either side of the island.

Two more scouts were killed in these attacks.
George Culver was shot in the head and killed outright.
"Wild Bill" Wilson was hit in the abdomen and died in
agony. Still, the scouts held out and the Indians were
unable to overrun the island.

Because the Indians had known for several days
that the white men following them numbered only about
fifty men, the Cheyennes had expected this to be an easy
battle. In anticipation of quickly overpowering the
whites, some of the Dog Soldiers had brought their families to a hillside a short distance from the Arikaree
River. It was like a giant arena where they could watch
the fight and cheer for the easy destruction of this small

enemy force. After the third Cheyenne attack was repulsed by the withering gunfire from the little island, the women and children were sent away.

Chief Roman Nose was not among the Dog Soldiers making the initial attacks. The Indian leader stayed in his tepee about three miles from the battle front. If the other warriors found it unusual that the great chief avoided the battle, they presumably attributed the absence to the anticipated ease of victory against so few of the enemy. At about noon, however, the Indians at Beecher Island were feeling a decided lack of inspirational leadership. Several of the lesser chiefs rode back to the village and confronted the absent Roman Nose.

The battlefield delegation pleaded with Roman Nose to come and join the battle, saying his arrival on the battlefield would inspire the warriors and permit them to defeat the surprisingly strong enemy. The chiefs also told Roman Nose that he was needed to personally lead the battle, because the Indians were getting discouraged and frightened at the unexpectedly stiff resistance from the white men. (They presumably were also discouraged by their unexpectedly high casualty rate.)

Roman Nose hesitated. Some accounts say several of the lesser chiefs concluded at that moment that Roman Nose was frightened, perhaps made soft by his enormous power and reputation. These accounts say two of the chiefs taunted Roman Nose, asking him whether he was afraid to go into battle.

Whatever transpired at the chief's tepee, the Dog Soldier leader finally told the gathered chiefs that if he entered the battle that day, he would certainly be killed.

The answer took the chiefs by surprise. After all, this was the man who had laughed at death and taunted the enemy in earlier confrontations. Ignoring his surprising response, the delegation from the battlefield pleaded with Roman Nose. One said, "All those people fighting out there feel that they belong to you." Roman Nose responded, "I know that I shall be killed today."[9]

There were several seconds of stunned silence after this second protest. Then the warrior chief quietly explained why entering a battle that day would surely claim his life.

When he was a boy, Roman Nose won the "manhood battle" by beating all the other twelve-year-old boys in a contest marking the rite of passage to warrior status. In recognition of his impressive victory, an old medicine man gave Roman Nose a magic war bonnet. The great medicine man told Roman Nose that as long as he observed certain traditions, the bonnet would make him impervious to the white man's weapons.

It had always worked just that way. After all, if the legends were true, it was the magic bonnet that once permitted Roman Nose to dash through a circle of covered wagons without being shot. Later he rode completely around encircled wagons, taunting the soldiers who were shooting at him. His horse was blasted from beneath him, but Roman Nose escaped unscathed. The magic had saved Roman Nose from certain death when shot in the chest at point-blank range, during the recent battle of Fort Wallace.

But, alas! The magic worked only so long as Roman Nose did certain things and avoided doing others. Among the taboos that must be observed to preserve the magic was an absolute rule: Roman Nose must never eat any food prepared in, or served from, a metal container.

The medicine man instructed Roman Nose that any broken taboo could be overcome and the magic restored, but only if the chief went through a lengthy and difficult purification ceremony. The restoration ceremony required thirty days of fasting and praying. If a taboo were broken and the purification process not completed, Roman Nose would certainly be killed the next time he went into battle.

Roman Nose explained that he had unwittingly violated one of the taboos on the night before this battle. He had been a guest in the lodge of another warrior—one who was not familiar with the rules for keeping the magic intact. The warrior's wife gave Roman Nose some buffalo meat, which he consumed. It was not until after dinner that he learned how the meat had been cooked: in a metal skillet taken from a wagon train, attacked and destroyed several weeks earlier. To the famous war chief, his violation of the taboo meant he would surely die in his next battle—unless he first went through the lengthy purification process.

The other chiefs must have believed in the magic. They knew that Roman Nose had led a charmed life and had thumbed his nose at danger in the past. In fact, it seems likely that the great magic bonnet and all of its taboos were common knowledge among the Dog Soldiers. Nonetheless, the other chiefs pleaded with Roman Nose to come lead the attack. They told him that his Dog Soldiers might be routed by a relative handful of whites if he did not personally lead the fight. Such a defeat would have been humiliating to the fiercest of the Cheyenne warriors.

Perhaps the chiefs intended that Roman Nose merely show up as an inspiration to the troops, while remaining out of rifle range. Perhaps they hoped that a little bit of the magic remained. It is not possible to know what Roman Nose, himself, planned to do. After a brief hesitation, however, the big chief agreed to come to the battlefront.

MAJOR FORSYTHE WAS WATCHING through binoculars when Roman Nose appeared atop the ridge a quarter mile away. Forsythe recognized the famous enemy chief at once. Even in his weakened condition, Forsythe noted in his diary that he was awestruck by the huge warrior. Forsythe wrote,

> He was a man of over six feet, three inches in height, beautifully formed, and—save for a crimson silk sash knotted around his waist and his moccasins on his feet—perfectly naked. His face was hideously painted in alternate lines of red and black, and his head crowned with a magnificent war bonnet, from which—just above his temples and curving slightly forward—stood up two black buffalo horns, while its ample length of eagle feathers and herons' plumes trailed wildly in the wind behind him...[10]

Roman Nose rode slowly and majestically up and down the line of warriors facing Beecher Island. At last, he stopped in the midst of the warriors. Shaking his fist toward the white men, he gave a loud war hoop and kicked his horse in the ribs. His big gray mare leaped forward and raced directly at the island, with hundreds of whooping warriors following close behind.

Forsythe shouted at his men to hold their fire until he gave the order. The scouts crouched in their shallow pits, rifles cocked and ready.

As Roman Nose began the charge, the Indian snipers opened up on the island. The Indians were shooting as fast as possible to keep the soldiers pinned down. There was chaos on the island—bullets ricocheting from trees and rocks or thudding into the bodies of the fallen horses that the men were using as breast-works. The scouts crouched, and waited.

The instant the sniper fire stopped, Forsythe shouted, "Now!" All the men rose and opened fire. Their shooting was once again extremely effective. Great gaps appeared immediately in the Indian lines—but the charge continued unabated, and Roman Nose was still in the lead.

Closer he came, racing at break-neck speed toward the river. The scouts knew that Roman Nose would not turn away and ride past them. The big chief—impervious to injury—was seemingly determined to ride directly onto the island.

On the far right side of the Indian line—the left side to the soldiers—rode Medicine Man, another famous and highly respected Cheyenne war chief. He was second in command to Roman Nose. Chief Medicine Man was hit on the third or fourth volley from the island, and tumbled from his horse. The other Indians ignored his death and raced onward, close on the heels of their respected leader.

Roman Nose and the fastest of his followers were almost on top of the island. At the last second, one of the scouts leaped to his feet. Ignoring the rain of Indian bullets, this scout stood with his legs spread, apparently oblivious to the battle raging around him. The soldier took careful aim and gently squeezed the trigger.

The bullet flew straight and true. It smashed into Roman Nose's chest with an almost audible thud, and blood splattered from a gaping wound. The force of the bullet knocked the giant warrior backward from his horse. The chief crashed in a heap at the edge of the river bed, only fifteen or twenty yards from the nearest white man—and did not move again.

Time seemed to stop. All eyes were on the chief, who had cheated death so often in the past. Nothing seemed to move. Men on both sides expected Roman Nose to leap to his feet—but there was no movement. The legendary Dog Soldier leader would never move again.

It became obvious to everyone on both sides that the great Roman Nose was dead, and the impact on the Indians was instantaneous. It was as if the wind had suddenly been sucked from the sails of the Indian warship. Remaining warriors broke off their attack, split into two groups and headed far away from the island in opposite directions. Even before they vanished over the low hills or into the trees there was a noticeable change in the Indians. They seemed suddenly to lose their desire to overrun the island, or to even continue the fight.

(The book *Death on the Prairie* says that the brave scout who risked death in order to fire the shot that killed Roman Nose was Jack Stilwell. Unlike other accounts of the Beecher Island battle, this book also says that Roman Nose managed to crawl from the battlefield and died later that evening in his own tepee. Virtually all other accounts of the battle, including official government records and the diaries of Major Forsythe and Sid Schlesinger, say Roman Nose was killed outright, and that the soldiers saw him fall dead.

Several accounts of Roman Nose's death say all the white men were shooting at once, and no one knows whose shot actually killed the famous Cheyenne chief— in spite of the brave actions of the scout who stood up to fire at Roman Nose. Among the accounts which do not credit the kill to any one individual are those eye witness accounts written by Major Forsythe and the young Sigmund Schlesinger.)

AS THE CRESTFALLEN INDIANS HEADED AWAY from the island following Roman Nose's death, the scouts on the island rose to their feet and cheered. Simultaneously they emptied their rifles at the retreating Indians. When the weapons were empty, the men pulled their Colt revolvers and also emptied them at the warriors— even though the distance was clearly too great for the pistols to have any effect.

Forsythe suddenly could be heard shouting above the din of battle, ordering the men to take cover. They had barely responded when the Indian snipers opened fire again, raking the island with gunfire. Under cover of this nonstop sniper fire, several warriors raced forward to retrieve Roman Nose's body, and carried it away.[11]

Twice more that afternoon, the Cheyenne warriors attacked Beecher Island—but something had clearly gone out of the attack. Both of these later charges were broken off well before Indians reached the island, although the warriors on the hillside continued their deadly sniper fire without letup until it was too dark to see.

IN SPITE OF THE DEATH OF ROMAN NOSE and the lessened ferocity of the attacks, Major Forsythe knew his scouts were in serious trouble. The chief's death may have severely impacted the Indians, but it did not cause them to leave the battlefield. The scouts were still surrounded and still under attack. They could not leave, and they could not hold out much longer where they were. Their biggest problem was the lack of medical care, and the fact that they were cut off from their food supply. They simply could not outlast the Indians. Forsythe had not intended to be caught in a battle of attrition, and knew that he could not win this battle under the current circumstances.

Courtesy Colorado Historical Society
George Forsyth
This photograph was taken several months before Major George Forsyth's heroic confrontation with Roman Nose at Beecher Island. Forsyth's calm and determined leadership saved his command and ended the career of the most notorious of Cheyenne Dog Soldiers.

When darkness came that night, Forsythe called for volunteers to go for help at Fort Wallace, about sixty-five miles away. He warned that the trip was so dangerous any volunteer would probably be killed within minutes of leaving the island. Without hesitation, every able–bodied man volunteered to undertake the dangerous mission.

Forsythe selected two of the men—Pierre Trudeau, who at forty-two was the oldest man on the island, and Jack Stillwell, a lad who had just turned nineteen. After somber farewells the two men left the island at about 2:00 a.m., walking backwards in their stocking feet. They hoped that by walking backwards any Indian who later spotted their tracks would believe them to have been made by Indians wearing moccasins, walking toward the island.

Trudeau and Stillwell moved as quickly as they dared, scooting from hiding place to hiding place, fully expecting to be discovered and killed at any moment. They were afraid to stand up, even in the darkness. After getting a hundred yards or so from the island the two scouts turned and faced toward the front. Crouching, they began moving as rapidly as they could down the rocky stream bed. After covering only a few dozen more yards they decided that they were making too much noise and simply presented too great a target in that stooped position. They dropped to their hands and knees and began crawling.

Within minutes their knees and the palms of their hands were cut and bleeding, but they appeared not to notice. Pausing to rest and listen every few seconds, the men continued their arduous journey throughout the night—but had covered only two miles before sunup. At first light, they hid in tall grass at the edge of the river bed, making themselves as invisible as possible.

Still fearing detection at any moment they found they could not sleep. They were still close enough to the island that they could easily hear the sounds of the battle throughout that first day of their dangerous mission.

On the second night, the two scouts walked upright, but encountered three Indian patrols. Each time they dived to the ground at the edge of the river bed and hid in the grass hanging over the bank. They hardly dared to breathe until the Indians had passed by their position. Because of these constant interruptions and the need keep out of sight, they managed to cover a total distance of less than five miles before the predawn light forced them to again find a hiding place.

On the third night they encountered only two Indian patrols. Gaining increased confidence now, the two scouts covered about seven miles before dawn, and were now fourteen miles from Beecher Island.

Feeling that they were far enough away to be out of the range of Cheyenne patrols, the two scouts pressed onward—even after daylight. To their delight they saw no sign of the enemy and were able to make good time. Then, walking across the open prairie about the middle of the morning, their luck changed. They spotted a group of Indian warriors riding directly toward them.

The two dived into a shallow buffalo wallow and laid flat on their stomachs. They fully expected to be seen and killed at any second. Six or so Indians rode within two dozen yards of them, passing so close that the scouts could hear the breathing of their horses. The scouts could hardly believe their luck when the Indians passed on by without seeing them.

As they lay in the pit, Stillwell claimed that a rattlesnake—apparently startled by the Indians' horses—slithered over the side of the wallow only a few inches from his face. Stillwell was chewing tobacco at the time, and says he aimed a squirt of tobacco juice at the snake's head, which turned it aside.[12]

After the braves had ridden well past the buffalo wallow, the two scouts lay quietly for what seemed like an enormously long while. Finally they raised up and looked carefully around. Seeing no one, they scrambled out of the wallow and hastened from the area.

At last, on the afternoon of the fifth day, Trudeau and Stillwell stumbled into the Cheyenne Wells, Colorado, stagecoach relay station, thirty miles west of Fort Wallace. The exhausted men blurted out their story to a surprised station master, who immediately rushed them to the fort to sound the alarm.

Trudeau was physically spent from the long ordeal and collapsed after entering the fort. He was hospitalized, and took a week to recover his strength. Stillwell, however, was strong enough to volunteer to lead a rescue party back to Beecher Island.

BACK ON THE BESIEGED ISLAND, of course, no one knew whether Trudeau and Stillwell had been captured, shot, or had become lost. It was almost too much to hope that they had gotten through to summon help. Major Forsythe later confided that he assumed the men had been killed. After a second day of fighting that virtually duplicated the battles of the first, Major Forsythe again asked for volunteers to go for help.

Chauncey Whitney and A.J. Pliley were selected this time, and soon crawled off the island. They had traveled only a short distance when they spotted a line of Indians stretched across the creek bed. Deciding they could not possibly make it past these warriors, they reluctantly returned to the island. When they crawled back at about 3 a.m., the unanimous opinion on the island was that the first two scouts must have been captured and killed. The men presumed that the line of Indians was to make certain no one else tried the same thing. Some of the soldiers struggled to hold back their tears of frustration. Many spent the next hours writing final farewells to loved ones.

At dawn, the Indians attacked again. And again, concentrated fire from the scouts broke up the attack. The routine continued throughout the long day.

Years later, when Schlesinger dictated his memoirs about that awful time trapped on Beecher Island, he said,

I have often been asked whether I have killed any Indians, to which my answer must truthfully be; that I don't know. The conditions were such, speaking for myself, that I did not consider it safe to watch the results of a shot, the Indians being all around us, shooting at anything moving above ground. At one time I threw a hat full of sand that I had scraped up in my pit to the top of the excavation, exposing myself more than usual, when a hail of bullets struck my hill of sand, almost blinding me! This will explain why I did not look for results.

My plan of observation was to work the barrel of my carbine, saw fashion, through the sand from the edges on the top of my hole downward, obtaining by these means a sort of loophole through which I could see quite a distance; also taking a general observation by suddenly jumping up and as quickly dropping back into my hole, which enabled me to take a shot, or as many as the size of the target warranted, without undue exposure and yet be in touch with the general situation. In such instances I have seen Indians crawl behind a knoll and saw several times two horsemen drag a body away between

them. Indian boys came from behind a knoll shooting arrows at us. I saw bodies of Indians both on
foot and horseback, coming toward us. These I considered good targets.[13]

On the third night, Forsythe scribbled a desperate
appeal for help and once again called for volunteers to
carry the message to Fort Wallace. Pliley again volunteered and was again chosen, and was accompanied this
time by John Donovan. After three days of assaulting
the island the Indians had become somewhat more lax,
permitting these two men to get through without difficulty. They walked upright almost from the time they
left Beecher Island, and saw no Indians whatsoever. Of
course, they did not reach Fort Wallace for three days,
and no one on the island knew whether they had gotten
through either.

On the day before the second pair of volunteers left
the island, the Indians charged the scouts only twice,
keeping up just enough sniper fire to make certain the
scouts were pinned down. Nonetheless, the constant
shooting and pressure was beginning to take its toll
among the white men. The scouts were exhausted from
the strain of the ordeal and were desperate for food,
although they had at least found that they were able to
get water from the stream or by digging pits in the sand.

Four of their number were now dead: Dr. Moores,
Lieutenant Beecher, G.W. Culver, and William Wilson.
Several others were seriously wounded, including Major
Forsythe. The days were blistering hot, and the dead
(both horses and men) were rotting in the warm sun-
shine. The rancid air made it difficult to breathe. Most of
the men tied scarves around their noses and mouths to
make it easier to tolerate the awful stench of decaying
flesh.

Ironically, autumn weather in the West is subject to huge temperature swings—from blistering hot to icy cold in just a matter of hours. On this occasion the hot weather that rotted dead flesh quickly changed to the other extreme.

Sid Schlesinger said of that third full day that the horrors of the situation were almost overwhelming to the men:

> They were hopelessly outnumbered. While the day had been blistering hot, a steady cold rain set in at night. Worst of all, starvation confronted them, starvation which could only be allayed by chunks of horseflesh from the decaying animals.[14]

Shortly after nightfall Forsythe talked with the soldiers about the danger of starving to death. He said it was vital that they find something solid to eat. The men had not eaten particularly well on their long journey before the island ordeal began, and some of the men were already showing signs of starvation. Several others were ill from eating the raw strips of flesh from the dead horses. Forsythe asked for a volunteer to leave the island in a search for food. Schlesinger volunteered.

A few minutes later Schlesinger crawled from the island in a desperate effort to find anything that might pass as food. The first thing he found was not food, however. Instead, he found three dead Indians lying within 10–12 feet of the pit where he had been crouching for the past three days. He had no idea when the Indians had been killed, or by whom. In keeping with what had become custom, Schlesinger scalped the three braves and tossed the bloody scalps back into his own rifle pit before continuing his quest for food.

Schlesinger was rewarded almost immediately; he spotted a fox (some accounts say coyote, which is more probable) stalking some other animal, which was not visible to Schlesinger. A rifle shot was risky, but Schlesinger felt he was near enough to the island to take the chance. He shot the fox, grabbed its lifeless form, and quickly dragged the animal back to the island. The ravenous men were delighted with the fresh meat, and feasted that night on their first meal in three days. Forsythe said later the bones were boiled three times to make certain everything that could be eaten had been fully extracted.

Although the scouts were unaware of it, most of the Indians probably withdrew from the battlefield that night. By the morning of September 21, the fifth day of the battle, only a few dozen snipers remained behind to harass the scouts. It apparently had become Cheyenne strategy to keep the scouts pinned down and simply starve them to death rather than continue what had turned out to be most costly frontal assaults. Several friendly Indians later said this had been the Beecher Island battle plan. The lack of frontal attacks on the island was welcome, but did nothing to dramatically improve the increasingly severe conditions facing the scouts.

For the soldiers, in fact, the ordeal on the island was becoming increasingly unbearable. After the fox was devoured they had no more fresh food of any kind. The trail food in their haversacks was completely exhausted by the sixth day. The air was foul, and because of the lack of sufficiently cold weather, flies and maggots infested the dead horses. (The dead men had been buried in shallow graves, scooped out of the island's sand during the nighttime hours).

On the morning of the sixth day, Major Forsythe again called the ragged men together. He told them that because so few Indians were believed now to be guarding the island at night, most of the scouts could probably reach safety if they were to make a dash for freedom sometime after dark. He said the strongest of the men—those who had not been wounded—needed to take advantage of the opportunity and save themselves. Forsythe said he expected the healthy men to leave the island that night.

The scouts looked at Forsythe as if he had lost his mind. Every one of the men flatly refused to leave, knowing that to do so would mean certain death for Forsythe and the other injured survivors who could not travel, and in some cases, could not even defend themselves. (The wounded men most likely would have committed suicide, rather than submit to Indian capture and torture.)

WHEN TRUDEAU AND STILLWELL ARRIVED at Fort Hays, an alarm was telegraphed to all forts in the area. Colonel George C. Carpenter and a newly arrived detachment of "buffalo soldier" (Negro) troops were just setting up camp near Cheyenne Wells, Colorado. These men were immediately ordered to ride to the rescue of Forsythe's scouts. A second group of soldiers, under a Colonel Bankhead, was dispatched from Fort Wallace with Jack Stillwell acting as their guide.

Shortly after both groups had left by separate trails for Beecher Island, scouts Pliley and Donovan arrived at Fort Wallace. Donovan was given a horse and was sent to catch up with Colonel Carpenter, to lead him to Beecher Island. Some sources say that at first both Pliley and Donovan refused to go back to the island. Then Lieutenant Hugo Johnson, in temporary command of the Fort, offered Donovan and any other man on base $100 to catch the troops, go with them to the island, and rescue the scouts. According to these reports, a total of six men accepted the offer, including Donovan. They caught up with Colonel Carpenter on the Republican River and quickly led his troops in the right direction. (Other sources do not mention the bribe to get these men to go back to Beecher Island. Given the fact that those on the island were close friends of Pliley and Donovan, it seems unlikely they had to be bribed to ride back to the battlefront.)

Sunday afternoon, September 27, 1868: Beecher Island, Colorado. Sniper fire had been sporadic all day long—just enough to keep the scouts pinned down. By this time several of the men were near death because of their wounds or starvation, and all of the men were resigned to die. They had been on the island for ten days with little food and almost no sleep. Some of the men could no longer stand up.

When the weary defenders talked to one another the subject was always the same: at what point it would become necessary for the men to kill themselves in order to avoid capture and torture. Indian torture was always too awful to contemplate; the scouts could only guess at how much worse it would be for the men who had killed Roman Nose! Yet somewhere deep in their souls burned a lingering desire to hang on just a little while longer. No one was sure why they waited. They knew it was unlikely that any volunteers had reached safety, or that help was on its way. Still, the men clung to life—and hope.

When Colonel Carpenter's soldiers first rode into sight late Sunday afternoon, the Beecher Island scouts were so exhausted they barely reacted. Even after they fully understood that they were being rescued, many of the men were too weak to stand and cheer or to walk out to meet the soldiers.

The remaining Cheyenne snipers hastily fled as the troops arrived, but many of the warriors were caught and killed in running battles with soldiers who gave chase. Only a handful of Cheyenne warriors got away; none were captured.

Doctors accompanying the relief column immediately started tending to the scouts on the island. Many of the wounded were in terrible shape. One man, Louis Farley, had a severe leg wound infected with gangrene. Doctors amputated his leg, but Farley died a few hours later in spite of the effort.

One of the survivors of the battle was the old scout Sharp Grover. He had survived two improbable brushes with death in the past year—shot in the back by supposedly friendly Indians and then pinned down for ten days on Beecher Island. He was not to be so lucky, however, fighting the whites. Grover was shot to death a few months later in a barroom brawl at Salina, Kansas.

Forsythe's losses were relatively light in view of the probability that all would have died had their rescue been postponed by only a few hours. Five scouts had been killed, sixteen wounded.

Indian losses were never determined, since the warriors had carried away most of their dead and injured. George Bent later claimed that only two Indians died in the fighting, although no one believed him. Schlesinger personally scalped three dead warriors within fifteen feet of the island, and all had seen Roman Nose and several other Indians die on the battlefield. Major Forsythe said he counted the bodies of thirty-two Indians at the height of the first day's fighting. He estimated that at least fifty (and probably many more) were killed. The

Cheyennes eventually admitted losing seventy-five dead
and "many" wounded.

In the wake of the rescue, Major Forsythe was lav-
ish in his praise for all the men—especially for Sid
Schlesinger. In his own book written many years later,
Forsythe (who turned out to be something of a poet and
apparently somewhat of a bigot, as well) wrote of
Schlesinger:

> When the foe charged on the breastworks
> With the madness of despair,
> And the bravest souls were tested,
> The little Jew was there.
>
> When the weary dozed on duty,
> Or the wounded needed care,
> When another shot was called for,
> The little Jew was there.
>
> With the festering dead around them,
> Shedding poison in the air,
> When the crippled chieftain ordered,
> The little Jew was there.[15]

Schlesinger's handwritten diary entries were rea-
sonably, and understandably, rather terse. Among them
were these:

> Thursday, September 17. About 12 Indians carched
> on us, stampeedet 7 horses 10 Minuts after about
> 600 Indians attacktet us Killt Beecher Culver &
> Wilson. Woundet 19 man and Killt all the Horses

We was without Grubb & Water all Day dug Holes in the sand whith our Hands.

Friday, September 18, 1868. in the night I dug my hole deeper cut of meat oof of the Horses & hung it up on the Bushes, Indians made a charge on us at Day brake, but retreatet Kept Shooting nearly all day they Put up a White Flag, left us at 9 o clock in the evning Raind all night.

Saturday 19 the Indians came back again Kept sharp shooting all day 2 Boys startet for Fort Wallace Raind all night.

Sunday 20. Dr. Moores died last night Raining part of the Day snow about 1 inches thick Indians Kept sharp shooting.

Monday, September 21, 1868. scalpt 3 Indians which were found about 15 Feet from my hole consealt in Grass.

Tuesday 22 Killt a Coyote & eat him all up.

(No additional entries were made in the diary.)[16]

Notes
1. Maurice Mattloff, ed., *American Military History* (Washington DC: Office of the Chief of Military History, United States Army, 1969), 301.
2. Ibid., 305–6.
3. Ibid., 308.
4. Wayne C. Lee and Howard C. Raynesford, *Trails of the Smoky Hill* (Caldwell, ID: The Caxton Printers, Ltd., 1980), 123.

Other sources give slightly different figures. Merrill J. Mattes, *The Beecher Island Battlefield Diary of Sigmund Schlesinger* (Lincoln: Historical Society of Nebraska), says the men were paid a flat fifty dollars per month to join the unit, and an additional twenty-five dollars per month if they supplied their own horse.

5. *The Beecher Island Battlefield Diary of Sigmund Schlesinger*, 4.

6. *The Beecher Island Battlefield Diary*...says the Indians stampeded seven horses, but the official report of Major Forsythe gives the figure reported here.

7. Virtually all accounts, including Schlesinger's diary, say that Lieutenant Beecher was killed in the early moments of the fighting. *Trails of the Smoky Hill,* however, says that Beecher was killed in the sniper fire immediately after Roman Nose was killed several days later. According to the latter account, "As the Indian charge swept on past, the soldiers cheered...but at that moment, Lieutenant Beecher crawled over to Colonel Forsythe and said, 'I've been hit bad. I think I'm dead.'" The book says Beecher became delirious within moments and died at sundown. The source of this information is unclear.

8. Paul Wellman, *Death on the Prairie* (Lincoln/London: University of Nebraska Press, 1962), 75. This book also says the physician was named Dr. Morehead.

9. *The American Heritage Book of Indians* (New York: Simon & Schuster, 1961), 346.

10. *Death on the Prairie,* 76.

11. *Trails of the Smoky Hill,* 128–9

12. As improbable as this story seems, it is repeated in virtually every account of the Beecher Island battle.

13. *The Beecher Island Battlefield Diary*..., 6

14. Ibid., 9

15. Ibid., 8–9

16. Ibid., 9–10

A smothered passion for revenge agitates these Indians, perpetually fomented by the failure of food, the encircling encroachments of the white population, and the exasperating sense of decay and impending extinction with which they are surrounded. A desperate war of starvation and extinction is imminent and inevitable, unless prompt measures shall prevent it.
William Bent

[Indians] abhor labor. The women do the drudgery. They are an indolent community, lay around, pilfer and beg. They are great lovers of whiskey and sugar, and think it very strange that I have not allowed it to be bought and traded for such commodities as they have to sell; the braves will often offer a good pony or mule for one bottle of whiskey. They are very licentious, they worship the sun, earth and smoke, and swear by the pipe.
BIA Agent Albert Boone

–SIX–

Incredible Survival

THE FINAL DAYS OF THE CIVIL WAR had been difficult ones for John German's family. Their little farm in Fannin County, Georgia was in the middle of one of the last battles between North and South. It wasn't a significant fight. No great or lasting victories were won. It was not a turning point in the war, or even the area campaign; it was merely another bloody fight between American brothers.

But while the confrontation was insignificant in terms of history, it was life changing for the Germans. The battle devastated the family farm. Trees were shattered by cannon balls; buildings were either demolished by gunfire or burned. Cattle and other livestock, that weren't killed in the battle itself, were confiscated by the soldiers for food. Crops were trampled and ruined.

For a time after the war ended, John German tried to rebuild his farm—but it was no use. The war destroyed not only the land, but the will of the family who lived there. There was no money, so they could not replace their animals or buy seed to replant their crops. Without money, they could not buy lumber to rebuild their house and barns. For nine years after the war, the family struggled to make it work, but it simply was not to be. Eventually the Germans concluded that their only hope was to simply head west and start a new life on the frontier of Colorado.

Besides John German, the family consisted of eight other persons. There was Lydia, his wife, plus six daughters and one son. The girls were Rebecca, twenty; Catherine, seventeen; Joanna, fifteen; Sophia, twelve; Juliana, seven; and Nancy Adelaid—called "Addy"—who was five. The only boy was Stephen, nineteen.

Making the trip to Colorado was a considerable undertaking for anyone in the middle 1870s; it was especially difficult for the Germans. John sold most of what little he owned to buy a sturdy covered wagon and a team of oxen. Into the wagon the family piled what personal goods they had left: a mirror, a chest of drawers, three beds, bedding and clothing. They also brought along their last livestock: two cows and a calf, and a crate containing five chickens.

The family headed north out of Georgia and then turned westward, walking first into southern Missouri. From there they headed due west across southern Kansas, making straight for the Colorado Rockies and their dreams of a new life. The first part of the trip was not all that difficult. The roads were fairly good and folks along the way were friendly and helpful.

The further west the family traveled, however, the more difficult the roads became and the more isolated the Germans felt. Following the railroad tracks to Fort Hays was easy—but they soon found that both the tracks and the road petered out west of the little Kansas community. Folks in town suggested the family follow the still-visible trail formerly used by the Butterfield stagecoach wagons, advising them that both grass and water would be more plentiful on that southern route than along the main, more northerly road to Denver. The well-meaning advice was to produce disastrous consequences for the Germans.

Usually the two smallest German girls rode in the covered wagon alongside their mother, who drove the team. Sometimes, though, the youngsters walked with the older children and their father as he drove the cows along behind the wagon. Frequently, Stephen and John walked ahead of the wagon with their long-barreled, single–shot rifles at the ready just in case they scared up a rabbit for dinner.

Thursday, September 10, 1874. Shortly after lunch the Germans met two men on the trail, heading in the opposite direction. The strangers told the family they would likely reach Fort Wallace the following day. The men said the trail was fairly well marked and easy to follow. Buoyed by the optimistic news, the Germans pushed on in good spirits. When evening came, the family made camp on the banks of a small stream.

Friday, morning, September 11. The Germans arose early, as was their custom. Following a hearty breakfast (thanks to eggs from the traveling chickens) Stephen and Catherine went out to round up the cows which were grazing a short distance away. Since the cows were ahead of the wagon, John signaled to his wife to start the team forward. Just as they began moving, though, the air was suddenly filled with the yelps of Indians. A number of warriors charged out of a ravine. The war party consisted of seventeen Cheyenne braves and two

squaws, led by Chief Kicking Horse. The chief had a reputation for violence, and for failing to keep his promises.

The Indians made short work of their attack. They
headed straight for John German, and before the husband and father could even raise his voice or his rifle, he
was shot in the chest and killed. Mrs. German, who
leaped from the wagon and ran to her husband's side,
was killed with a tomahawk blow that crushed her
skull.

Twenty-year-old Rebecca grabbed an ax from the
wagon and struck the warrior who had just killed her
mother. The brave was badly hurt, but it is not known
whether he was killed. Another warrior shot and killed
Rebecca.

Stephen and Catherine, still a short distance from
the wagon, turned and tried to run to some nearby
bluffs. They were quickly overtaken by Indian braves
riding ponies. One of the warriors drove a lance through
Stephen, probably killing him outright.

Catherine was shot in the hip by an arrow and tumbled to the ground. A big warrior was instantly at her
side. Jerking the arrow from her hip, he threw her onto
his horse and raced back to the wagon.

Some of the other Indians now rounded up the two
cows, the calf, and the oxen. Still others in the raiding
party ransacked the covered wagon. Some of the items
were tied to their horses, and the others were simply
tossed out onto the prairie.

Little Addy was crying hysterically at the side of the
wagon. One impatient warrior, apparently irritated by
the noise she was making, raised his rifle and pointed it
at the child's face. At the last instant one of the squaws
leaped in front of the girl, no doubt saving her life. The
woman dragged Addy and her next older sister, Juliana,

away from the wagon and announced that she was claiming the two children as her own property.

The three older girls were forced to line up at the back of the wagon—Catherine, seventeen, her hip bleeding profusely from the arrow wound; Joanna, fifteen, and Sophia, twelve. Several of the braves began to argue over who owned the three girls. At the height of the argument, one of the warriors jerked on Joanna's bonnet and it tumbled from her head, revealing her long, golden hair. The brave dragged Joanna to the side of the wagon, stabbed her with his knife and then scalped her—apparently to merely possess the golden-haired trophy.

The four surviving sisters were dragged onto horses behind the braves. After setting the wagon ablaze, the Indians rode away, heading south. The entire attack probably lasted no more than ten minutes or so, but every detail was permanently etched on the minds of the four surviving sisters.

The Indians drove the three German cows ahead of them, but after about three hours they stopped, killed all three of the animals, and had a feast. They offered food to the four children, but the girls—overcome by grief and shock, and expecting at any minute to be killed or, even worse, raped and then killed—were unable to eat.

After a two-hour break, the Indians pushed on. In a little while it began to rain. The children were cold and wet, and the two smallest girls cried, but the Indians continued riding. The four sisters were too stunned to take notice as to where they were going, or even in which direction they were traveling.

When nightfall drew near, the Indians made camp. The older girls, Sophia and Catherine, were petrified with fear of what the night would bring. Their fears

Courtesy Colorado Historical Society
Catherine and Sophia German
This photograph of Catherine (on the left) and Sophia German was
found in the burned remains of the family's covered wagon.
Although barely teenagers, the sisters endured multiple rapes and
beatings from their captors. Throughout the ordeal, they attempted
to protect their two younger sisters, who also survived the Kansas
massacre and became captives of the Cheyenne.

would prove grotesquely true. A short time after dark several braves grabbed the two older girls. The sisters were dragged into a nearby grove of trees and their clothing was ripped off. Then the braves took turns raping the youngsters.

The following day, the Indians killed a buffalo and once again ate a hearty meal. This time the older girls forced themselves and their sisters to eat, also. That night was a duplicate of the first.

On the third day, the Indians stole several horses and two more cows from a ranch they passed. By this time, the Indians permitted Catherine and Sophia to ride their own horses alone, although the animals were led by warriors. The two smaller girls still shared horses with the squaws.

On the sixth day (or maybe it was the seventh; the girls lost track of time) the Cheyennes and their captives crossed the North Canadian River in western Oklahoma, then turned westward into the Texas panhandle. They were now approximately 230 miles southwest of Fort Wallace, Kansas.

For days the Indians continued on the move. Sometimes they stole cattle or horses by day. At night they camped along the nearest available stream, and always Catherine and Sophia were ravaged during the night. In spite of everything, the older girls clung tenaciously to their determination to survive and to protect their little sisters.

SOMETIME IN OCTOBER—the girls believe about four weeks had passed since their capture—the group camped one night in the Texas panhandle. Just before dawn the following morning the squaws awakened and began preparing breakfast. The two youngest sisters, Juliana and Addy, were sent into a grove of underbrush and small trees to gather firewood. Suddenly the older girls could hear a distant rumble, as if many horses were running. The girls hoped—and the Indians feared—that the noise might be approaching soldiers. The Indians broke camp in haste, abandoning many of their supplies, and raced away in the semi-darkness. In their panic to escape, the Indians rode off without the two smallest girls. Sophia and Catherine were beside themselves with fear and anger, but the Cheyennes ignored their hysterical pleas.

Throughout that day the Indians pushed onward with their two remaining captives, trying to put considerable distance between themselves and what they assumed were pursuing soldiers. After several days with no sign of soldiers, the Indians concluded that they were not being chased after all. They slowed the pace of their travel. However, they continued to ignore the pleas from the older German girls to go back for the children. Eventually, the older girls concluded that their younger sisters were probably dead.

In actual fact, when the Indians broke their camp and rode away in haste that morning seven-year-old Juliana simply took charge. She wasn't sure why the Indians left or whether they would be back, but in the meantime, she knew she needed to care for her five-year-old sister.

Thus began one of the all-time most improbable and incredible tales of survival.

Holding Addy's tiny hand, Juliana began walking along across the prairie. In a short time she found an old wagon trail and began following it. Sometime later that day, she came upon an abandoned army camp. When the soldiers left the camp several days earlier they fortunately had not been very thorough in their cleanup efforts. Juliana poked around the debris and found some hardtack and stale bread. Nearby she found some wild berries growing on a bush. A stream flowed lazily past the camp site, offering water to quench the girls' thirst.

The two lonely little girls set up camp, and then they waited.

September 30, 1874. A buffalo hunter found the bodies of the five German family members on the trail in western Kansas. He notified the next stagecoach relay station, which, in turn, telegraphed the grim news to Fort Wallace. Soldiers soon recovered and returned the bodies of the murder victims to Monument Station, where they were buried.

In the charred debris that had once been the family's covered wagon, one of the soldiers found the German family Bible. From it, he determined that there had been seven children in the family—four of whom were obviously missing. The army concluded that the missing girls probably were kidnapped by the same Indians who slaughtered the rest of the family.

Lieutenant Charles C. Hewitt of the Nineteenth Infantry was placed in charge of a massive search and rescue effort. He was given orders to "stop at nothing" in his effort to locate the missing children. While army officials telegraphed the grim news all over the country, Hewitt and 200 soldiers set out to try to follow the faint remains of the trail, left by the Indians nearly three weeks earlier.

At the same time, General Nelson Miles joined the search out of Fort Sill, Oklahoma. He took eight companies of the Fourth Cavalry and five companies of the Tenth Infantry to scour the Texas panhandle.

The army had recently received reports that a "sizable" Cheyenne village had been established somewhere in the Texas panhandle. Such a village would probably contain hostile young warriors, who resisted moving to reservations with older Indians. These "defiant attitudes" typified warriors who would murder and kidnap.

Led by Seminole and Tonkawa scouts, Miles searched at length for this rumored Indian camp. The general presumed the missing children would either be in that camp, or that Indians in the village would know where they were. After nine days, Miles' search was rewarded. Seminole scouts spotted a huge Indian village, hidden in a deep canyon, a short distance ahead.

The canyon was the famed Palo Duro Canyon in Texas. It was so deep that there was no apparent way to get from the prairie down to the canyon floor where the tepees were erected. Major Ranald McKenzie, commanding the leading element of the army, stood on the ledge and scratched his head. Eventually McKenzie ordered Lieutenant W.A. Thompson to take a patrol and scale down the face of the sheer canyon walls. At the same time McKenzie took the main body of troops further to the east to find a faster or better way to the bottom.

Lieutenant Thompson and his men began working their way down the rugged canyon walls in the pre-dawn light. There was no trail. In some places the men had to stand facing the canyon wall, their toes on narrow rock ledges no more than two or three inches wide. Eventually, one of the soldiers kicked loose a sizable rock, which bounced noisily down the canyon wall and crashed heavily into the valley below.

A lone Indian brave was guarding a herd of horses in the floor of the canyon. Hearing the rock tumbling down the canyon wall, he glanced up and saw the dozens of soldiers working their way toward the bottom. The Indian let out a loud whoop, alerting all the other Indians in the area. Cheyenne warriors emerged from every tepee, with their rifles in hand. At the same moment, women and children scrambled up the canyon in the opposite direction.

Almost simultaneously, the soldiers scaling the walls reached the bottom of the valley, and Major McKenzie thundered into view (riding up the canyon from an easier approach he had found two miles away). Now there were several hundred soldiers against possibly several dozen braves—a rear guard trying to cover the escape of their fellow warriors. A brief, but fierce battle transpired between the soldiers and the Indian defenders, who were firing from positions of concealment among rocks on the canyon walls. Although the warriors were too few in number to inflict serious casualties, they were successful in delaying the soldiers' advance. When the shooting finally stopped, dozens—possibly hundreds—of Indians had seized the opportunity to escape in the opposite direction.

The army later reported having suffered no casualties of their own in the brief battle. General Miles' report said that the Indians had suffered heavily. The bodies of four warriors were recovered from the main village where the first shots were fired, and many others were probably carried away by the retreating braves. The Indians themselves claimed that only those four men died in the attack, but that many Indian women and children were killed by the soldiers.

Even without inflicting major casualties, however, the fight accomplished one of the army's goals. The soldiers drove a large number of "uncontrolled" Indians from their hiding place. The troops destroyed more than 400 tepees, captured 1,400 Indian horses, and burned most of the Indians' supplies. It was a major blow to the Cheyennes still living on the plains.

Within twenty-four hours, the same soldiers located and destroyed five smaller Indian camps near Canon Blanco on the Red River.

Some accounts of these battles, including the one written by Paul Wellman, say that Major McKenzie had no way to care for the 1,400 Indian ponies seized in the Palo Duro Canyon. To keep the Indians from having the ponies, McKenzie ordered them destroyed. Wellman says the horses were slaughtered on a flat plain the next day.[1]

Friday, October 9, 1874. Troops under the command of Colonel George P. Buell found a large and apparently just-abandoned Indian village in the same general area. Buell burned the village's 500 tepees and seized 900 horses left behind by the fleeing Cheyennes. Several other small villages were destroyed over the next several days.

None of these raids, unfortunately, produced the missing girls. However, the raids succeeded in sending a strong message to the Indians. The clear warning was that the army was bound and determined to hunt down the Indians responsible for the kidnapping, and would stop at nothing until the children were released.[2]

Tuesday, October 20. Tired of constantly running from the soldiers, Dog Soldier Chief White Horse surrendered to Colonel Thomas H. Neill. White Horse was accompanied by twenty-five fellow Cheyennes, most of them women and older men. Chief White Horse claimed that he and many others really wanted only peace with the whites, but had been forced to accompany the militant Dog Soldiers on their recent raids. He said he had escaped from the Dog Soldier camp specifically to surrender. (A common complaint by the Indians was that the most militant Dog Soldiers threatened to harm them and their families unless they participated in raids against white men.)

White Horse told Colonel Neill that Chief Grey Beard was the leader of the militant Dog Soldiers; a lesser chief, Medicine Water, was leading a smaller element of hostile braves. It was this smaller group, White Horse said, that had attacked the German family. He said that Medicine Water had also earlier wiped out the Hennessey wagon train and a large railroad survey party. White Horse reported that all of the Dog Soldiers were now camped together somewhere in the panhandle region of Texas.

According to White Horse, Chief Grey Beard knew the US soldiers were after him. In fact, reports of the army's search were the subject that dominated conversation in every Indian village. Grey Beard kept constantly on the move to avoid capture, but White Horse said that the end of the chase may be near; Grey Beard's horses were exhausted.

As if to confirm the report, Grey Beard raided a Caddo camp a day or so after this conversation took place. The raid was believed to be an effort to seize fresh horses, to permit the Dog Soldiers to continue running from the soldiers. The Caddos discovered the plot and drove away the Cheyennes. Three of Grey Beard's raiding party were killed, and six others took advantage of the opportunity to escape from the war party. They went to a reservation in western Oklahoma and surrendered to the US Army.

Tuesday, October 27. A small war party attacked a ranch in the southwestern corner of Kansas, making off with seventy-five horses. Pursued at once by a army patrol and a sizable civilian posse, the Indians escaped in a running gun battle. Two white civilians were killed in the fight. During the chase, however, the Indians were forced to abandon the horses. The army found evidence that the Indians involved were Cheyenne Dog Soldiers, possibly those of Medicine Water's tribe.

THE TWO OLDER GERMAN GIRLS were being held at the camp of Cheyenne Chief Stone Calf. The girls were completely unaware that a massive search for them was underway. They assumed that no white person even knew of their abduction or the murder of their family.

The older girls were now the property of Stone Calf, who traded six of his best horses for them. Catherine's hip was fairly well healed by this time, and during the day the girls were forced to do the work of squaws. If their work was not satisfactory, they were beaten.

But the difficult work and the squaws' beatings were nothing compared to the nightly horror they endured. Both were ravaged by one or several warriors every single night. Incredibly, the girls clung to their determination to survive. They were driven by the hope that they might someday provide eyewitness testimony to bring justice to the murderers of their family.

Stone Calf and the other Dog Soldiers, though—feeling the heat—had to keep on the go virtually all the time. The longer they ran, the more tired Stone Calf's tribe became. The army was obviously relentless in its search and showed no signs of giving up the hunt. Surprised at the tenacity of the search, Chief Stone Calf became increasingly alarmed for his own welfare. He was especially concerned because of the abandonment of the two littlest German girls nearly two months earlier. Eventually Stone Calf ordered several warriors to go back and see if they could locate the children.

To their total amazement, the children were found: emaciated, cold, and dirty, but alive. They were still living in the rubble of the abandoned army camp, just waiting for someone to come along and tell them what to do. Both of the children were recaptured by the warriors, and returned to Stone Calf's camp on November 7—just about eight weeks after they were first abandoned.

Friday, November 6, 1874. Soldiers were everywhere. Army patrols crisscrossed the country constantly, searching for the German girls. There seemed to be no place anyone could go without seeing soldiers. The pressure was being felt not only by the Cheyennes, but also by the Kiowas and any other Indians trying to avoid moving to the reservations. The Dog Soldiers were generally hated by the other Indians now, because they blamed the Cheyennes for the terrific military pressure.

The Dog Soldiers themselves were tired and edgy. Furthermore, they were alarmed at the numbers of other Indians flocking to the reservations to surrender. It seemed that the only Indians left in the panhandle were those being sought by the army, making it increasingly more difficult to avoid capture.

On the morning of November 6, Lieutenant H.J. Farnsworth and twenty-eight men of the Eighth Cavalry were patrolling near the southwestern Kansas border with Colorado and Oklahoma. They were attacked by approximately 100 Cheyenne warriors. In the brief fight that followed, one soldier was killed and six were wounded. The Cheyennes carried off their casualties but Farnsworth counted at least four Indian dead: all Dog Soldiers.

Sunday, November 8. Lieutenant Frank Baldwin was on patrol in the Texas panhandle. He encountered some friendly Indians who reported that a small group of Cheyennes camped on McClellan Creek "might have" some white children hostages.

The report was encouraging. Although there had been other, false reports about white captives, the lieutenant later said he had "special feeling" about this one. Baldwin decided that if the children were in the reported camp, his only hope of rescuing them alive was to take the Indians by surprise.

Accompanied by Troop D of the Sixth Cavalry and Company D of the Fifth Infantry, Baldwin encircled the sizable Indian encampment in the predawn hours of Monday, November 9. As soon as it was light enough to see, Baldwin gave the signal and the soldiers raced into the village.

Unfortunately for the soldiers, the Indians had heard them coming. Warriors raced from their tepees or crouched behind rocks and in low-lying places, firing weapons at the troops. The ensuing battle lasted several hours, until the surviving Indians finally managed to escape down a stream bed.

When the battle ended, Baldwin was disappointed. There had been no sign of any white girls during the long battle. Soldiers searching the abandoned tepees found no trace of the children. Baldwin felt betrayed.

Long after the battle stopped and the last of the tepees had been searched, soldiers stood in the abandoned village talking about the battle. Suddenly, an Indian brave stood up in a clump of bushes at the edge of the village. The warrior fired his rifle at a bundle of buffalo robes lying beside a tepee. He missed—and soldiers returned his gunfire, killing the brave.

When the soldiers examined the pile of robes that had been the Indian's target, they were astonished to find little Juliana German was rolled up inside! The terrified child said her younger sister, Addy, should also be somewhere nearby—that she had just been sent to gather firewood when the shooting started.

Soldiers fanned out quickly to search for the five-year-old. They located her moments later—innocently continuing to gather fire wood just as she had been instructed before the battle began.

The two little girls were nearly starved, and could hardly comprehend that they were safe. The soldiers fed the children and then tenderly took them back to Camp Supply. There the youngsters were turned over to the wives of the officers and slowly nourished back to health.[3]

Before leaving the scene of the battle, however, the soldiers destroyed the Indian village. They set fire to more than 100 tepees and to many stacks of food, robes, and other supplies. They also seized 200 horses.

At virtually the same time, troops under Colonel J.W. Davidson struck a somewhat smaller Indian village a few miles away, on the Texas–Oklahoma line. They burned fifty lodges and then chased the Indians, who fled without a fight. After trailing them for three days, the soldiers finally caught the Indians and fought a brief skirmish.

After a short fire fight, most of the Indians once again escaped through a stream bed. This time, however, they were forced to abandon all of their pack animals, which had been carrying badly needed supplies, including many buffalo robes.

A severe sleet storm struck the area a few hours later. The storm was so bad that the soldiers expressed concern over the safety of Indian women and children, who now had no protection from the elements.

For the fleeing Indians, though, there was one silver lining to the cloud: the sleet storm forced the army to temporarily suspend its search. When the storm abated, scouts could find no trace of the missing Indians.

After the two smallest German girls were rescued, friendly Indians told the army that the older girls were also still alive—or least had been a few days earlier. The army asked them to pass the word to whomever held the girls that their search would never be abandoned. They also said that the longer it took to find the girls, the harder it would be on their captors.

Now the army got really tough with the Indians still living off reservations. Troops were to do everything they could to make it impossible for the various Cheyenne villages to receive food or supplies. Additionally, pressure was applied to "compliant" Indians. Nonessential items were also withheld from those already living on the reservations; they were given only the absolute minimum of necessities. Thus, the military hoped to pressure other Indians to assist them in finding the German girls and winning their release. At the same time, the army pushed even harder in the massive search operation.

Sunday, November 29. Troops located and destroyed a small Indian village at Muster Creek, but apparently inflicted no casualties.

Thursday, December 3. The same group of soldiers found a village of about twenty-five tepees on the Sweetwater River. The Cheyennes in the village surrendered and asked to be taken to the reservation. They were desperate for food; the army's campaign was apparently having its desired effect.

Tuesday, December 8. Dog Soldier Chiefs Eagle and Hawk Leader surrendered themselves and nine of their warriors at Camp Supply. They admitted they simply could not keep running any longer.

Monday, December 14. Chief Little Shield and fifty warriors surrendered to the army. They told General Nelson Miles that the two older German girls were now being held by Chiefs Medicine Water and Sand Hill. According to Little Shield's men, the girls had frequently been traded for ponies or food among the various Cheyenne camps. They said the tribe now holding the girls hoped the white government would eventually pay a large ransom for the sisters.

Saturday, January 2, 1875. Chief Stone Calf was tired of running. Physically exhausted, and his horses nearly starved, Stone Calf sent a warrior to Camp Supply to bargain with the army. The problem was that since he had traded Sophia to Gray Beard, Catherine was his only bargaining chip. He agreed to surrender both the girl and himself, and did so that afternoon. Catherine was rushed back to the fort and began receiving medical attention.

With one of the girls still missing, soldiers once again stepped up their pressure on the Indians.

Sunday, January 3. Units of the Sixth Cavalry surrounded Gray Beard's Camp—the village where Sophia was apparently being held. The troops made no effort to attack the village; they merely positioned themselves to cut off the camp's food and water. Then the soldiers waited.

More than a month passed. The Indians knew they were surrounded, and that they could not leave their village. Although they were hungry and cold, and without even basic necessities, the Cheyennes refused to surrender. The army was afraid to move in; if the German girl was still alive, they feared she would be murdered. The tense standoff continued.

Tuesday, February 9. Grey Beard sent word to the soldiers surrounding his village that he was prepared to give up. However, he would do so only in exchange for favorable surrender terms. These terms included a promise that he would not be prosecuted for killing the surveyors he attacked nearly a year earlier. If that offer was unacceptable, he offered an alternative plan: he would swap the one German girl in his possession for several Cheyenne warriors being held by the army.

(Because of the cultural differences, Indians rarely understood that kidnapping and rape were serious crimes. On numerous occasions, Indians were amazed that white men got so angry about the treatment of women. Gray Beard thought the only crime he had committed was murder, and therefore sought only to avoid prosecution for killing the surveyors. In his view, the German girl was simply an item of barter to trade for his captured warriors.)

The army rejected Grey Beard's offer, refusing to make any deal whatsoever. Soldiers continued to surround Gray Beard's camp, preventing them from getting food or supplies.

Another two weeks dragged by.

Friday, February 26, 1875. Six months after the grisly German murders in Kansas, Grey Beard finally capitulated.[4] Shortly after sunup, the chief and several other warriors walked from their village and surrendered unconditionally to the soldiers surrounding them. The final hostage was found moments later by soldiers dashing through the Cheyenne village.

When they were finally released, both of the older German girls—like their younger sisters—were barely alive. Catherine had just turned eighteen and stood about five feet, five inches tall—but she weighed only eighty-five pounds. Both girls appeared to be in shock, and had dazed looks in their eyes; neither could talk, and both bore the scars and bruises of numerous beatings.

Despite their awful physical and mental condition, all four girls responded quickly to loving care of the officers' wives. Before long, it was difficult to get them to quit talking. Understandably furious, the older girls were eager to identify the braves who had raped them virtually every night of their long captivity.

Ultimately, Catherine and Sophia positively identified seventy-five Indians involved in their captivity and torture, or the murder of their family. All of these were subsequently convicted and sentenced to lengthy prison terms in Florida.[5]

Under the watchful, loving care of the military doctors and officers' wives, the girls eventually returned to health. All four of the sisters lived to be elderly; Juliana died in 1960, at the age of ninety-two.[6]

Notes

1. Paul Wellman, *Death on the Prairie* (Lincoln/London: University of Nebraska Press, 1962), 122.
2. Donald Berthrong, *The Southern Cheyennes* (Norman: University of Oklahoma Press, 1963), 385.
3. *Death on the Prairie*, on page 124, claims that both girls were found in Chief Grey Beard's tepee. This information does not agree with official records, and the source of that information is unclear.
4. *The Southern Cheyennes,* on page 401, places this date as March 1, although army records indicate the earlier date is accurate.

5. *The Southern Cheyennes* claims the girls identified only four Indians, but that appears to be in error. Army records indicate the girls identified four Indians who specifically took part in the murder of their parents. The remaining seventy-one warriors they identified as those who held them captive and raped or otherwise mistreated them. *Death on the Prairie,* on page 125, confirms this higher figure as do various other accounts.

6. There are several excellent accounts of the German odyssey. We found Wayne C. Lee and Howard C. Raynseford's *Trails of the Smoky Hill* (Caldwell, Idaho: The Caxton Printers, Ltd., 1980), 214–19, to be especially helpful in researching this story.

The Indians were angered by the constant streams of emigrants who moved down the Santa Fe and Platte River Trails on their way to California and Oregon. The caravans of covered wagons made such noise, what with the creaking wheels, the shouts of mule skinners, the cracking of whips, the bellowing of cattle, and the general hubbub which always accompanies the white man wherever he goes. As a result the buffalo and antelope moved out of the country. It was ruined as a hunting ground.

Paul I. Wellman,
DEATH ON THE PRAIRIE

...low, mean, cunning, cowardly, selfish, and treacherous; these are the characteristics of the whole Indian race.

BIA Agent Thomas Fitzpatrick

–SEVEN–

The Fetterman Massacre

IN THE SPRING OF 1865, the entire frontier was caught up in a continuous bloody confrontation, pitting whites against Indians. The Sand Creek Massacre was four months old, the Indian attack on Julesburg and Fort Segwick three months old. Each side, seething with anger, had a burning passion for revenge.

The trouble was especially severe in Wyoming, Nebraska, eastern Colorado, and western Kansas. Cheyennes, Arapahos, Kiowas, Kiowa–Apaches, and even Comanches were on the war path. The braves danced nightly, either in preparation for war or in celebration of some bloody new battle. Fresh white scalps were commonly found in tepees across the Great Plains.

But the warriors wanted more than just a local war on whites: they wanted the entire Indian nation to join in a sort of holy war against these interlopers. Angry Cheyennes from Colorado's Arkansas Valley carried their war pipes far to the north, where they enlisted the support of the Teton Sioux, including Sitting Bull. The

Sioux and the Cheyenne were the two largest, and most warlike, of the Great Plains tribes. Although in the past they had often been enemies, they were now united as one against the white man.

Actually, smoking the war pipe was hardly necessary for the Santee and Teton Sioux (including the most hostile branch of the tribe, the Brules). These Sioux tribes already considered themselves to be at war with whites, and many were veterans of earlier battles. Most of the Sioux living in Nebraska, the Dakotas, Wyoming, and Montana at this time were Santee Sioux. They had either been through the 1862 uprising in Minnesota or the army's subsequent punitive campaign of 1863. Driven to central Wyoming and Montana, they boiled with anger against the white man.

One of the most outspoken of the Sioux war chiefs was Red Cloud. In 1862 he joined the Santee war parties in North and South Dakota. The Santees were fighting bitter hit–run battles with soldiers who had pursued them out of Minnesota. Already a recognized war chief, Red Cloud added to his reputation for fierceness and cunning as a participant in the biggest Santee battles of 1863 and 1864.

In July of 1865, Red Cloud rode with (and may have even led) attacking Sioux warriors who devastated an army supply train on the Niobrara River, in extreme northwestern Nebraska. The battle ended in a draw; after fighting inconclusively for several hours, the Indians signaled they wanted to council with the soldiers. They offered to let the army wagon train go on unmolested if a ransom was paid. Colonel Sawyer gave them sugar, coffee, tobacco, and rice, and the Indians withdrew.

Chief Red Cloud had no illusions about this minor victory, or about the flood of white intruders flocking to

Courtesy Colorado Historical Society
Chief Red Cloud
Gentle by nature, Red Cloud could be the toughest of the Indian warriors when conditions dictated. He participated in numerous battles with whites throughout Colorado, Kansas, Nebraska, Wyoming, and Montana. Red Cloud personally commanded the siege of Fort Phil Kearney, probably participated in the annihilation of the Fetterman brigade, and was among the council of chiefs who planned and executed the Indian defense of Little Big Horn.

the West. Red Cloud was among the most consistently outspoken Indians opposing all white men, everywhere.

His opposition continued even when he was seemingly preoccupied with intertribal warfare. During a time when he was badly wounded from a battle with rival Crows, Red Cloud spoke out against whites from his tepee (where he was recovering). He urged his tribe to never sign or accept any agreement to permit white men to enter "Sioux country." Red Cloud was determined that north–central Wyoming and southeastern Montana (the Powder River basin) would remain the exclusive domain of his people.

Early in 1866, the white man called for another peace council with the Sioux and northern Cheyenne, to be held at Fort Laramie. The council's main purpose was to allow General Henry B. Carrington to inform the northern tribes of the government's intention to open new roadways through parts of South Dakota, northwestern Nebraska, northeastern Wyoming and southern Montana. Road building, of course, also necessitated building a series of forts along the way to guard future travelers and settlers.

In addition, new roads meant increased traffic, and traffic would scare away the buffalo herds as it did in the Smoky Hill basin of Kansas.

In short, there was nothing the Indians wanted less than a new treaty encouraging white immigration.

When the Fort Laramie conference finally convened in March the army expected no serious resistance. Military leaders even expressed pleasure at the number of Sioux and Cheyennes in attendance. About twenty chiefs and several hundred other Sioux and Cheyennes gathered to hear General Carrington's opening address. Carrington later commented that he thought his remarks were conciliatory and completely inoffensive.

The Indians, however, interpreted his words differently. In the midst of what the white men felt was a calm and peaceful discussion, Chief Red Cloud suddenly leaped atop a table where maps were displayed.

As startled white onlookers watched in amazement, Red Cloud shouted that (brevet) General Carrington was a "white eagle." (This was an apparent reference to the colonel's insignia the newly-promoted general still wore on his dress uniform.) He said that Carrington had come to steal Indian land. Red Cloud also shouted a warning that if the white man ever crossed into Sioux territory (meaning the Powder River Valley) he would be attacked. After an angry harangue lasting several minutes, Red Cloud jumped from the table and stormed out of the council. Scores of followers accompanied him as he left the meeting. Over the next twenty-four hours, almost all remaining Indians struck their tepees and vanished from the Fort Laramie area.

The anger of the Indians and their decision to walk out on the council both surprised and disappointed General Carrington. He had hoped the meeting would lay the groundwork for a new understanding between whites and Indians. However, the walkout in no way altered the plans to build railroads, roads, and a fort.

Shortly after the collapse of the Fort Laramie talks, General Carrington personally led several hundred soldiers into the Powder River Valley to select a site for the new fort. Army engineers soon found an ideal location— near the confluence of the Powder River and Piney Creek. Here the General ordered construction of what was to be the main fort in the region, Fort Phil Kearney.

To Red Cloud and other Sioux, the decision to build the fort—in defiance of Indian warnings at Fort Laramie—was the same as an open declaration of war. Red Cloud called a war council and began planning ways to stop the construction, and drive the white man from the region. Among those attending the council was a young Oglala Sioux brave named Crazy Horse.

Thousands of angry Sioux and northern Cheyennes attended Red Cloud's council; some estimates say as many as 1,200–1,500 gathered along the Little Goose River. Not all of them were warriors, of course—but if even a third were fighting men, they represented a significant fighting force.

Day after day the chiefs met, discussed strategy, and made plans. Night after night, the warriors danced to the war god, preparing for battle with the white soldiers.

As soon as the army actually began construction of the fort, the Sioux and Cheyenne warriors made good their threat; they attacked. Actually, the opening skirmish was comparatively minor, but the Indians made their presence known.

And they didn't let up. The Indians harassed the builders constantly, surrounding the fort on a permanent basis and attacking whenever the opportunity presented itself. This siege—almost unheard of as a tactic of the Indians—was apparently under the personal direction of Chief Red Cloud.

Wednesday, July 19, 1865. Soldiers began digging a foundation for the main barracks building at Fort Kearney. Red Cloud's warriors struck less than forty-eight hours later. At dawn on Friday, July 21, warriors stampeded the army's horses and opened fire on the soldiers' and engineers' tents. In the firefight that followed, two soldiers were killed and three others wounded. As usual, there was no way to determine Indian casualties.

That afternoon Indians attacked a sutler's[1] supply train several miles from the fort, and six white men accompanying the train were killed. The Indians captured most of the supplies, plus a number of horses and mules.

Over the following two weeks, five additional supply trains were attacked, horses and mules taken, and fifteen white men killed. By that time, General Carrington realized he was in for a long-term struggle, and sent for reinforcements.

Carrington cautioned his soldiers to always be on the alert. He warned especially that the enemy would seize any opportunity to capture and torture them.

The general's warning became a matter of fact almost at once. Any man who fell behind while on routine patrol was killed by lurking Sioux warriors, as were any who carelessly wandered out of sight while on guard duty. Supply trains, if not heavily guarded, were attacked, destroyed, the animals driven off, and the men with the train were killed. Frequently, soldiers were captured alive, then horribly tortured and mutilated. Night sentries were picked off if they permitted themselves to be silhouetted by a bright moon.

Sometimes a captured soldier would be tortured at nighttime only a short distance from the fort, with the victim's agonized screams continuing for hours. Soldiers inside the fort would lie awake, firearms ready, listening to the horrendous sounds of a comrade dying a gruesome death. Although no one talked about it, it surely had an enormous psychological impact on the soldiers.

Capture and torture was feared far more than death itself. The soldiers always seemed resigned to the possibility of being killed in battle, but no one was ever prepared for the torture. Most of the men carried a pistol, specifically so that they could commit suicide if faced with inevitable Indian capture.

The possibility of dying a tortuous death was real, and the determination to avoid it at all costs was entirely understandable. Army General Richard I. Dodge told of one common mode of torment employed by these Sioux and northern Cheyenne:

> A favorite method of torture was to stake out the victim. He was stripped of his clothing, laid on his back on the ground and his arms and legs, stretched to the utmost, were fastened by thongs to pins driven into the ground. In this way he was not only helpless, but almost motionless. All this time the Indians pleasantly talked to him. It was all a kind of a joke.
>
> Then a small fire was built near one of his feet. When that [foot] was so cooked as to have little sensation, another fire was built near the other foot; then the legs and arms and body until the whole person was crisped. Finally, a small fire was built on the naked breast and kept up until life was extinct.[2]

Before the year ended, Sioux attacks had killed more than 200 soldiers and army engineers—154 of them in the final six months of the year alone. They also wounded twenty others, ran off about 700 horses and mules, and staged more than fifty separate assaults.[3]

These constant attacks took a mounting toll of soldiers. They also left the white men worn out from sleepless nights and the strain of constant vigilance.

In spite of Indian attacks, the fort had to be built. One of the biggest problems (for the army engineers and construction crews) was that the wood needed for construction had to be hauled from a forest about seven miles away. Unless the wood cutting parties were accompanied by a sizable military escort, they most certainly would be attacked. Sometimes the attacks came even if many soldiers were present.

Into this tense and deadly situation rode a brazen young army captain, who was destined to go down in history. The captain was William J. Fetterman, a highly respected and skilled soldier, who was also a decorated Civil War veteran.

Fetterman had little respect for—and virtually no fear of—the Indian enemy. His fearlessness was probably due to a lack of knowledge; he had never before seen or fought the fierce Sioux and Cheyenne warriors. In his ignorance, Fetterman also let it be known that General Carrington was "too soft" on the Indians. In his opinion, if the general was only a little tougher, the Indians would give up their siege of Fort Kearney. Fetterman would soon have an opportunity to test his theory.

Wednesday, December 9, 1865. An army lookout on a high hill, a half mile south of the fort, began to signal wildly. His signal meant that the wood cutting wagon train was under attack. Captain Fetterman, a less seasoned captain named Fred H. Brown, and Lieutenants William Bingham, Benjamin Grummond, and George C. Wands were dispatched with forty enlisted men to rescue the wood train.

As the rescuers thundered over the hill, the surprised Indians broke off their attack and fled. Fetterman signaled for his troops to give chase. He intended to teach these Indians a lesson they would not soon forget.

Given what the army already knew about chasing Indians—lessons such as the one taught to Captain O'Brien at Fort Segwick and Julesburg eighteen months earlier—Fetterman should have been suspicious of this Indian retreat. He apparently was not.

Onward the soldiers raced, slowly gaining ground. Eventually, the warriors rounded a small hill and it appeared Fetterman would soon catch them. As the eager soldiers rounded the same hill, however, they found themselves facing hundreds of Sioux warriors. Captain Fetterman had ridden into a trap!

About fifteen of the soldiers, lagging behind the other men, were separated and cut off from Fetterman's command. The captain knew at once that he was outnumbered, but also realized that he had vastly superior firepower. In a move that was either extremely brave or extremely foolish, the brazen Fetterman ordered his soldiers to slowly advance toward the Indians. Surprisingly, this boldness worked. The Indians—possibly surprised at Fetterman's unanticipated advance and uncertain how many other soldiers might be following this initial group—broke off the confrontation, and quickly rode back into the hills.

Even with the Indian retreat, however, Fetterman's command was not unscathed. Lieutenant Bingham, Sergeant Jeremiah Rogers, and five enlisted men were killed in the brief skirmish.

Captain Fetterman returned to the fort. Although chagrined to have ridden into the Sioux trap, he was more confident than ever that a show of force would make the Indians retreat. That night at the officer's mess, Fetterman boasted, "Give me eighty men and I'll ride through the whole Sioux nation."[4] He would soon get his chance.

Friday, December 21, 1866. Once again an army lookout began signaling that the wood cutting crew was under attack. General Carrington ordered Captain James Powell to ride to the rescue, but Fetterman intervened. He pleaded for an opportunity to atone for his earlier error in leading the charge against the attackers. Carrington agreed to this change in command.

Captain Fetterman was given forty-nine men from the Eighteenth Infantry, twenty-seven more from the Second Cavalry, plus Captain Phillip Brown who wanted to ride along for the adventure and experience. He was also joined by Lieutenant Grummond, who volunteered to lead the cavalry troops. Two veteran civilian Indian scouts also volunteered to join the soldiers. Ironically, the forty-nine plus twenty-seven soldiers, two officers, and two civilians gave Fetterman eighty men: the exact number he mentioned two weeks earlier when he pledged to "ride through the whole Sioux nation." (If anyone noticed the irony at the time, it is not recorded.)

As Fetterman's troops mounted their horses, General Carrington seemed to have some premonition of disaster. The general ordered him to do whatever it took to relieve the wagon train and drive the Indians off. Recalling how the captain nearly rode into an Indian trap on his last opportunity, the general added, "under no circumstances are you to pursue them beyond Lodge Trail Ridge" (the hill beyond which Fetterman was attacked earlier in the month).

Fetterman's troops thundered out of the fort and over the first hill. As soon as they cleared the initial rise they could see the small Sioux attacking party. The Indians had already broken off their attack on the wood cutters and were riding off in the opposite direction. Fetterman spurred his horse and charged after the disappearing warriors in hot pursuit. When his troops reached Lodge Trail Ridge, Fetterman again signaled them to continue the chase.

No one is quite sure what prompted Fetterman to immediately disobey his orders. Presumably he continued pursuit because, as he reached the ridge, Fetterman spotted about ten braves milling around in the valley just below him. They must have seemed such an easy target, and they had, after all, just attacked an army supply train. What Fetterman could not know (but given his recent experience, certainly should have suspected) was that all of the hills, valleys, and forests around them were crammed full of Sioux warriors.

As Captain Fetterman and his eighty men raced on down the hillside, the ten Indians fled, riding in a criss-cross pattern. That pattern was their signal that it was time to attack. Within seconds, Sioux and Cheyenne warriors poured out of their hiding places and were on all sides of the troops. The attack was so sudden that Indians were dashing directly through the lines of the completely startled soldiers before the soldiers could even fire a shot.

Instantaneously, the Indians had separated the troops into two distinct groups. Captain Fetterman, Captain Brown, and the forty-nine infantrymen were in one group of men; Lieutenant Grummond's cavalrymen and the two civilian scouts were in the second. Army casualties mounted quickly.

Captain Fetterman was one of the first to go down—knocked from his horse in the first rush of the Sioux. Captain Brown also went down in the initial Indian charge as did several soldiers. Lieutenant Grummond desperately tried to rally his cavalrymen, but then he, too, was shot down.

Panicked and leaderless, the remaining soldiers tried to retreat back up the ridge, but it was no use. There were simply too many Indians. No matter which way the panic-stricken soldiers turned they encountered more braves; Cheyenne and Sioux were on all sides. The Indians were so efficient in their attack that within a matter of minutes it was all over and the shooting stopped. A sudden, eerie silence enveloped the battle-field.

BACK AT THE FORT, the men waited in breath-holding suspense—especially after realizing Fetterman had disobeyed orders and rode on beyond Lodge Trail Ridge. Hearing the sudden outburst of gunfire moments later, the men at Fort Kearney knew a fierce battle was underway. General Carrington dispatched Dr. Barry Hines (the camp physician), an orderly, and five others to try to join the troops—assuming there would be some casualties.

In a few minutes, the medical team returned to the fort, unable to continue toward Fetterman's position because of the enormous number of Indians in the area.

Now General Carrington was really alarmed. He rounded up every man he could spare who was able to carry a gun. "Every man who could carry a gun" turned out to be fifty-four soldiers. The general ordered Captain Robert TenEyck and these men to ride out and see what was going on with Fetterman's command.

General Carrington and the others at the fort watched anxiously as TenEyck rode to the top of the first ridge. Immediately the troops halted. In a few seconds the captain sent a lone rider racing back toward the fort with an ominous message: there were Indians everywhere, but no sign of Fetterman. TenEyck pleaded with Carrington to send howitzers.

In recounting the day's events sometime later, Captain TenEyck said that when he topped the ridge he estimated 2,000 Sioux warriors were milling around in the valley below—chanting, cheering, prancing back and forth. There was no sign whatsoever of Captain Fetterman or any of the soldiers who had followed him into battle. TenEyck held his ground until two mountain howitzers and their crews arrived to support him.

It was already late afternoon. While TenEyck waited for reinforcements, the Indians suddenly vanished from the valley below. After several minutes, TenEyck cautiously rode down the hill toward the valley, afraid of what he might find. As he rounded the first little curve in the trail his worst fears were realized. Suddenly he found himself in the midst of a scene of terrible carnage.

There in a small glen lay the bodies of Captain Fetterman, Captain Brown, and forty-seven enlisted men. All of the victims had been stripped of their clothing, scalped, shot full of arrows, slashed open, and otherwise mutilated. Many of the soldiers' heads had been bashed in.

Captains Fetterman and Brown both had bullet holes in the side of their heads, and powder burns were visible on their temples. Many people believe that after being wounded in the first rush of the enemy, the two captains committed suicide rather than face possible capture and torture by the Indians. An alternative explanation is that after they were killed in the first rush, Indian warriors had walked among the victims administering the *coup de grace*—a tactic that was not altogether uncommon (see chapter 11).

Captain TenEyck rode no further. It was beginning to get dark and he had no desire to be out in the valley with 2,000 enemy warriors after nightfall. He ordered his entire command back to the fort.

General Carrington doubled the fort's normal guard that night. Virtually everyone expected the Indians to follow up on their tremendous success in the valley by launching an all-out attack against the fort. They did not do so, however, and the night passed without incident although virtually no one in the fort slept.

Sheer terror gripped the fort that evening. The intensity of their fear became apparent in view of the remarkable orders General Carrington issued: he ordered that the wives and children of the officers be placed into a single, one-room building under triple guard. The guards had strict orders. If the anticipated attack developed and if Indian warriors penetrated the fort's outer perimeter, the guards were to shoot and kill all of the women and children! This would assure their mercifully fast deaths, rather than permitting them to be captured and tortured by the "savages."

The following morning, Captain TenEyck and his troops returned to the valley. The remaining soldiers of Fetterman's command were found in three little groups, and all had suffered the same fate as those discovered the evening before. On the battlefield, TenEyck also found ten dead Indian ponies, and sixty-five "great pools of blood;" where, he presumed, Indian warriors had paid the supreme price.[5]

The last of the bodies had barely been returned to Fort Kearney when snow began to fall. Within two hours, the snow was unusually heavy and the wind was blowing at gale force. By early afternoon there was a full-scale Christmas week blizzard.

The storm was both good and bad news for those in Fort Kearney. It almost certainly meant the Indians would not attack, since warriors almost never fought during a storm. However, the weather also would make it extremely difficult for whomever General Carrington sent out for help, and there was no question that someone must go. Carrington desperately needed reinforcements, and the only way to get assistance was to send someone to Fort Laramie—nearly 250 miles away, with all of those miles controlled by the enemy.

When Carrington asked for volunteers to make the nearly impossible ride for help, he was met with a long period of stony silence. Every man knew it was highly unlikely that anyone could get through. If the storm didn't kill him (and his horse), the Indians most certainly would.

After an agonizingly long time, one man finally stepped forward. The volunteer was John "Portugee" Phillips, a grizzled old fur trapper and army scout. Some say Phillips volunteered out of sheer pity for the widows and children of the murdered officers. Their sorrowful, terror-stricken sobs emanated from the heavily-guarded building where they were being kept.

Whatever the reason, Phillips stepped forward. As the only volunteer, he was quickly accepted to undertake the mission. Phillips made quick preparations and was ready to go less than an hour later.

Out into the night Phillips crept, leading General Carrington's own horse. The horse was an unusually fine animal, loaned to Phillips for this desperate mission because of his strength, intelligence, and endurance. Phillips and his mount were almost immediately swallowed by the vicious snow storm, literally vanishing as soon as they stepped through the gate.

Phillips expected to be killed at once. He kept waiting for the arrow or gunshot, and was surprised when none came. After walking about a half mile, he mounted the horse and set off in what he hoped was the right direction. In the storm he could see no landmarks and had no trail to follow; he trusted the horse to remain on the trail.

The storm howled on unabated through the night. It continued through the next day, and the next, and the next. Snow was often three feet deep, with drifts higher than a man's head. Phillips was dressed in the warmest clothing the army had, yet still he suffered constantly from the cold. Ice formed on his mustache and eye lashes, making it impossible to see. At times he let the horse go wherever it wanted, but he never stopped moving.

Some days he could travel only a few miles because of the deep snowdrifts and howling wind. He was able to find streams of water for both he and the horse to drink, but could find no food anywhere. Even when the snow quit falling, his lot did not improve significantly. The clearing skies brought sharply colder temperatures and the constant threat of snow blindness. Still, Phillips and the horse pushed onward.

Monday, December 31, 1866. A gala New Year's Eve party was underway at Fort Laramie. All the officers at the base and their wives were gathered in the mess hall. The tables had been cleared away to provide room for dancing. An army band was playing for the entertainment of the crowd. The room sparkled with holiday decorations, and a long table was filled with holiday treats.

Suddenly, the door was flung open and a snow laden gust of wind swept into the building. The band stopped playing. Everyone turned their eyes to the door, and must have been startled, perhaps even frightened, by what they saw. Through the door stumbled a mountain of a man, completely covered with ice and snow. His hands and feet were frozen stiff, making it difficult for him to stand up, and he was so cold he could not talk. Outside the door, his once magnificent horse collapsed in the snow and lay gasping for air. The animal died within minutes.

When at last the man had warmed up enough to speak, Portugee Phillips blurted out his story. When he finished, he was carried to the base infirmary where they put him into warm robes and piled on the blankets. Fortunately, Phillips was a strong man and survived the ordeal, but it took five agonizing weeks before he was well enough to leave the hospital. It was a full year before he was well enough to again leave Fort Laramie. The government eventually awarded Phillips a $300 bonus for making the desperate ride. But the trapper's ordeal did not end when he finally reached Fort Laramie. In future months and years, Phillips was subjected to constant harassment from angry Indians, who resented him for getting through to Fort Laramie. At one point, Sioux warriors attacked Phillips' ranch near modern-day Cheyenne, killing about fifty head of cattle. When Phillips finally died in 1883, the government gave his widow another $5,000 as compensation for the slaughter of the cattle and other losses he suffered as a consequence of his bravery and his incredible ride.

It took nine more days—until January 8, 1867—to equip a relief column and for the column to battle back through the deep snow to Fort Kearney. When the soldiers finally arrived, the Indians still had not struck, and the fort was safe—for the moment.

Months passed. Winter gave way to spring, then to summer. Possibly because of the heavy troop reinforcements at Fort Kearney, the Indians became less and less visible. Even so, they continued to harass every man who left or entered the fort. Crazy Horse rode regularly with warriors making hit-and-run raids, and appeared to enjoy the sustained effort against Fort Kearney.[6] Even though the Indian attacks became less frequent, there were still occasional major battles.

Friday, August 2, 1867. Captain James Powell led thirty-six woodcutters and soldiers to the forest seven miles from Fort Kearney on another tree-cutting assignment. The men planned to remain at the site for several days. Powell divided the soldiers into three groups: one party of twelve men, a second crew of thirteen, and a third band of eleven. During the first few hours Captain Powell received several reports that Indians were nearby. The captain was nervous, and ordered preparations be made "just in case."

Captain Powell's preparations were meticulous. He unbolted the beds of fourteen wagons and stood them on their sides to form a circle around the men's tents. The wagon beds created a wooden wall that not only kept Indians from seeing inside the circle, but offered protection against arrows, and at least some protection against bullets.

Another wagon—this one still on its wheels—was placed across the only opening in the circle. The wagon could be pushed aside with some difficulty to allow men in and out. Finally, all other wagons were placed in a second and larger circle a few feet outside the wall formed by the wagon beds. The new barrier created a second line of defense. The one obvious problem with these arrangements was that they offered no protection for the soldiers' horses.

The anticipated Indian attack finally came in the pre-dawn light of the following morning. Their first target was the army's herd of horses. Cheyenne and Sioux warriors sneaked in among the animals and stampeded them.

Several soldiers were already up, and a few were outside the protective circle of wagons when the Indians struck. These men dropped what they were doing and raced desperately for the circle of wagons. Four of them didn't make it. All four, struck by gunshots and arrows, fell outside the wagon-gate. The remaining thirty-two soldiers squeezed inside the walls of their makeshift fort and prepared to fight for their lives.

Unable to see past the wall of wagon beds, the Indians couldn't be sure how many soldiers were inside the circle. Chief Red Cloud was personally directing the attack, and seemed a little unsure about the best way to penetrate the soldiers' defense. He eventually decided to use a frontal assault.

With Red Cloud were Crazy Horse, American Horse, Big Crow, High Backbone, and several other noteworthy Sioux and Cheyenne warriors. The Indian force consisted of hundreds (possibly thousands) of warriors.

As they mounted their first charge, the Indians anticipated they would be met by a single volley of gunfire from the soldiers, followed by a period of silence (and safety) while the soldiers were reloading. That had always been the pattern of past confrontations. The interim during reloading would provide a time for the Indians to overrun the defenses. What the Indians did not know was that these soldiers were armed with the new seven-shot Spencer repeating rifle. This time, there would be no pause after the initial volley.

The Sioux and Cheyenne warriors tore out of the woods, bearing down on the wagons. The crack of many rifles, firing simultaneously, rent the air. Several warriors tumbled from their horses. But to the surprise of the Indians, there immediately were more shots—shots without pause—and more of the Indians fell. In a matter of seconds, the Sioux charge faltered, then broke off altogether. The warriors scampered back into the woods on both sides of the little circle.

Confused by the unexpected barrage of gunfire (unlike anything they had ever encountered before) Red Cloud sent for reinforcements. When they attacked a second time, the approach was entirely different. This time, warriors snaked on their bellies through the tall grass and got as close as possible to the makeshift fort. Thanks to the destruction of the Fetterman detachment the previous year, the Indians had some excellent firearms of their own; but fortunately for the army, they were all single-shot rifles. One of the Indians opened fire, followed instantly by all the others.

The soldiers quickly answered the gunfire, but as instructed by Captain Powell, picked their targets carefully to conserve ammunition. Even with the limited response from the soldiers, the Indians were taking casualties while the army was not.

After some time, Captain Powell signaled his men to stop shooting altogether and to remain absolutely quiet. The Indians, surprised at the lack of return fire, took several more shots at the circle of wagons. Apparently, they believed they had killed or wounded all the men inside. A few minutes later, the Indians charged out of the woods on foot in a "flying wedge," aiming straight for the opening in the little fort.

They were still about twenty yards away when Powell gave the order to open fire, and thirty-two Spencer rifles answered his command. Although several of the lead Indians fell, the others continued coming. They headed straight at the wagons: straight into the virtual wall of lead from the soldiers' rifles. The attack lasted only seconds, but it seemed like several hours. Time after time the leading warriors fell, but others took their places and kept coming. Soldiers nearest the doorway swore they could see the whites of the Indians' eyes. They were grabbing for their knives, assuming that hand-to-hand combat was a second or so away, when the Indian attack finally faltered then collapsed altogether.

The Indians were within eight or ten feet of the fort before the charge was finally broken. Survivors turned and ran back into the woods, leaving the ground littered with their dead and dying.

The lull was temporary. In a matter of minutes, the Sioux charged a third time. Now they were on horseback, moving much more rapidly than before. Eventually, however, the end result was exactly the same. By the time the lead horse was within a dozen yards of the wall, the gunfire was impenetrable. The Indians broke off the attack and once again fled into the woods—and once again left the battlefield littered with dead and dying warriors.

The warriors decided they could not penetrate the fort and did not charge again, but they were not yet ready to give up entirely. Following their normal custom, they wanted (at the very least) to first retrieve their dead and wounded. Their purpose was threefold: it kept the white man from knowing the extent of his success, but it also provided opportunities to treat the wounded and give the dead proper burials.

Red Cloud sent forth his warriors a fourth time. They came crawling through the grass, dragging ropes with nooses tied in the ends. The braves would slip a loop around the foot of a dead or wounded comrade, jerk on the rope, and other Indians would drag the body back into the woods.

Suddenly, a bugle could be heard playing "Boots and Saddles," and a relief column of soldiers came thundering into the glen. The men were on routine patrol when they heard the gunfire and raced to Powell's defense. The Indians simply could not cope with so many soldiers. They turned and fled, leaving Powell's men safe at last.

In the wake of the battle, the army counted three dead and two wounded soldiers.[7] Indian casualties are uncertain, but between the bodies found on the battlefield and bloody drag marks found in the grass, the army estimated that 150 to 180 Indians were at least knocked down. Most of them were probably killed in this lopsided battle.[8]

WINNING THIS SKIRMISH did not mean the winning of the Fort Kearney war. The Indians continued to harass the base and to take a steadily mounting toll of soldiers. Eventually people began to question whether this isolated fort was worth the price being paid.

The following spring, April of 1868, the army and the Bureau of Indian Affairs convened another council at Fort Laramie. This time, the army was more prepared to listen to Chief Red Cloud. After only a few days of talking, a new agreement was struck. Under the new plan, the Sioux and Cheyennes would permit the construction of the Northern Pacific Railroad across North Dakota, Montana and Idaho. In exchange for that concession, the army agreed to abandon Fort Phil Kearney and to stay out of the Powder River Basin. The agreement was formally signed on November 6, 1868.

Even before the formal signing ceremony, though, the army kept its part of the bargain. On Saturday, August 8, 1868, a long column of soldiers rode out of Fort Kearney, followed by wagon loads of military supplies. Many of the men were saddened to leave the fort. Nearly all felt betrayed by the army's agreement to abandon the post, for which so many men had given their lives.

The soldiers were not yet a mile away when Indians entered Fort Kearney and set it ablaze. Clouds of smoke poured into the air, and the column of soldiers riding toward Fort Laramie could see evidence of the burning fort for several hours.

The closure and destruction of Fort Phil Kearney was a great victory for Red Cloud and his Sioux and

Cheyenne army. It was one of the very few major victories the Indians would enjoy in this protracted battle with the white men.

Notes

1. A sutler was a private individual or company under contract to supply food and other items to the army. The sutler also usually ran a "general store" adjacent to major army bases at which the soldiers could buy various personal items for themselves. The loss of a sutler supply train had a profound and immediate impact on soldiers in the area.
2. Paul Wellman, *Death on the Prairie* (Lincoln/London: University of Nebraska Press, 1962), 36. The Indian had perfected the "art" of torture. How well a brave could inflict prolonged pain on a captive was a measure of his ability and worth was a warrior. There are documented reports in which a captured Indian from one of the southwestern tribes—possibly Apache— actually ridiculed his captors for their inability to torture him effectively. The doomed brave gave his captors explicit instructions as to how better to inflict pain and suffering, which he then endured stoically until death.
3. Ibid., 34.
4. This comment is well documented in official military records and other locations; it is reported in *Death on the Prairie* on page 38, and is quoted in nearly all histories of Fort Phil Kearney.
5. There are numerous accounts of the "Fetterman Massacre." This version contains the information that seems to be universally accepted as accurate, and corroborates information contained in formal US Army documents.
6. Some accounts say Crazy Horse also participated in the Fetterman Massacre, although that information is not verified.

7. Although many popular versions of the battle indicate as many as seven soldiers killed, the official army version of the battle [Maurice Matloff, ed., *American Military History* (Washington DC: Office of the Chief of Military History, United States Army, 1969), 307–8] lists the military casualties as three dead and two wounded. The army report says several thousand Indians were involved in the attack.

Commenting on the fighting ability of trained soldiers as compared to the ability of largely undisciplined and untrained Indian warriors, the book says that "...in the Wagon Box Fight, Captain James Powell, with thirty-one men armed (with converted breech-loading Springfields and several repeating rifles) and stationed behind wagon boxes removed from their running gear, held off an investing force of several thousand Sioux and Cheyennes for a good four hours, withstanding mounted and dismounted attacks by several hundred warriors at various times, with only three killed and two wounded.

8. Ibid., 307–8. In commenting on the Fetterman massacre and the Wagon Box Fight that followed, the army is careful to note that accurate Indian casualty figures are impossible to even estimate; "It is risky to deal in statistics concerning Indian participation and casualties in western campaigns. Accounts vary widely, are founded on shaky evidence, and require some balancing and juggling merely to reach a general order of magnitude, much less an accurate assessment of the facts in a given situation. There is no doubt that the Sioux and Cheyennes suffered serious casualties in the...Wagon Box fight."

Indians will sell anything they own—hors-es, blankets, anything—to obtain whiskey. In ranking the good things of this world in order of rank, [the Indians] say that whiskey should stand first, then tobacco, [then] guns, horses, and women.

Gaines P. Kingsbury,
US Army Lieutenant

We have had some experience of it [white man's education]. Several of our young people were instructed in all your sciences, but when they came back to us they were bad runners, ignorant of every means of living in the woods, unable to bear either cold or hunger; they knew neither how to build a cabin, take a deer or kill an enemy; they spoke our language imperfectly. They were totally good for nothing.

Unidentified chief,
quoted by Benjamin Franklin

-EIGHT-

The Battle of Adobe Walls

SATURDAY, JUNE 27, 1874, 6:00 A.M. An unusually large Indian war party attacked a group of white buffalo hunters, at the southwestern Kansas trading camp called Adobe Walls.[1] The attack was carried out by perhaps as many as 300 Cheyenne, Comanche, Kiowa, Arapaho, and Kiowa–Apache warriors. The buffalo hunters had just arisen and were going about their daily routine when the warriors suddenly poured out of a ravine, shooting rifles as they came. The leader of the war party was believed to be Cheyenne Chief Isatai.

Adobe Walls had at one time been an important trading post, but it had been abandoned and fell into disrepair. The camp now consisted of the ruins of several original buildings, plus four still usable structures: a lumber storage building, a small general store, and a house (all constructed of logs) and a saloon built of sod. During hunting season, the four buildings were occupied by traders. The camp served as a central exchange point, where white hunters could either trade or store their buffalo hides and obtain supplies to continue the hunt.

Under normal circumstances only seven or eight white men would have been at Adobe Walls this time of year. That relative handful would be operating a blacksmith shop, a small general store, and a saloon. By sheer coincidence, however, about twenty-five well-armed buffalo hunters arrived at Adobe Walls a few hours before the attack began. The Indians did not expect to meet with stiff resistance, and the presence of the additional men laid the groundwork for a classic battle.

The night before the attack began was unusually hot and humid. Those at Adobe Walls had trouble sleeping, although none seemed certain as to why. Many of the men later recalled that the horses seemed unusually restless. Subsequent to the attack they reasoned that the horses were probably reacting to the Indian war party that was closing in on Adobe Walls.

There were twenty-eight men and one woman at Adobe Walls that night. The lone woman was Lucille (Mrs. William) Olds, who helped her husband run a small restaurant at the rear of the general store.

At about two o'clock in the morning, one of the wooden beams supporting the saloon roof suddenly gave way with a loud crack. The broken pole crashed heavily to the floor and the ceiling sagged ominously. The noise awakened everyone in camp. They quickly discovered the sagging roof, which was threatening to collapse at any moment, and everyone set about making emergency repairs.

At precisely the moment the beam broke, the Indians surrounding Adobe Walls were preparing to sneak into camp and set fire to the wooden buildings. Now, because all the whites were up and moving around, the Indians feared discovery. They had to pull back and delay their initial raid. The emergency repairs were completed just as the sun began to brighten the morning sky.

One of the men who worked through the night repairing the broken support beam was Bill Dixon, a seasoned buffalo hunter. Dixon was walking to his flat bed wagon moments later to prepare for the day's hunt. As he walked, he noticed a "large, dark mass" approaching the camp. Initially Dixon thought the mass was a herd of buffalo, but after a few seconds realized that it was an Indian attack.

Two other white men had already gone to a second wagon parked slightly further from the camp's buildings than was Dixon's. Brothers Frederick and William Shadler hoped to get a short nap in the cooler bed of the wagon before starting the day's work. They were just lying down when they spied the attacking Indians.

The two men leaped from the wagon bed and started running toward the buildings of Adobe Walls. They were too late getting started; both were quickly overrun by the attackers. Dixon says that as the brothers ran toward the main buildings of Adobe Walls the Indians caught up with them and "ran them through" with lances.

Dixon, being considerably closer to the buildings, reached them well ahead of the Indians. He scurried inside the walls of the complex, screaming a warning as he ran. The hunters and others at Adobe Walls knew immediately what was happening and reacted instantly. Several sprang to windows or doors and began shooting in the direction of the Indians. Others knocked adobe chinking from between logs and began firing through the cracks.

The hunters had excellent weapons, and all were good shots. The combined fire from buffalo rifles and

Sharpes repeating rifles turned back the Indian assault just before it reached the front gate.

If this had been a "normal" Indian attack (or an attack launched a few years earlier) the Indians would simply have begun riding round and round Adobe Walls, lobbing occasional fire arrows at the buildings. This was not a normal attack, however. Isatai and his warriors were determined to kill every person in the compound, regardless of the consequences.

Instead of backing off when the whites began shooting back, the Indians milled around in momentary confusion, then resumed the assault. Dozens of braves dashed inside the main gate. They rode straight for the buildings where the fort's inhabitants had taken shelter moments earlier. After a short time the Indians managed to surround the four buildings.

In the early moments of the attack, all of the whites were either already inside a building, or ran to the building closest to them. That meant that the whites were divided into several groups. Nine of them were in the saloon. These nine had plenty of food, water, and whiskey—but not much ammunition. Eleven others, well armed and supplied with ample ammunition, were in the general store. They also had adequate food, although water was not readily available. The six remaining men and Mrs. Olds were inside the small house. They were well armed, and had adequate supplies of everything they needed: food, water, and ammunition.

In the opening moments of the battle, the glass windows shattered in all four of the structures. Warriors on foot raced up to the doors and tried to smash them open, but the well-constructed buildings did not give way to the pounding. Several Indians tried to crawl through windows, but were blasted from the openings by the big buffalo guns of the men inside. The whites were shooting from every conceivable position in the buildings, and the Indians were hard hit by the rifle fire.

At this point two of the hunters made a grievous error. When several of the Indians began withdrawing toward the gate, Billy Tyler and Fred Leonard stepped outside the building to get a better shot at them, thus laying themselves open to Indian gunfire. Within seconds a bullet smashed through Tyler's chest. Leonard dragged his friend back inside the building, but Tyler bled to death a few moments later.

After a confusing several minutes of fierce fighting—a time that seemed forever to the whites, the Indians suddenly began to withdraw. They dragged their dead and wounded back outside the walls.

The first round of the battle was over, a victory for the defenders. However, no one supposed that the Indians were gone for good.

Several minutes passed with agonizing slowness, and not a sound could be heard from outside the compound. The whites breathed heavily and frequently checked their weapons, waiting for the inevitable. The silence was shattered as the Indians burst through the gates for a second time, making another rush at the buildings. Once again the warriors were mowed down by the murderous, concentrated fire of the hunters. After a brief period the Indians withdrew a second time, again dragging their casualties with them.

After two attacks, shortage of ammunition for the men in the saloon was becoming critical. There was no ammunition for some of the rifles in the building, and only limited amounts for the other weapons. As the Indians retreated from the compound a second time, the door of the saloon was thrown open. Billy Dixon and James Hanrahan sprinted across the courtyard toward the general store and the invaluable supply of bullets contained therein.

The Indians, apparently taken by surprise, fired no shots at the compound for a few precious seconds. The men were half way to the store before the Indians opened up. Bullets smashed all around them, kicking up dust at their feet and sending wood chips flying around their faces. The men were lucky; they reached the store and dived inside through a smashed window without being hit.

Because of a shortage of manpower in the store, and the danger of making the return crossing, Dixon decided to remain and help defend the store. Hanrahan would have liked to stay, but knew he needed to take ammunition back to his companions in the saloon.

Filling several bags with cartridges, Hanrahan crouched at the door. At a lull in the shooting, someone threw open the door and out he ran. Crouching as low as his could, Hanrahan zig-zagged across the dusty court yard, puffs of smoke and clods of dirt rising all around him. Once again, however, the Indians all miraculously missed.

Over the next several hours the Indians launched frequent new attacks against the compound, but each ended the same way. Occasionally the Indians got inside the compound, and even reached the buildings from time to time, but were eventually driven back. Each time, they dragged dead and wounded warriors with them.

One reason for their failure was that the warriors had unwisely adopted the white man's tactic of first blowing a bugle to signal the start of each charge. The bugling alerted the buffalo hunters to each new attack, permitting them to be fully prepared for the charge that followed.

By the middle of the afternoon, the braves decided they were not going to be able to overwhelm the whites. The warriors withdrew to higher ground some distance away and began plotting a new strategy.

Then the Indians made another serious mistake; they decided to engage the white men in a long-range rifle duel. The Indians were equipped mostly with old smooth-bore, single-shot rifles and a few carbines. The buffalo hunters had the huge .50 caliber "buffalo guns," shooting 125 grains of powder and 600 grains of lead.

In addition to the advantage of better weapons, the hunters were the most skillful shots on the frontier. These were men who were accustomed to making good on long-range shots and proud of their deadly accuracy. What the hunters did over the next several minutes may still be a world record for long range shooting. Everyone in the camp swears the story is true.

A band of a dozen or so Indians were sitting on their horses atop a ridge about a mile from the buildings in the fort. The whites watched the Indians and began to debate whether a buffalo gun could reach out far enough to hit one of them. Billy Dixon, the best shot in the crowd, wagered that he could hit a brave even at that distance. Others urged him to try.

Dixon picked up his favorite buffalo gun. Twice he took aim, then lowered the rifle and adjusted his sights. On the third try, he finally squeezed the trigger. The hunters watched for what seemed to be an eternity, and nothing happened. They were disappointed.

Just as they started to turn from the window, believing he had missed, the brave on the ridge suddenly shot backwards off his horse—obviously struck by the bullet. Later the men found considerable blood and other indications that the Indian had, in fact, been killed by the shot. Several years later, a surveyor measured the distance from the window to the spot at which the Indian was hit. The distance was 4,614 feet—just 666 feet short of a mile! Possibly as a result of this remarkable shot, Indians thought the white man's gun had mystic pow ers. The braves began calling the Sharpes the "shoot today, kill tomorrow gun".

In spite of their continuing setbacks, the Indians attacking Adobe Walls did not discourage easily. Undeterred by the fact that they could not penetrate the buildings and had suffered heavy casualties trying to do so, they continued to surround the camp and shoot at anyone who moved. These mostly ineffective sniping attacks continued for eight long days. Since the Indians were held at long range, the whites were able to move between buildings with some ease. During those eight days they suffered no serious shortages of food, water, or ammunition.

On the sixth day of the siege, the whites suffered their fourth casualty. William Olds accidentally killed himself with his own rifle. The weapon discharged as he was climbing down a ladder from an attic window, from which he had been shooting at the Indians.

In the middle of either the third or the fourth night (no one could remember which), several of the buffalo hunters slipped out of the camp and ran for help. They reached an army outpost the following afternoon, and a small army patrol was dispatched to rescue Adobe Walls from the Indians.

When the attacking Indians spotted the troops approaching the following day, they beat a hasty retreat. Leaving behind the bodies of six dead, the braves later claimed that was the number killed in the confrontation. Virtually everyone else believed the toll of dead was much higher, with perhaps twenty to thirty other Indians wounded.[2]

The rescuing soldiers didn't give up merely because the Indians ran. They began to trail the retreating war party. A few miles from Adobe Walls they found the scalped body of rancher William Watkins. Indian Agent John Miles joined the army patrol and rounded up several civilians to help. There were now perhaps forty men in the group chasing the several hundred warriors.

A few miles from where the dead rancher was discovered, the patrol found a still-burning wagon train, and the bodies of four white men. Wagon master Patrick Hennessey, identifiable only because of a ring he wore, was found tied to a wagon wheel and burned to death. George Gand and Thomas Calloway had been shot and then scalped; Ed Cook was simply shot.

The war party was apparently not aware of the soldiers and civilians still on their trail. The Indians were moving quickly, but took time to stage almost daily attacks as they worked their way in a generally south-southeasterly direction. On Wednesday, August 26, the Indians overwhelmed a railroad survey party, killing and scalping nine people.

By now, the pursuing posse had grown considerably. No longer primarily a civilian posse, the search was now being led by Colonel Nelson Miles. Miles was one of the best and most experienced Indian fighters on the frontier. He was accompanied by eight companies of the Sixth Cavalry, four companies of the Fifth Infantry, and thirty-nine Indian scouts.

On the afternoon of August 27, the pursuers topped a ridge and saw about 200 warriors attacking a group of eleven buffalo hunters in a small valley below. Before the soldiers could take action, they saw the Indians chase down one frightened buffalo hunter, and run him through with a lance. The soldiers charged down the hillside and into the hunters' camp, driving the sur-

prised braves before them. They managed to kill one
Cheyenne and wound another before the remaining
Indians fled.

Sunday, August 30, 1874. Advance elements of Colonel
Miles' search party, under the command of Lieutenant
Frank D. Baldwin, rode into a narrow valley on the
Sweetwater River. At the entrance they were attacked
by "large numbers" of Cheyenne warriors. (Estimates as
to the number of attackers varied widely; *The Southern
Cheyennes* says there were about 600 Cheyennes in the
attacking war party; *Death on the Prairie* estimates the
number at 200.) Dismounting quickly, the fifty soldiers
and scouts formed a small circle and held the Indians at
bay.

Apparently believing these were the only soldiers in
the area, the Indians quickly surrounded the patrol.
They were not aware when the main body of troops
arrived moments later.

Colonel Miles ordered Lieutenant Colonel J.W.
"Black Jack" Davidson and Colonel Ranald S.
MacKenzie to form a skirmish line. "Forward!" shouted
Miles. "If any man is killed, I will promote him to corpo-
ral."[3]

When the Indians spotted the much larger group of
soldiers attacking, they broke off their attack and hastily fled. Pursuing soldiers fought skirmishes with rear
guard warriors over the next five hours, but the main
body of Indians managed to cross the Red River. There
they split into several groups, most of them heading
southwestward into the Texas panhandle. The soldiers
were exhausted by this time (as were their horses), and
had to break off the pursuit and return to camp.

Over the next several weeks, sizable Indian war
parties attacked settlers, travelers, and outposts

throughout the region almost daily. Presumably, these Indians were from Isatai's camp of hostile warriors. During the month of July alone, about 200 whites were killed in these attacks in eastern Colorado, western Kansas, the Texas panhandle, and parts of Oklahoma.

Soldiers tracked the Indians and gave chase when possible, but pursuit was usually ineffective. The Indians, spread out in small groups, were able to strike and disappear quickly. Both the soldiers and their horses were quickly exhausted from these chases.

Frustrated by his failure to wipe out the Indians, Colonel Miles (now breveted to the rank of general) eventually withdrew to the Sweetwater River near the confluence of McClellan Creek. His supplies were running low—an attack on his wagon train on September 8 destroyed several wagon loads of food—and the horses were too weary to continue. Miles wrote a letter asking for reinforcements and supplies, and dispatched six men to carry the message to Camp Supply, Oklahoma.

The volunteers for the dangerous ride to Camp Supply were all frontier veterans. The six soldiers were joined by Billy Dixon, the hero of the Battle of Adobe Walls, and another well-known civilian army scout, Amos Chapman. Other men in the group were Sergeant Z.T. Woodhull and six enlisted men from the Sixth Cavalry.

The messengers did their best to escape detection by the Indians, but there were just too many warriors in the area. On the second day out, the messengers were spotted by a Kiowa war party of perhaps 100 braves. The Indians instantly attacked the small group of men.

When the Indians charged, the eight messengers leaped from their horses and scrambled for cover. One soldier, Private George W. Smith, tried to lead the horses to cover. He was shot through the chest and dropped to the ground, unmoving and apparently lifeless. Amos Chapman was also hit immediately, a bullet smashing his left leg. Private John Harrington was shot in the left arm, and Sergeant Woodhull was hit in the left thigh. That left only four of the eight volunteers unwounded.

Yet, in spite of their injuries, the little party fought back desperately. Spotting a shallow buffalo wallow nearby, those able to do so dove into its meager protection. The wallow was only ten inches deep, but afforded some cover. The men began firing back, but they were in desperate trouble. Neither Chapman nor Smith was able to move, and Chapman called out that his leg was too badly broken for him to change positions. Dixon, Woodhull, Harrington, and Private Peter Rath opened fire to keep the Indians at bay while they tried to figure out how to rescue their injured companions.

As the 100 Kiowa warriors scampered to surround them, Dixon noticed Chapman trying to pull himself along the ground to reach the buffalo wallow. Dixon rose to his feet in a crouched position (to present the smallest possible target) and ran to Chapman's side.

Throwing himself to the ground beside the wounded man, Dixon ordered Chapman to climb onto his back. Then, although Chapman was much larger than he, Dixon raised to his feet again and hastened back to the wallow. As he dove inside, the Indians fired everything they had in a vain effort to stop the rescue.

The Indians, possibly angered by the successful rescue of Chapman, launched a frontal assault on the wallow. The white men, however, were excellent shots, well armed, and all were battle veterans. Firing carefully with their repeating rifles, they picked off a half dozen of the attackers. As the leaders fell, the remainder of the Indians broke off the charge and retreated. This time it was the warriors who sought places of concealment, from which they continued shooting.

The battle continued all morning. Twice more the Indians leaped onto their horses and raced toward the wallow, but were driven back both times. Sniper fire was almost nonstop.

The day was unusually hot, and the soldiers soon began to suffer terribly from a lack of water. (One supposes the Indians also suffered, although there is no record of their reaction to the heat.)

The battle site was a grisly scene. All of the soldiers' horses had now been shot to death. A number of Indian bodies cluttered the grassy valley between the wallow and the trees, from which most of the Indians were shooting. Most of the surviving soldiers were in considerable pain, caked with blood and dirt. The situation appeared hopeless.

About the middle of the afternoon, a sudden, heavy thunderstorm swept across the valley. Welcome sheets of rain poured down. The storm not only provided badly needed water to the men, but it also temporarily obscured them from the enemy.

As the storm began to abate a few minutes later, someone in the wallow noticed the body of Smith. The dead soldier had been carrying a cartridge belt, and ammunition in the wallow was becoming scarce. If there was going to be an opportunity to get the ammunition belt, this was the time.

Private Rath scrambled over the side of the wallow and scurried to the dead man's side. Starting to yank off the cartridge belt, Rath was astounded to see the "dead" man move a little bit. Rath grasped the arms of the badly wounded Smith, and hustled back to the wallow, dragging him behind.

Shot through the chest, Smith did die within moments of being pulled back to the wallow. Even in death, however, Smith helped to defend their position. Dixon propped up the dead soldier, so that the top of his head and his rifle were visible from outside—making the Indians think there was one more defender.

When darkness finally brought a halt to the day-long sniping, Rath volunteered to go for help. He slipped over the side and vanished. The men waited quietly, hoping Rath had defied the odds and gotten through the line of Indians. To their disappointment, Rath reappeared after two hours. Unable to find any trail in the darkness, Rath was reluctant to wander around without having a clue where he was going.

But that was the bad news. The good news was that Rath had found no trace of the Indians.

At sunrise, Dixon set out to get help. He also found no trace of the Indians. About an hour later Dixon encountered an army patrol led by Major Charles Price.

Price and fifty soldiers flew to rescue the surviving messengers. They were given first aid and food, Smith's body was buried. Those who lived through the attack were taken back to Fort Sill.

The story of the "Battle of the Buffalo Wallow" drew widespread attention. One year later, the United States Congress awarded the Congressional Medal of Honor to the five white men who survived this battle.[4]

Notes

1. Paul Wellman, *Death on the Prairie* (Lincoln/London: University of Nebraska Press, 1962), says on page 105 that Adobe Walls was located in the extreme northeast corner of the Texas panhandle. Virtually all accounts say this attack occurred in extreme southwestern Kansas. It appears likely that there were two places

called Adobe Walls—this one and another abandoned William Bent/Ceran St. Vrain trading post in Texas. The Texas location is certain; it is the spot at which Kit Carson later had a major battle with Indians.

It also appears likely that one of the places was called "Adobe Wells" and the other "Adobe Walls"; several old documents indicate this may have been the case. Unfortunately, history seems to have lost track of which was which.

2. There are several well-documented accounts of the Battle of Adobe Walls. This account includes most of the commonly accepted facts of the battle, especially those that could be verified through US Army records. We found *Death on the Prairie*, pages 107–11, to be especially complete and helpful in our research.

3. *Death on the Prairie,* 113.

4. The description of this phase of the incident relies on several battle reports and published accounts. The information found in *Death on the Prairie*, pages 114–17, confirms much of the information.

If I were an Indian, I often think I would greatly prefer to cast my lot among those of my people who adhered to the free open plains, rather than submit to the confined limits of a reservation, there to be the recipient of the blessed benefits of civilization, with its vices thrown in without stint or measure. Stripped of the beautiful romance with which we have been so long willing to envelop him, the Indian forfeits his claim to the appellation of the "noble red man." We see him as he is—a "savage" in every sense of the word; no worse, perhaps, than his white brother would be similarly born and bred, but one whose cruel and ferocious nature far exceeds that of any wild beast of the desert. When the soil which he has claimed and hunted over for so long a time is demanded by this to him insatiable monster [civilization], there is no appeal; he must yield, or it will roll mercilessly over him, destroying as it advances. Destiny seems to have so willed it, and the world nods its approval.

General George A. Custer,
My Life on the Plains

–NINE–

Custer Enters the War:

Washita

ARGUABLY THE BEST INDIAN FIGHTER of all time was also one of the most flamboyant and most controversial. He was George Armstrong Custer, young, blond, dashing, daring, and—some say—stupid. Custer seemed to constantly hover between being idolized and vilified, loved and hated. He was first the hero, then the villain: a winner, then a loser. He would score an impressive victory, and follow it up with some inexcusable indiscretion. He was promoted and demoted, held up as a shining example, and then held up to ridicule.

First gaining fame in the Civil War, Custer was later sent to the Great Plains to battle the likes of Cheyenne Dog Soldier Roman Nose and the other militant Indians. Although never trained as an Indian fighter, he immediately scored several impressive victories and soon became the darling of the whites on the Great Plains.

Custer served in the Indian–fighting role for more than eleven years. More accurately, he was an Indian fighter for about ten years, with one year off in the middle of his assignment because he had been suspended without pay. But that comes later in the story.

One of the first documents dealing with General Custer the Indian fighter is in the nature of a formal 1867 complaint—not about him, but from him. Immediately after the Civil War the US Army was plagued with desertions from its ranks. The desertions made it difficult to keep up pressure against the Indians. Many men who wanted to hunt gold in Colorado, for example, would enlist in the army under an assumed name in the East, knowing that as soon as they were trained they would be shipped to one of the Indian-fighting posts in the West. When they arrived at their assigned post, they would quickly go AWOL and head for the hills.

General Custer complained to his superiors, in the fall of 1867, that he was losing so many men it was difficult to field a decent fighting force. Custer blamed more than "gold fever" for the AWOLs; he complained that at least some of the numerous desertions were due to "this terrible army food." He charged that the frontier troops were still being issued left over Civil War rations!

Desertions were epidemic. Nearly 800 men deserted from the Seventh Cavalry alone in a twelve–month period between July of 1866 and June of 1867. A newspaper at Junction City, Kansas, reported that thirty soldiers deserted in a single night.

In spite of his troubles, though, Custer vigorously pursued his assignment: to carry on an active campaign aimed at crushing Indian hostilities in western Kansas and eastern Colorado. He would later also fight in Oklahoma, the Texas panhandle, Nebraska, Wyoming, and Montana.

There was plenty of hostility to crush. Indian attackers had grown increasingly brazen. In late 1866, well before the Battle of Beecher Island, the army began planning a campaign that would hopefully put an end to the trouble without further fighting—but a plan that prepared to wage battle if necessary. The strategy called for a massive military show of force that would encourage Indians to voluntarily report to the many reservations now dotting the West. Hopefully, the Indians would turn in their weapons and agree to live forever as wards of the US government. But to make certain there was plenty of Indian cooperation, the army sent word that any who did not voluntarily go to a reservation would be considered an enemy, and would be killed.

Wednesday, April 3, 1867. After a series of long delays, the army finally began its "show of force" march through the heart of the frontier. This first march was to cover extreme western Kansas and east-central Colorado. Word of the army's presence "in force" quickly circulated among plains Indians, and the reaction was as varied as the people. Many of the tribes (most, perhaps) who were camped anywhere close to the Smoky Hill country now headed for the nearest army base to make certain they were not mistaken as "hostiles."

Many others (presumably those Indians who had no intention of abandoning the disputed land) began setting fire to the rangeland ahead of the troops. They hoped that the fires would deplete the forage for army horses around the Indian villages, forcing the soldiers to remain at a distance.

The fires were set, the grass was burned. The army kept coming.

Saturday, April 13. General Winfield Scott Hancock, new commander of the Division of the Missouri, personally led several hundred troops into Colorado. One of his senior officers was General George Custer. As the troops camped on the Colorado–Kansas border, Indian messengers appeared and told General Hancock that Sioux Chief Pawnee Killer and Cheyenne Chief White Horse wanted to council with him. Hancock agreed, and set the meeting for the following morning at nine-thirty.

When nine-thirty came the next morning, General Hancock stood waiting for the Indians. After several minutes, Chief Pawnee Killer rode up on his pony— alone—and said all of the other chiefs had been delayed, but would arrive at any time. Pawnee Killer then departed, saying he would return with the other chiefs in a few minutes.

Ten-thirty came. Then it was eleven o'clock, and still no other chiefs arrived. At noon, Hancock gave up, ordered his troops to mount, and began moving along the trail.

As the column crested another hill a few moments later, they found themselves facing a huge line of warriors in full battle dress. Hundreds of Cheyenne and Sioux were lined up side-by-side, stretching all along the crest of a ridge on the far side of a shallow valley. Lieutenant General Custer called it one of "the most impressive and most awe inspiring military displays I have ever seen."

The Indian battle line stretched for over a mile. Along the front line were mounted scores of grim-faced warriors in war paint, each carrying a lance. Each lance was topped with a feather or a pennant.

Immediately behind this front line was a second, and the warriors in the second line had rifles ready, revolvers shoved into waist bands.

Then there was a third tier of braves. These warriors carried bows and arrows at the ready.

The Indians had carefully selected for themselves the highest ground in the area, giving them a distinct advantage if fighting broke out. They stood in absolute stony silence, neither moving nor speaking, but staring resolutely at the line of soldiers approaching across the little valley.

General Custer was impressed. He wrote that the soldiers had paused for a ten–minute break just before meeting the Indians:

At 11 a.m. we resumed our march and had proceeded but a few miles when we witnessed one of the finest and most imposing military displays it has ever been my lot to behold. An Indian line of battle was drawn directly across our line of march, as if to say "this far and no farther." Most of the Indians were mounted; all were bedecked in their brightest colors, their heads covered with their brilliant war bonnets, their lances bearing the crimson pennant, bows strung, and quivers full of barbed arrows. In addition, each warrior was supplied with either a breech-loading rifle or revolver, sometimes with both—these latter obtained through the wise foresight and strong love of fair play which prevails in the Indian department.

For a few moments appearances seemed to foreshadow any thing but a peaceful issue. General Hancock, coming in view of the wild fantastic battle array, which extended far to our right and left and not more than a mile in our front, hastily sent orders to the infantry, artillery and cavalry to form a line of battle.

...Bright blades flashed from their scabbards into the morning sunlight and the infantry brought their muskets to a carry. After a few moments of painful suspense, General Hancock, accompanied by General A.J. Smith and several other officers, rode forward and [speaking] through an interpreter invited the chiefs to meet us midway for an interview. In response to this invitation, Roman Nose, bearing a white flag, accompanied by 10 other chiefs, rode forward to the middle of the open space between the lines, where we all shook hands, most of them exhibiting unmistakable signs of gratification at this apparently peaceful termination of our encounter.[1]

In truth, although the Indian battle line was very impressive, it is clear that the warriors were no military match for the troops. Whereas the Indians probably numbered no more than 600, about a third of whom were armed only with lances or bows and arrows, the army force included 1,100 heavily armed and well-trained soldiers. The army also had another 300 Pawnee scouts, who were also well-armed. In addition, the army had a number of artillery pieces at the ready.

When the soldiers first topped the hill and witnessed the great line of warriors, General Hancock signaled for his soldiers to disperse and prepare for battle. At that particular moment, however, Indian Agent Wynkoop, who was with the troops, rode forward by himself. Chief Roman Nose and several other war chiefs recognized Wynkoop and rode out a few paces from the line to meet him.

As edgy soldiers and warriors fingered their weapons nervously, Wynkoop, who was generally liked by the warriors, told the Indians that the army intended them no harm and would not fight unless attacked. He spoke softly to Roman Nose and reassured the chief that his women and children were safe, and would not be attacked by the soldiers. After a brief time he convinced Roman Nose and several lesser chiefs to ride back to a point halfway between the lines to meet personally with General Hancock.

Roman Nose was as impressive as ever. As already described elsewhere, he was extremely large—various descriptions say he was between 6'1" and 6'4"; he weighed over 200 pounds, but was all muscle. Today he wore a bright, feathered war bonnet (probably the "magic" one that protected him in battle), and splashes of colorful war paint. In his arms he cradled a rifle; in his waist band were four Colt revolvers, and slung across his back was a bow and a quiver of arrows.

Whites often said that Roman Nose seemed always to be angry and defiant—and he appeared on this day to be even more angry than normal. Although he immediately denied that he wanted war, the Cheyenne chief repeatedly warned General Hancock that he was prepared for battle in spite of the odds against him.

General Hancock also talked tough. He said the army would not tolerate threats, and demanded Indian compliance with the white man's rules. The talks went on for some time, and at one point an angry Roman Nose raised his rifle and pointed it toward the general. It was a tense moment that could easily have triggered open warfare. Instead, Chief Bull Bear, half-breed George Bent and fur trader Ed Guerrier all intervened and got Roman Nose to calm down.

The Dog Soldier chief finally lowered the weapon after Guerrier pointed out that Hancock's death would certainly cause the soldiers to destroy the Indian village. If they did so, he warned, they would certainly kill all the women and children therein.

In the end, Roman Nose agreed that General Hancock could visit his village and see for himself that it was peaceful. Hancock mentioned specifically that he wanted to chat with the women and children, to reassure them of the army's peaceful intentions. The Indians finally parted to allow the army officers through their lines. But when Hancock rode into Roman Nose's village a few minutes later, he found it totally deserted. The women and children had been evacuated while Roman Nose was delaying the soldiers.

General Hancock was furious, and felt he had been double-crossed by the Indians. He ordered Roman Nose to catch the women and children and bring them back to the village for talks. Roman Nose refused, saying his ponies were too hungry and weak to chase after them. Hancock told Roman Nose that he could borrow army horses, but he must return the women and children.

Roman Nose agreed to this demand and sent a number of his men on army horses to retrieve missing Indians. Before leaving, he warned General Hancock that it would probably be the next day before everyone was back in the village. General Hancock and his men pulled back a quarter of a mile and camped for the night, awaiting the return of Roman Nose and his followers.

About midnight, General Hancock began to get suspicious that the Indians were not coming back at all: that Roman Nose had double crossed him. Hancock stormed out of his tent, shouting and rousting several of his aides, then ordered his soldiers to surround the Indian village. When the sun rose the next morning, the soldiers entered the encampment and found it entirely deserted except for one elderly Indian man, a woman, and a teenage girl. The three Indians were apparently neither Sioux nor Cheyenne.

The girl, probably a slave captured in some earlier Indian war, had been beaten and showed other signs of brutal treatment. According to General Custer, the girl said she had been repeatedly raped by the Dog Soldiers. Army surgeons who examined the girl confirmed her story.

Several weeks later, however, Indian Agent Wynkoop reported that he believed the girl had also been raped by some of the soldiers who found her. He later filed a written report with the Bureau of Indian Affairs, making his suspicions into a formal accusation. All of the soldiers steadfastly denied Wynkoop's allegation, and numerous officers (including Generals Hancock and Custer) said that at no time was the girl out of the sight of the highest ranking officers long enough for such attacks to have occurred. Wynkoop and fellow Indian Agent Leavenworth stood by their charges, however. They also insisted that any subsequent trouble was the army's fault, because it sent soldiers into the Indian area in the first place, and because the soldiers had abused the girl.

General Hancock was furious at Wynkoop's assertions that the girl had been assaulted by his troops, and the two exchanged harsh words. But Hancock couldn't dwell on the BIA accusation; he had more pressing matters to worry about at the moment. Hancock was outraged to find Roman Nose's village deserted, and furious that Roman Nose had taken advantage of the army's generosity to get away on army horses.

The general wondered aloud whether he should burn the Indian village in retaliation for Roman Nose's deception. Agent Wynkoop argued against it. Wynkoop said such action would only harden the Indian position and give them new reason to attack.

Sunday, April 14, 1867. Primitive communication prevented General Hancock from immediately learning of new trouble that occurred five days before his meeting with Roman Nose and Tall Bull. Big Creek Relay Station, located eighty miles east of Monument Station in west–central Kansas, was burned to the ground. The station's stock tender was nailed to the side of the barn. Branches piled up around him were set on fire, and he burned to death. Other buildings at the station were also destroyed by fire, and all of the horses were run off.

Monday, April 15, 1867. Within hours after discovering that the Indians had vanished from their village while Roman Nose delayed the troops, Hancock ordered Custer to go after Roman Nose. Custer was to bring the chief and his tribe back to the village. Accompanying Custer were 400 cavalry troops, fur trader Ed Guerrier (to act as interpreter if the Indians were located), several Pawnee scouts, and "Wild Bill" Hickok to act as guide.

The troops moved rapidly, but the Indians had a good head start. Over the next three days, Custer and his men found numerous burned ranches, fences cut, and evidence that both horses and cattle had been taken by the Indians they were trailing.

On the morning of April 18, Custer found the Lookout Relay Station burned to the ground. The bodies of three men were tied to a fence. All had been horribly burned, then slashed open, and their intestines pulled out. Evidence at the scene suggested the mutilation may have been done while the men were still alive. Lookout was only twenty miles or so from the Big Creek relay station, burned a few days earlier.

Courtesy Colorado Historical Society
James Butler "Wild Bill" Hickok
Wild Bill Hickok was a man of mixed reputation. At various times, he was a gunfighter, army scout, lawman, teamster, showman, and cowboy. A known participant in some of the most famous Indian battles of the Old West, his name is associated with dozens more.

To his credit, General Custer apparently tried to be careful about placing blame for the Lookout attack. His official, hand-written report to General Hancock said he could not be sure who had raided the station and killed the men, although he noted that the depredation occurred "squarely in the middle" of the trail left by Roman Nose and his warriors. Custer dispatched a messenger to take the report back to General Hancock.

Sunday, April 19. When General Hancock read the message from General Custer he became livid. He rescinded his earlier instruction and ordered that Roman Nose's village be burned to the ground at once. Two hundred fifty-one lodges were destroyed by the fire started by Hancock's troops. The general ordered that the three Indians who had been living in the village be taken to Fort Dodge as army prisoners. Unfortunately, the girl was so badly beaten that she did not survive the trip.

The Cheyennes being trailed by General Custer now resorted to their normal tactics when they were being followed—they began splitting into smaller and smaller groups. Eventually, Custer decided there was no use to pursue them further and ordeded his command to return to General Hancock.

The unexpected delay left the troops in a difficult situation. Hancock could no longer continue his march across the plains. Forage was extremely sparse, and Hancock knew his horses would soon be in trouble if he remained on the prairie. He ordered his troops to return to Fort Riley.

Monday, April 22. Tired of life on the trail and pressed by other assignments, General Hancock placed General Custer in full command of the Smoky Hill Road from

Fort Hays to Denver. He ordered Custer to make the road safe for travel.

General Custer's appointment, as commander of one of the toughest and most troubled districts in the West, was a popular one—both with the soldiers and with the general public. In spite of modern history's unflattering judgements of Custer, he was immensely popular both during and after the Civil War. Notwithstanding the general's many brushes with authority, author Alvin Josephy says Custer was "idolized for his unquestioned courage and audacity" on the battlefield—both in the Civil War and in fighting Indians.

Custer clearly was brazen and fearless in battle, and seemed to lead a charmed life. In conflicts against Confederates from Bull Run to Appomattox, he had numerous close calls—and survived each of them. These brushes with death seemed to add to his mystique and popularity. On eleven different occasions during the Civil War, horses were shot from beneath Custer by enemy fire. Yet he was wounded only once, and that wound was not serious.

Custer again drew national attention and stirred the country's imagination when he became the first Union officer to ride aloft in one of the new observation balloons. He also was the youngest general in the Union Army, and personally led the attack that killed the famous Confederate general, Jeb Stuart. (Stuart, incidentally, was a former Indian fighter. He was first injured in battle while fighting Indians in Colorado, in 1858.)

Custer, like many other extremely active men, quickly grew bored with any period of inaction—and inaction was the hallmark of his 1867 assignment. What previously had been the hot spot of the Indian war suddenly became very quiet. Some historians argue that the mere presence of Custer in the region drove the hostile Indians elsewhere. Custer was said to have been extremely disappointed a short time later when Roman Nose was killed in the famous battle at Beecher Island (see Chapter 5).

Whatever the reason for the quiet in eastern Colorado, the lack of action where Custer was and the great amount of action elsewhere soon got him into trouble. Late that summer he was courtmartialed on charges of "deserting his post, failure to determine the welfare of some of his men, and using military equipment for personal reasons."

The charges were filed after Indians attacked the army post where Custer's wife was staying, some seventy-five miles from Custer's Colorado campsite. When he learned of the attack, Custer ordered his men to return immediately to the fort—even though that would put them miles from their assigned positions.

Custer force-marched his troops to try to reach the post quickly. Along the way, he fought a running battle with a sizeable band of Indians, and two of his men went down. Because of his hurry to check on the welfare of his wife, Custer continued moving—without stopping to recover the bodies of the dead men.

When Custer finally arrived at the post, he found that his wife had already been evacuated to another fort. Still concerned, Custer ordered his men to stay put, then rode his army horse to the second fort to check on his wife.

Convicted in February of 1868 of all charges filed against him, Custer was sentenced to a one year suspension from duty without pay. He was also ordered to leave the frontier, and demoted to his pre–war rank of captain. Custer and his wife returned to their family home in New Rumley, Ohio, to serve out the one–year suspension.

Custer no doubt agonized over this embarrassment—and over the fact that he missed out on the most important battle yet in the Indian war. The famous Roman Nose died in the dramatic Battle of Beecher Island while Custer stayed on the family farm.

But trouble was again building in Colorado.

Wednesday, September 23, 1868. A small military wagon train was attacked along the Santa Fe Trail in the far southeastern corner of Colorado. The fifteen men with the wagons were all killed.

Two hours later, a twenty-one–wagon military supply train was attacked five miles away. This time the wagons were successfully cir cled and about forty well armed men managed to keep the Indians at bay. The battle raged for four long days before the attackers finally withdrew and the weary defenders were able to flee for safety.

Responding to the continued fighting, General Alfred Sully set out with nine companies of the Seventh Cavalry. His mission was to locate and attack "hostile" Indians camped on the Cimmaron River, south of the Santa Fe Trail in western Oklahoma and the Texas panhandle.

On the second afternoon of Sully's march, two slow-moving soldiers became separated from the main column of troops. The laggards were still in sight of the others, however, when about fifty Indians thundered out of the underbrush, grabbed the startled soldiers, and rode away—with the victims screaming in terror. Sully's troops gave chase, and the Indians eventually shoved the kidnapped soldiers from their horses—but not before killing one and badly mauling the other.

The main body of soldiers continued their pursuit of the Indians, who were quickly identified—presumably with accuracy—as Cheyenne Dog Soldiers. The soldiers chased the band of warriors onto a rock-strewn hillside, then engaged them in a fierce fire-fight. Although the Indians were armed with Spencer single-shot rifles, they nonetheless managed to keep the soldiers at bay for more than twenty-four hours.

Eventually these Indians were reinforced by the arrival of perhaps fifty additional warriors. Apparently, the second group happened upon the battle by pure chance. The soldiers now found themselves trapped in a narrow valley between the first group of warriors and these newly-arrived reinforcements. The soldiers were soon surrounded at the battle site, on the banks of the North Canadian River along the Oklahoma–Texas border.

Despite the additional braves, the Indians were still probably outnumbered by soldiers. The soldiers also had better weapons with significantly more fire power. On the other hand, the Indians had the advantage of having selected the battle site; the warriors occupied the high ground on either side of the river valley where the troops were pinned down.

General Sully ordered his troops to dismount and fight on foot. The battle that followed raged for more than two hours and the soldiers appeared to hold the upper hand. Finally, the Indians successfully disengaged from the soldiers and rode away. Twelve dead braves were found on the battlefield and there were indications that more had been wounded or killed.

Thursday, October 1. Militant Cheyenne Dog Soldier Chief Tall Bull and about sixty of his warriors swept through a small army camp on the Republican River, catching the soldiers there completely by surprise. One soldier was killed, three were wounded, and twenty-six army horses were taken.

Tuesday, October 6. Three hundred braves attacked a wagon train just seven miles west of Fort Lyon, Colorado, wounding one of the eleven men with the train. More importantly, they kidnapped a pioneer woman, Mrs. Clara Blinn, and her two small children. They also seized all forty-six horses that were with the train.

The survivors told an army rescue patrol that the attackers were led by Kiowa Chief Satanta. Satanta was rapidly gaining a reputation as one of the most fierce chiefs on the Great Plains. He was also one who hated the whites with an unbending passion. In the wake of the recent death of Roman Nose, the army considered Satanta now to be the most dangerous Indian in the West.

Chief Satanta would always deny his involvement in the raid near Fort Lyon, but Satanta was not the most trustworthy man on the Great Plains. Strong evidence, including eyewitness reports from both Indians and whites, suggests he was there.

It was not unusual for the Kiowa chief to deny something that others accepted as true. Satanta often practiced the "big lie" technique—lying just to see if he could get by with it, and then boasting to others about his ability to deceive.

Satanta especially enjoyed seeing how many lies he could get by with in his conversations with the gullible white man. In *Death on the Prairie*, Paul Wellman quotes reports of the Historical Society of Kansas, describing Satanta as follows:

Before a peace commission the old rascal grew very pathetic as he warmed to his subject. He declared he had no desire to kill white settlers or emigrants, but that they ruthlessly slaughtered the buffalo [there was truth in the charge] and left the carcasses to rot on the prairie. He also said white hunters set fires which destroyed the grass and cut down the timber on stream margins to make large fires while the Indian was satisfied to cook his food with a few dead and dried limbs.

"Only the other day," said he with the moving power of his voice playing at its finest, "I picked up a little switch on the trail. It made my heart bleed to think that so small a green branch, ruthlessly torn out of the ground and thoughtlessly destroyed by some white man would in time have grown to be a stately tree for the benefit of my children and grandchildren."

After the pow-wow was over Satanta got a few drinks of liquor into him and his real thoughts asserted them selves; "Didn't I give it to those white men?" he exulted. "Why, I drew the tears from their eyes! The switch I saw on the trail made my heart glad instead of sad for I knew there was a tenderfoot ahead, because an old plainsman would have used a quirt or spurs. When we came in sight he threw away his rifle and held tightly to his hat for fear he would lose it!"[2]

Tuesday, October 13, 1868. General Sully ordered two companies of soldiers to pursue the larger group of fleeing Indians. The pursuing troops—the best in Sully's command—were rapidly gaining on the Indians when the soldiers blundered into a trap. As the cavalrymen dashed through a narrow canyon in hot pursuit of the enemy, they were suddenly surrounded by Indian warriors and cut to ribbons. Surviving soldiers were sent running back toward Sully's lines in a virtual rout. As the soldiers fled, the Indians rose to their feet, thumbed their noses and slapped their buttocks in derision.[3]

Saturday, October 17. Two hundred Cheyennes attacked two companies of the Tenth Cavalry, under the command of Major General Eugene Carr. Carr, who had been transferring men and equipment from one fort to another, circled his wagons and held the Indians at bay for six hours. Then the Indians suddenly withdrew for no apparent reason. There was no report on army casualties in the skirmish; the Indians left four dead on the battlefield.

General Carr followed the warriors for a short distance. He had to stop pursuit when the Indians touched off a range fire, which not only slowed the pace of the soldiers but also completely covered the trail of the escaping braves.

Sunday, October 18. A 100–man detachment of black "buffalo soldiers" had finished escorting General Carr to join the Fifth Cavalry on Beaver Creek, and was heading back to Fort Wallace. Captain Thomas Graham and two enlisted men were scouting about a half-mile ahead of the main body of troops.

Suddenly the three men found themselves surrounded by about twenty-five Indians. Other troops rode to the rescue, and found themselves in the midst of about 600 Indians! The soldiers dismounted and stood in a circle atop a little knoll. Fortunately for them, they were armed with new repeating rifles and were able to lay down a withering barrage of gunfire.

The Indians appeared startled by the amount of resistance the 100 troopers were able to offer. After suffering many casualties in only a matter of minutes, the Indians pulled back to a safe distance and tried to regroup.

With the Indians was a warrior called Medicine Man, who was literally that—the tribe's producer of magic. After chanting mysteriously for several minutes, he told the braves that they were now protected by a magic spell he had cast. To prove the strength of his magic, Medicine Man raced his horse almost to the line of soldiers and then turned to ride once around the perimeter of the circle.

The troops concentrated their gunfire at this brazen target, and literally blew Medicine Man off his horse. Seeing the magic man killed, the startled braves turned and fled from the scene. They left "multiple dead and wounded" on the field.

Back at Fort Leavenworth, the army's anti–Indian headquarters, General Sherman was furious. The brazen, continuing attacks sweeping the plains enraged him. He was also furious at the federal government for waffling in dealing with this trouble. Sherman renewed his demands: either all whites should be ordered out of the frontier area, or the army should wage all-out war.

Sherman told Secretary of War John Schofield that "all" Cheyenne and Arapaho tribes were clearly and openly at war with whites in Colorado and western Kansas. He said that even those who had not yet taken up arms were supporting those who had done so. Furthermore, he said, all tribes refused to turn over the murderers, rapists, and thieves among them.

Secretary Schofield agreed with Sherman, and granted him permission to "put a stop to this thing, once and for all." Sherman immediately put together a plan:

three separate columns of troops would converge simultaneously on the Oklahoma land where the Indians were camped for the winter.[4] He planned to wipe out those he called the savages, and stop the Indian trouble once and for all.

Ironically, on the same day that Sherman finally received the authority for the all-out pursuit of the hostile warriors, hundreds of Indians voluntarily surrendered at Fort Cobb. Those who gave up said they were tired of war and were ready for peace. Since it was getting to be late autumn, the new desire for peace should have been expected. Indians hated to fight in cold or stormy weather, and almost all wintertimes were calm! Those who surrendered, however, reported that thousands of others from virtually all tribes were gathering supplies to begin a new offensive.

Friday, November 20, 1868. Cheyenne "peace chief" Black Kettle, a survivor of the Sand Creek Massacre, reported to Fort Carr. Black Kettle said he no longer had control over anyone in his tribe except the 180 women, children, and old men who had chosen to accompany him to the fort. But as for those 180, Black Kettle promised that from this time forward they would live at peace with the white man. He said they would not associate with those Indians waging war, nor would his group permit hostile braves to live in their camp. This promise was similar to the one Black Kettle made shortly before the infamous Sand Creek Massacre in Colorado. After that battle it was learned that while most of the Indians in the village probably were peaceful, there were also substantial numbers who continued to attack, kill, rob, and otherwise harass the whites.

As Black Kettle once again promised peace for himself and his tribe, he also warned that other Indians had renewed their war against the white man. The new declaration, he said, was because a group of Kansas farmers had fired on peaceful Indians the previous year. It was the fourth different reason Black Kettle had given for continuation of the all-out war. He earlier blamed the war on General Hancock's burning of a village, John Chivington's attack on Cheyennes at Sand Creek, and the shooting of an apparently drunk warrior by guards at Fort Lyon.

The truth appears to be that these four incidents were not the cause of the continuing war. Rather, the continuing warfare was symptomatic of the Indians' frustration, anger, distrust, and fear. These were the emotional costs the Native Americans paid for the invasion of the North American continent by white Europeans. The expanding white population in the East, and then the growing settlements in the West contributed to the Indians' perception that everything they ever had was about to be lost.

General Sheridan ordered Black Kettle and all other peaceful southern Cheyennes to report to reservations in Oklahoma. But Sheridan also warned his superiors that at least as many hostile Indians had not surrendered as the peaceful ones who had.

Sheridan began mapping "one massive last campaign" against those Indians who stubbornly resisted "settlement." He wanted his best men on this operation. After thinking it over, Sheridan sent for General George Custer, whom he called "my best Indian fighter." Custer had served only nine months of his one year suspension, but Sheridan waived the remainder of the penalty. He needed Custer, and to get him, Sheridan ended the suspension. Ordering Custer to report back to duty, Sheridan also once again breveted him to the rank of general. Custer was quick to accept the appointment, and returned to the front.

The recall of General Custer was just one step of Sheridan's action plan to wipe out hostile Indians, once and for all. To augment army regulars already fighting the Indians, Sheridan also called up the Nineteenth Kansas Volunteers—1,200 men under Colonel Samuel J. Crawford. In addition, he called up dozens of Indian scouts and frontiersmen to assist in the new campaign. He "promoted" General Sully to a desk job and gave the field command to his trusted friend, General Custer.

Monday, November 23, 1868. General Custer wasted no time getting underway. On November 23, in the middle of a driving snow storm, he took eleven companies of soldiers and left Camp Supply. Custer's goal was to find hostile Indians who had attacked several white ranches in central Oklahoma, seventy-five miles south of the Colorado–Kansas border.

The soldiers marched southward into the heart of the Indian Nation, targeting the south Canadian River basin in western Oklahoma. That's where Custer expected to find hundreds of hostile Indians spending the cold winter months. The area of Custer's search was along the ill-defined border that supposedly separated Indians who had submitted to the white man's control from those who defiantly remained independent and free.

Four days later—Thanksgiving morning, 1868— Custer found a large, new Indian trail, and began following it along the south bank of the Washita River. He presumed that a fresh trail this time of year could only be made by Indians who had never settled down in a peace camp; that would mean they were hostile.

Within an hour, he spotted a large Cheyenne village—just as the Indians in the village spotted the soldiers. Custer and his officers later said the Cheyennes in the encampment opened fire on the approaching troops, and the Battle of Washita was joined. As the gunfire erupted, Custer's regimental band struck up "Garry Owen," lending an ironically festive atmosphere to the fierce battle.[5]

Within minutes of those opening shots, Custer's men gained the upper hand. Indian women and children were fleeing in terror, and the braves had been driven into the trees where a fierce, sometimes hand-to-hand battle was being waged.

What Custer did not know was that this was the smaller of two Cheyenne villages located within a half mile of one another. The women and children who fled from this village ran to the second to appeal for help. Cheyenne braves, accompanied by a few Arapaho and Kiowa warriors, responded to their cries, armed themselves, and raced back to face the soldiers.

Several Indian braves ran out of the trees at the first village and dashed into a ravine. These escaping Indians were followed closely by Sergeant Major Joel H. Elliott and fifteen of his men. They were in a fight and obviously meant to kill or capture the braves.

Elliott and his men had ridden only a short distance when they were met and overwhelmed by the hundreds of warriors responding from the second village. All sixteen of the soldiers were quickly killed and mutilated.

In a short time the situation at the first village had changed dramatically. Instead of chasing fleeing Indians, Custer realized he was badly outnumbered by Indians who were now on the offensive. Custer had 700 men, but he estimated that the Indians numbered two to three times that many.

As darkness approached, Custer began pulling his troops back through the village they had captured hours earlier. Before leaving, however, Custer's soldiers ransacked the area. They learned that the village was not entirely peaceful, as claimed by Indians. From its tepees, the soldiers brought considerable evidence that clearly linked these Indians to a series of recent bloody attacks. Amazingly, the village was the home of the old "peace chief" Black Kettle. Just weeks before, Black Kettle had pledged that he and his followers had stopped attacking whites forever. He also said he was through associating with those who still fought the white man, and would never associate with them again. Yet, in Black Kettle's village General Custer's soldiers found mail taken from stagecoaches, attacked just two weeks earlier. They also recovered numerous items which they traced to specific homes and relay stations, ransacked and burned over the preceding three months. The soldiers also found pictographs, or drawings, which depicted many of the bloodiest Cheyenne raids—including several that involved rape and torture.

Worst of all, they found Mrs. Clara Blinn stabbed to death in one of the tepees. In the opening seconds of the battle, the soldiers saw a Cheyenne woman plunge a knife into the belly of Mrs. Blinn's two-year-old son. The baby was dead when soldiers reached him. Mrs. Blinn had been dead for a half hour or so when they found her. The soldiers also found several white scalps in various tepees.[6]

During the battle, Custer's men captured 900 Indian ponies and seized a considerable amount of arms and ammunition. The general reported fifty-three women and children were captured. One hundred three Indian dead were counted on the battlefield, including Chief Black Kettle. Subsequent investigations verified that Chief Black Kettle and his family were among those who died in the Battle of Washita. In the end, Custer and his troops were forced to evacuate the area, in the face of strong counterattacks by hundreds of hostile braves from the second village.[7]

General Custer and his troops returned triumphantly to Camp Supply shortly after the Washita Battle. They were personally greeted there by a smiling General Philip Sheridan. Osage scouts led the parade of soldiers as they rode back through the gates of the fort, waving the scalps of Cheyenne warriors—including one identified as that of Chief Black Kettle. General Sheridan issued a proclamation commending Custer and his men for the "gallant and efficient" service.[8]

General Sheridan said the mere fact that the soldiers had recovered white scalps, assorted loot from a series of Indian raids, and the pictographs of Indian depredations made it "clear to one and all" that Chief Black Kettle had talked of peace while continuing to participate in horrendous crimes. Those crimes included murdering and pillaging, that he so often specifically denied.[9]

Custer's attack on the Cheyenne village and the killing of Black Kettle, however, were not universally praised. As was the case with Colonel John Chivington's raid on Sand Creek a few years earlier, mounting criticism followed closely on the heels of initial praise and celebration. Those who criticized Custer most loudly were the same men and organizations who had been successful in disgracing John Chivington.

The BIA denounced the raid as an "unprovoked attack by the army against Indians who were trying to live at peace with the white man." Iowa Senator James Doolittle called the raid a "travesty." Custer's attack ultimately led to another open split: between the military and local whites on one hand, and the Bureau of Indian Affairs (and Congressmen and senators who had faithfully supported the BIA) on the other.

BIA Superintendent Murphy—who just four months earlier had called on the army to destroy the Cheyennes and Arapahos—now said the army had made a terrible mistake by attacking the village of Cheyenne Chief Black Kettle. In spite of the scalps and loot found there, Murphy said that Chief Black Kettle was a "real friend of the white man."

Colonel Samuel Tappan, another outspoken critic, also said that Custer's raid was a mistake. Tappan said that even the proof of scalping, looting, and other attacks was not reason to raid the village on the Washita. If Black Kettle's people were involved in atrocities, Tappan said, they had been forced to commit the crimes because whites had failed to deliver the things promised under various treaties. He maintained that even if a few of the braves had been attacking whites, most of the villagers were peaceful and should not have paid the supreme price for the crimes of a few.

Former Indian Agent Wynkoop also denounced Custer's raid. Wynkoop said that Black Kettle had been a "truly noble savage, the spiritual leader of all the plains Indians, a man whose very word was law and whose advice was always heeded."

Newspapers throughout the eastern part of the country quoted Wynkoops' scathing denunciation of General Custer. Apparently, none of them remembered how a few weeks earlier, Wynkoop stated publicly that Black Kettle was no longer viewed as a leader by many of the Cheyennes, and was unable to control even the people of his own village. At the time, Wynkoop had called for whatever action was needed to control Black Kettle.

But if the newspapers were having a field day with the attack on Custer, the military seemed not to notice. General Sherman wired his personal congratulations to Custer, then told General Sheridan that "...if we get in a couple of more licks before Christmas, the Indians will beg for their lives."

Yet even with the support of both the western public and the US Army, the military severely criticized Custer behind closed doors. There were angry words over Custer's withdrawal from the village before determining the fate of sixteen missing men (led by, and including, Sergeant Major Elliott). This was the second time Custer was accused of such a failure: just one year earlier, Custer received an official reprimand for failing to determine the fate of two of his soldiers during another Indian battle.

The day after the Washita incident, General Sheridan dispatched a sizeable patrol to return to the battle site to account for the missing men. The search patrol found the bodies of the missing soldiers; all had been stripped of their clothing and jewelry, and were horribly mutilated. Several of the men had been decapitated, and some had arms and legs severed. Such behaviors had become customary among warring Native groups.

The soldiers apparently died in battle, and not as the result of torture. With the exception of one man, the dead were lying in a small circle where they had died while standing back to back, trying desperately to hold off Indians.

The one soldier whose body was not in the circle was Sergeant Major Elliott. Indians later said that Elliott was the last survivor, and the Indians had tried to capture him alive. Apparently realizing that he would be horribly tortured if captured, Elliott raised his arms as if to surrender, but had no intention of really doing so. In one of his raised hands, Elliott held his saber. When the Indians held their fire, Elliott walked toward their leader as if to give up, but when he got close enough he lunged forward and plunged the sword through the man's body. Other warriors, reacting instinctively, shot Elliott to death.

In view of the continuing deadly struggle between whites and Indians all along the frontier (and especially because of the evidences of atrocities found in the village), General Custer was strongly praised in the wake of the Washita battle. Many believed the destruction of Black Kettle's village would finally end more than thirty years of hostilities. Westerners almost unanimously praised Custer for killing the controversial Cheyenne chief and many of his warriors.

However, the Washita battle has been increasingly criticized in more recent years. *The American Heritage Book of Indians* seems to represent more modern and so-called politically correct feelings about the Washita River attack when it says,

> . . . Black Kettle had made unceasing and increasingly successful efforts for peace since the Sand Creek Massacre, believing there was no other hope of survival for his people. In the winter of 1868 his village...was treated to its second stealthy and totally unexpected attack by troops who were under orders to destroy a village and hang all the men and take all the women prisoner.[10]

The book sardonically comments that this battle might well be called "Custer's first stand."

UNFORTUNATELY, THE WASHITA BATTLE—like the many which preceded it, and some that followed—did not put an end to bloody raids and battles. Between July 1 and December 31, 1868, Indian raiders killed a total of 157 people in western Kansas alone. The dead included fourteen women and "a number" of children. In addition, four women and twenty-four children were kidnapped. Twenty-four ranches were destroyed, eleven stagecoaches and four wagon trains demolished, and 1,600 horses stolen.[11] History does not record the number of Indians killed in these confrontations.

After finding the bodies of Custer's missing patrol, General Sheridan was more determined than ever to stop the Indian trouble throughout the Great Plains. He sent several sizeable troop detachments with orders to "find and control" all hostile Indians from Oklahoma to Canada and Kansas City to Salt Lake. It was a sizeable undertaking, indeed.

When peaceful Indians learned of this newest military campaign, several entire tribes headed into the Wichita Mountains to distance themselves from any hostile Indians being sought by the army. These "peace Indians" made camp on open land, and constantly flew white flags from the center of their villages.

The army patrols were successful, almost at once, in capturing many Indians considered to be hostile. Among the first to be taken as prisoners were Chiefs Satanta and Lone Wolf. Some accounts say they were captured in a skirmish with well armed buffalo hunters at Anadarko, Oklahoma, although official army records give no details on the capture. After the chiefs were in custody the army sent word to their tribes that unless all their warriors surrendered by December 19, the chiefs would be hanged. The Kiowas surrendered five days later. General Sheridan told them that unless they made a lasting peace and separated themselves from trouble makers at once, he would "wipe them out." The Kiowas agreed to live peacefully "forever more" on an Oklahoma reservation.

By Christmas, thousands of Indians had gone to Fort Cobb to surrender and pledge that they were through making war—or to claim that they never had made war in the first place. General Sheridan listened to the chiefs, but showed little sympathy for their protestations of innocence. The general made it clear he didn't trust the Indians, no matter what they said.

"You cannot make peace now, and war again in the spring," he warned them. "Either you make a permanent and complete peace, or you go back out now and we will fight this thing to the bitter end. It is for you to say which way it will be!" He also told the chiefs that until all Indians surrendered, those already at the fort were under house arrest.

Thursday, December 31, 1868. Twenty-one chiefs of various tribes signed a formal peace pledge at Fort Cobb. General Sheridan noted that without exception, those Indians who surrendered were in terrible physical shape, and appeared to be near starvation. The Indians were also poorly clothed and seemed ill-prepared to deal with the bitter winter weather. His report said the Indians seemed relieved to have the peace agreement signed, and genuinely pleased to have access to the food supplied by the army.

But not all Indians surrendered, and when it became apparent that hundreds or thousands remained on the loose Sheridan extended the surrender deadline to January 15, 1869. When many tribes still had not given up by the later deadline, Sheridan ordered his soldiers to go find them and bring them in. Fortunately, the soldiers were not quite ready to begin such a mission. While they were still making preparations, several hundred Indians arrived at Fort Cobb to give themselves up.

In spite of the massive surrenders, Sheridan still wasn't satisfied. He commented that while thousands of Indians were now in custody, the worst and the most hostile were still at large—showing no signs of giving up. He worried that they might start a new wave of atrocities. His observation proved to be prophetic.

Friday, January 8, 1869. As if to give credence to Sheridan's warnings, Indian attackers once again destroyed the Big Timbers relay station on the Colorado–Kansas border. Less than twenty-four hours later Indians burned the Lake relay station in eastern Colorado. Two white men were captured, tortured, killed, and scalped.

Wednesday, January 20. More than 900 Indians, from tribes considered to be hostile, surrendered at Fort Cobb. By January 27, almost all Arapaho Indians had given up, but many Kiowas and Cheyennes (including their more warlike leaders) were still missing. Some of the Indians in camp reported that about eighty Arapaho warriors, who had not surrendered, were joining the several hundred Cheyenne Dog Soldiers in pledging that they would never give in to the white man's demands.

Tuesday, February 2, 1869. Once again, under orders, General Custer began a search for the unsurrendering Cheyennes. This time, however, the army hoped that the Indians could be talked into returning without more bloodshed. The army simply wanted to warn them one last time that they must surrender or "face extermination." Custer took only forty soldiers, to make it clear he had no intention of attacking anyone.

Custer's soldiers were guided by Chiefs Yellow Bear and Little Bear, who had earlier given themselves up and signed a new peace pledge. They quickly found where the Cheyennes and missing Arapahos had been camping, but the Indians were already gone. Custer returned to Fort Sill on February 7 without making contact. The army, frustrated and angry at their inability to find the hostile Indians, concluded that there was no longer any use in trying.

Tuesday, March 2. This time there would be no effort to display peaceful intentions. General Custer left Fort Sill with 800 veteran soldiers, determined to find hostile Indians and "permanently" put an end to their capability to wage war.

Saturday, March 6. Custer's scouts sighted smoke in the distance—a sure sign that an Indian village was ahead. Osage scouts went to investigate and returned shortly with word that there was a small Cheyenne village on a creek bank about a mile and a half away. Custer made preparations to attack, but the Indians in the village saw the soldiers coming before the assault could be launched. By the time the troops arrived, the village had been abandoned. Custer did his best to follow their trail, but the escapees had split into small groups and made tracking them impossible.

Monday, March 15. Nine days after losing track of the Indians from the first village, Custer's scouts spied a sizeable herd of horses grazing in a valley just ahead. Indians herding the horses also spotted Custer's soldiers and scurried into a heavily wooded area just behind the glen.

As Custer rode toward the herd, eight braves rode out to meet the soldiers and ask for a council. The eight said they represented more than 250 Cheyenne lodges on the Sweetwater River, and admitted that most of the lodges were occupied by Dog Soldiers. They also told Custer of another village of sixty lodges (about 200 people) a few miles further on. The braves said both villages were tired of war and wanted only peace. They asked Custer under what terms they would be allowed to simply surrender.

Custer told them he wished to meet with their chief, but he also ordered his troops to surround the nearest village to "encourage the chief to cooperate" in signing a formal peace agreement. When Custer rode into the village for a conference a short time later, he discovered that the Indians there were holding two white women who had been kidnapped earlier in Kansas—Mrs. Anna Belle Morgan and Miss Sarah C. White.[12]

Custer was angry that the self-proclaimed peace Indians were still holding white prisoners, and angrier still at the condition of the two women. Both were pale, thin, and haggard-looking. Both bore bruises and other marks of mistreatment. Custer tried not to display his emotions, but said later that he was so upset at the pitiful condition of the captives that he shook with anger.

The Indians didn't seem to notice Custer's emotional reaction to the presence of the women. They offered Custer a pipe, which he assumed was a peace pipe. Custer smoked it, but after he did so, one of the Indians told him it was merely a "parley pipe," meaning they were prepared to talk about some things, but not about peace.

This time Custer did not maintain his silence. He leaped to his feet and angrily told them the only subject for their conversation was to be peace. A medicine man then rose and poured ashes over the toes of Custer's boots, telling the general that the ashes would bring Custer and his men bad luck.

Custer angrily kicked the ashes from his boots and stormed out of the meeting. Returning to his troops, he wrestled with the dilemma he was facing. Custer felt he could not attack the village because of the presence of the two women prisoners, nor could he simply ride away—for the same reason. He called a staff meeting to discuss the situation.

A number of his junior officers argued that the women had been so debauched that they might not even want to live, and that under any circumstances, they were likely to be killed by the Indians the moment any pressure was applied. In fact, they reasoned, the only possibility of rescuing the women was in a lightning-quick, overpowering raid, grabbing the hostages before the Indians could kill them. The officers argued for an immediate attack, and sharply criticized Custer when he rejected the advice.

Instead of attacking the village, Custer sent patrols to probe for weak places in the Indian defense: specifically to determine whether the women could be rescued. The patrols returned without finding a way to save the women, but didn't come back empty handed! In a near-by wooded area they surprised and captured four Cheyenne chiefs, who had apparently been riding between villages and were unaware of the soldiers' presence. The captured chiefs were brought back to Custer.

General Custer was elated at this unexpected turn of events; he now had bargaining chips. Custer sent a messenger into the Cheyenne village to inform the

Indians that he was holding four of their chiefs. He offered to swap the chiefs for the two women.

The Indians replied that they were not interested in a trade for their own chiefs, but would release the women in exchange for a huge ransom of money, weapons, ammunition, and supplies. Custer reasoned that the ransom demand was planned before the arrival of his soldiers, and felt the Indians had not yet really reacted to the capture of the chiefs. Custer refused to pay any ransom.

Custer told his junior officers that he felt certain the Indians were bluffing, but he wasn't sure how to force their hand. For three days the stand-off continued. The soldiers continued to surround the two villages and hold the four chiefs as hostages, but there was no more direct contact with the Indians.

By the fourth day, Custer's patience had worn thin. Leading the four captured chiefs to a large old tree atop a high hill in plain sight of the larger Indian Village, Custer ordered that nooses be placed around the necks of three of the men, Fat Bear, Big Head and Dull Knife. Releasing the fourth chief, Custer told him to go tell Chief Little Robe that unless the women were released within fifteen minutes, he would hang the other three chiefs.

The chief disappeared into the village and there was an agonizing silence. Nervous soldiers checked and rechecked their weapons in the event the Indian response was an attack. To the great relief of Custer and the troops, the Indians brought the two women to the edge of their village a few moments later and sent a warrior to talk with Custer. The warrior said the Indians were now willing to trade the women for the three remaining Chiefs. But Custer had the upper hand and knew it. He sent back word that he was tired of bargaining with the Cheyennes and was no longer offering a trade. Either they release the women unconditionally, or the chiefs would be hanged.

The Indians hastily held a conference, then cut the ropes from the two women and turned them loose. The frightened women stumbled to the soldiers for safety, sobbing with relief and fear. They told Custer that the two villages were near starvation and were subsisting by eating dead ponies, mules, and dogs. Custer later said it was not difficult to believe that report; his own men had been living for the past four days on the meat from mules which died each day because of the lack of forage.

Custer sent word to the Cheyennes that he was taking the three captive chiefs back to Fort Sill, and that all Indians in the village must report to the fort within one week. If they failed to do so, Custer warned, the three chiefs would be hanged and soldiers would come back to wipe out the Cheyenne villages. Although Custer had won the showdown, the incarceration of the three chiefs soon led to unexpected tragedy with far-reaching consequences.

Three days later, the captured Cheyenne leaders were turned over to the custody of guards at Fort Sill. Someone at the base (exactly who made the decision is not clear) ordered the Indian prisoners be placed in the guardhouse for security. The captured chiefs either did not understand what was going on, or were simply unwilling to be placed in the guard house. When they saw guards walking toward them with fixed bayonets, they apparently believed they were about to be executed.

Pulling knives concealed in their loin cloths, the chiefs rushed the soldiers. In *Trails of the Smoky Hill*, Wayne C. Lee writes, "The Indians leaped on the guards with table knives that had been honed to razor sharpness." Chief Fat Bear stabbed an army sergeant before the startled troops could react. In the lightning-quick scuffle that followed, Big Head and a squaw who was standing beside the chiefs were shot to death. Dull Knife was stabbed to death with a bayonet and Fat Bear was knocked unconscious.[13]

The fatal outburst soon had a tragic impact—far beyond just the deaths of the two chiefs and the innocent bystander. A few days after the incident, other Indians from the Cheyenne village began arriving at Fort Sill to surrender. When they learned that two of the chiefs had been killed, they assumed they had been tricked by the soldiers. Chief Red Moon and about 120 of the Indians immediately left the fort, apparently to join Chief Sand Hill who had said earlier he would never surrender.

The following morning, the situation worsened further. A civilian teamster and an Indian brave got into a shouting match at Fort Sill, and the civilian was stabbed to death. The warrior involved in the stabbing and the occupants of twenty-two lodges—about eighty in all— fled Fort Sill and headed for Red Moon's camp. General Eugene A. Carr took a troop after the fleeing Indians in an effort to bring them back to Fort Sill. Carr and 150 soldiers gave chase. A few hours later he found the Indians camped on the Republican River.

Exactly what happened next is not clear, but fighting erupted almost as soon as the soldiers reached the village. In a series of sharp clashes that followed, the army inflicted heavy casualties on the Indians, destroyed one of their villages, recaptured stolen goods, and freed another captive white woman.

In total, Carr's brief campaign resulted in the deaths of at least seventy-five Dog Soldiers, plus another dozen Indian women and children—although that estimate was probably severely understated. His troops burned nearly 100 Cheyenne lodges, and seized tons of supplies—including food, robes, blankets, and other essential items. The troops also successfully released a woman named Mrs. Weichel from Cheyenne captivity.

In the tepee of Chief Tall Bull, soldiers found a necklace made of human fingers; it was not possible to tell whether the fingers came from white men, Indians, or both. They also found the scalps of "several" white women, 900 dollars in US paper currency, and several gold coins. The soldiers voted to give all the money to Mrs. Weichel, and army brass approved.

The series of confrontations involving General Carr's unit, which climaxed with the "Battle of Summit Springs," effectively crushed the Dog Soldiers as a solid-ified, effective Indian army in Colorado and Kansas. There would be continued raids and an occasional major battle—but for the most part, the really hostile Indians that had roamed the Central Plains were now either defeated or driven to other parts of the country. Most future Indian (and white) atrocities would occur in New Mexico, Arizona, Oklahoma, and Texas to the south, and in Wyoming, Montana, Nebraska and the Dakotas to the North.

Most of the comparatively few Dog Soldiers who survived Carr's relentless pursuit fled to the far north. There they joined up with the Sioux Indians in north ern Wyoming, Montana, and the Dakotas. Some of them would later meet General Custer one final time at a place called Little Big Horn. A few others split into numerous small groups and continued to camp in the Smoky Hill basin of western Kansas.

Notes

1. Wayne C. Lee and Howard C. Raynesford, *Trails of the Smoky Hill* (Caldwell, Idaho: The Caxton Printers, Ltd., 1980), 95.

2. Paul Wellman, *Death on the Prairie* (Lincoln/London: University of Nebraska Press, 1962), 88.

3. Donald Berthrong, *The Southern Cheyennes* (Norman: University of Oklahoma Press, 1963), 320.

4. Maurice Matloff, ed., *American Military History* (Washington DC: Office of the Chief of Military History, United States Army, 1969), 310.

5. Ibid., 310.

6. Paul Wellman, *Death on the Prairie*, 85, says that two white babies were murdered when the attack began.

7. As usual, the Indians said the toll of dead and captured was significantly lower than the figures reported by the army. More modern army figures (quoted in the *American Military History*, 310) say that Custer captured fifty-three Indian women and children and that "perhaps" fifty other Indians died in the battle. The report says that Custer lost twenty-one officers and men killed, and 123 wounded in the battle.

8. *The Southern Cheyennes*, 327.

9. Ibid., 328.

10. *American Heritage Book of Indians* (New York: Simon & Schuster, 1961), 346–7.

11. *Trails of the Smoky Hill*, 133.

12. Some accounts say this was a Mrs. White, and that her infant son was also a prisoner in the Indian village.

13. *Trails of the Smoky Hill*, 121.

The Only way to stop this evil [white men taking, buying or bartering for rights to traditional Indian lands] is for the red men to unite in claiming a common and equal right to the land, as it was at first and should be now—for it was never divided, but belongs to all. No tribe has the right to sell, even to each other, much less to strangers. Sell a country? Why not sell the air, the great sea, or the earth?

Shawnee Chief Tecumseh

We are great liars and thieves. We have killed. We have done all the evil that the Great Spirit forbids us to do—but we did not know those beautiful words you now use. In the future we will try to live better.

Unidentified Indian chief,
speaking to a Roman Catholic priest
at Fort Laramie, *circa* 1835

–TEN–

Disaster at Powder River

B Y 1876, GEORGE CUSTER was the unquestioned leading Indian fighter on the frontier. He had a worldwide reputation as the most daring, dashing and unconventional military man in America. His unorthodox life-style, including his brief suspension from duty, enhanced rather than harmed his reputation. Millions of people simply idolized this larger-than-life hero in spite of his frequent brushes with authority, and the continued criticism from those who held that he represented everything that was wrong with the way white men treated Indians.

In truth, those who were now developing a conscience about the white man's dealing with Indians were mostly those who lived far away from the frontier. Those persons living where the trouble continued steadfastly supported any sort of aggressive military action against the Indians.

By the mid 1870s, there were 35,000 Teton Sioux on the northern Great Plains. Most of them lived in the Dakotas, eastern Montana, northeastern Wyoming and northern Nebraska. Many of the Sioux remained openly hostile, and continued to physically attack whites whenever and wherever possible. Like the Cheyenne Dog Soldiers still "on the loose" in southern Colorado, western Oklahoma and the Texas panhandle, these northern warriors were involved in constant skirmishes. For the most part these confrontations were relatively minor— minor here meaning that only a few people on either side were killed in any given incident. No major uprising involving either the Sioux or northern Cheyennes had occurred for a period of many months. The so-called Indian trouble had fallen into a somewhat predictable routine. The frontier was like a noisy Saturday night on Denver's Larimer Street; you knew there would be some trouble, but it involved mostly people with whom you wouldn't associate anyway, and the law would quickly deal with it.

Yet, behind the scenes Indian hostility in the North was again boiling. Perhaps it was the simple result of the Indians being held virtually as prisoners on reservations, or that the warriors were no longer free to conduct their great annual buffalo hunting expeditions. Indians of all ages yearned for earlier times when life was not so complicated—a time when buffalo were plentiful and white men were scarce.

Many frustrations fueled the Indian's growing bitterness—and most all of them were the direct result of whites moving to the West. Time after time, the Native Americans were mistreated by whites—especially the white government, which negotiated treaties and then ignored the treaties. The white man's mistreatment of the Sioux in Minnesota was already well documented, and the Sioux now living in the Dakotas, Montana, and Wyoming (many of them refugees from Minnesota) had not forgotten.

Well before 1874, these northern plains Indians had been "given" the Black Hills area to be their land "forever." Yet, when word was received that prospectors had discovered gold there, the United States government ordered General George Custer to enter this Indian land and investigate the rumors. Custer sent back his report confirming the find. Then, to make certain the information was correct, the government sent its own assayers into the very heart of the Indian country. The assayers also reported back that gold had, indeed, been found. The government made no apparent effort to hide that fact, and the Black Hills Indian country was soon swarming with white newcomers, prospecting for gold.

The Sioux and northern Cheyenne protested loudly about this newest violation of treaty promises. In response, the government offered to buy back the land from them. After thinking it over, the Sioux and northern Cheyennes said they were willing to negotiate.

Having discussed it among themselves, the Indians asked $50 million for the land. The government counteroffered only $6 million. The Sioux reduced their demand to $20 million. The government said the $6 million was a "take it or leave it" offer—and the Sioux would not reduce the price further. Eventually the talks were broken off.

Still, the white prospectors came.

Fearing an outbreak of hostilities, and acting on behalf of the US Government, the army ordered leading Sioux and northern Cheyenne chiefs to attend a council on January 1, 1876. The timing seemed imprudent; the council was set during one of the most severe winters in history. The avowed purpose of the council was to discuss "a reasonable solution" to the problem of control of the Black Hills region and, hopefully, to avoid warfare.

The Indians refused to come to the meeting. The distance, they argued, was too great and their horses too lean to withstand such a trip in the middle of winter. Furthermore, their people were unprepared for a lengthy march through blizzard conditions; such a trip would kill their elderly and the young.

The army ignored their objections, and apparently really expected the Indians to come en masse to the council. When the appointed date arrived, no Indians showed up.

Local government officials were irate over this snub. The army was ordered to mount an expedition, search for the Indians, and force them to come to the meeting. Partially because the bitter weather made it difficult to get supplies, it took several weeks to outfit the military search party. The expedition finally got underway about the middle of February.

Thursday, March 16, 1876. Troops searching for the missing Indians crossed into Sioux territory along the Powder River—the land into which the Sioux had vowed never to permit whites. Numerous reports say that the weather in mid–March that year was the worst of an unusually bad winter. The temperature held at forty degrees below zero for several consecutive days. General Joseph J. Reynolds had carefully outfitted his ten troops of cavalry in preparation for the cold however, and they pushed onward in spite of the bitterness.

Late in the afternoon of March 16, army patrols located an Indian trail running parallel to a small creek. Troops began to follow the trail, hoping it would lead to some of the missing Indians. At about midnight, scouts reported back that they had located a sizable Indian village just ahead.

The village turned out to be the encampment of Chief Crazy Horse: already known as one of the toughest and ablest of the Indian leaders. He had fought at the siege of Fort Kearney, probably participated in the Fetterman massacre, and led several other raids and battles. Western writer Paul Wellman says Crazy Horse was to the Sioux as Robert E. Lee was to the Confederacy—brilliant, beloved, tough.[1]

General Reynolds ordered his troops to quietly surround the Indian village in the darkness of night. Although the purpose of the army's campaign ostensibly was to force the Indians into negotiations for the sale of their land, the obvious intent of the military campaign was to inflict major and highly visible punishment on the Indians.

Reynolds launched an all-out attack on the village at about the time the sun first appeared on the horizon. The preparations had gone without a hitch, and no enemy was in sight as the troops raced in among the tepees. The sudden appearance of the soldiers came as a total surprise to the Indians; most were still sleeping.

A teenage Indian boy had just emerged from his tepee when he was confronted by dozens of soldiers. Apparently believing he would be immediately shot, the boy pulled his blanket around him and stood perfectly still. He stared at the soldiers standing only a few feet away.

Captain John G. Bourke was standing near the boy and pointed a rifle at the Indian. However, Bourke could not bring himself to shoot the boy. After several awkward seconds, the captain took a step forward. Suddenly, the teenager let out a loud war-hoop. Instantly, the entire village was awake. Braves scrambled from each tepee, bringing their weapons with them.

The soldiers had already cut off access to the Indian ponies, so the warriors trying to get away could only flee on foot. They raced into trees and fired at the soldiers, but there were not enough of them to have a telling effect.

Chief Crazy Horse, however, had fled down the valley and escaped from the area. After a few minutes he recovered from his initial surprise. He rounded up several braves and began working his way back toward the village. Along the way he gathered more and more warriors until eventually dozens of Indians were in the party. Silently these warriors waded through the snow and bitter cold back toward the troops.

In the village, the troops thought all the Indians were gone. Just as the soldiers set fire to the now-empty village, the warriors under Crazy Horse opened fire from two high ridges on either side of the village. The Indians also managed to stampede many of the army's horses.

The solders' position among the burning tepees, under heavy fire, quickly became untenable. Many of men had shed their heavy coats because of heat from the fires; they now fled without the coats in order to escape the deadly rain of Indian gunfire.

Until this minute, the soldiers apparently had given no thought to the possibility of an Indian counterattack. Now as they fled into the woods, General Reynolds struggled to regain control of his troops. Fortunately, the soldier's horses and the captured Indian ponies were upvalley from the burning village. The troops quickly mounted the horses and fled.

Within minutes the soldiers had retreated back up the valley, safely out of the range of the Indian rifles.

Now, however, they faced an enemy even more dangerous than the warriors: the bitterly cold weather.

Long before he wanted to do so, General Reynolds had to stop and set his troops to gathering fire wood. Soon, a dozen huge fires were going to keep the lightly clad soldiers from freezing to death. Unfortunately, the fires not only put out heat, they emitted light and smoke as well. The lifesaving fires now served as a beacon to Crazy Horse and the warriors accompanying him. The Indians were moving quietly through the woods in the direction of the troops.

Within two hours Crazy Horse was at the edge of the soldiers' camp. This time it was the army that was taken completely by surprise. In one swift move, the attacking warriors managed to cut off and free their own horses (and seize many of the army's animals that had not bolted earlier), driving the animals swiftly away from Reynold's camp. They also managed to steal two of the army's provision wagons, and set fire to two other wagons.

In spite of their achievements, the Sioux were unable to take further advantage of the situation. The soldiers still had their weapons and fought desperately against attack. Crazy Horse was unprepared for prolonged battle at that time. In a matter of minutes the Indians had vanished from the area.

For the moment the troops were safe, but they had clearly suffered a humiliating and dangerous defeat. The soldiers had lost many of their horses and supplies, making it difficult to move and problematic whether they could find food. Even worse, because of the foolishness of the soldiers in discarding their coats it was plain that the men were in a life-and-death jam. They could neither continue the campaign against the Indians, nor safely retreat in the biting cold.

Realizing that they could not remain in the open during such harsh conditions, Reynolds ordered his troops to begin marching. Thus began a numbing, dangerous, bitter march for the survivors of this humiliating army error. Eventually the 150 cavalrymen plodded eighteen miles through deep snow and frigid weather to reach the safety of the main military camp.

When he learned what had happened to General Reynolds, General George Crook was beside himself with anger. The first contact between his soldiers and the recalcitrant Indians was supposed to accomplish either their punish or capture.

The clash had clearly ended in one-sided victory for the Indians. Crook and Reynolds weren't sure what to do next. While they waffled, the Indians took the initiative.

Two days after the half-frozen soldiers returned to camp, Crazy Horse sent a message to General Crook. The message was simple. "We do not want war with the white man," Crazy Horse said. "Keep your troops out of our country and there will be no trouble." But Crazy Horse's message also warned that if any soldiers ever again crossed the Tongue River, they would be immediately attacked.

General Crook bristled at this brazen threat. In spite of his anger and his eagerness to exact revenge upon Crazy Horse, General Crook took his time getting ready for the next outing. He wanted to be absolutely certain this time that he could inflict punishment (and would not be further embarrassed).

Crook gathered more than 1200 men, and made sure they were well outfitted. Perhaps to be certain that his soldiers could not make another foolish mistake about their coats, Crook also waited for warmer weather. Finally, on Monday, May 29, 1876, he moved out with

1200 soldiers for a second expedition against Crazy Horse.[2]

Friday, June 9. The Indians, fully aware of the approaching troops, were ready for battle. The minute the soldiers crossed the Tongue River, they came under attack from Sioux war parties.

Warriors, firing from carefully selected places of concealment among rocks and trees on a nearby ridge, inflicted no injuries, but did deliver a powerful message to the army. The surprised solders scrambled for cover as bullets smashed all around them. By the time the troops recovered from their initial surprise, however, the Sioux were gone. The Indians had no desire at this point for any major face-to-face battle. They simply wanted to make certain General Crook knew that if he pushed on, there would be a price to pay.

General Crook got the message, but did not intend to let US soldiers be driven away again. He pushed onward toward the Rosebud River, in south-central South Dakota.

The following day, the soldiers passed through Dead Canyon and stopped in the valley at the bottom of the gorge. Scouts were sent ahead to try to locate Sioux camps.

Unknown to Crook, the Sioux and their northern Cheyenne allies had already located the soldiers. Hundreds of Crazy Horses' braves were concealed in the rocks and trees, just waiting for the right moment to launch an attack.

Four of General Crook's Crow scouts climbed a bluff to look around. As they reached the top, they were jumped by several Sioux warriors. The gunshots fired on the ridge opened the Battle of the Rosebud.

Courtesy Colorado Historical Society
Unhorsed
This painting of the last seconds of life for a frontier soldier first
appeared in The Century Illustrated Monthly Magazine, in
January, 1892. Indians frequently outnumbered the soldiers in such
battles, and—thanks in part to a Confederate plot to supply
weapons to Great Plains Indians—were sometimes as well-armed
as the soldiers against whom they fought.

As startled soldiers reacted to the shooting, Crazy
Horse's warriors poured out of the rocks and trees on all
sides. There were hundreds of Indians—shouting and
shooting as they raced toward the troops. The Crows and
Shoshonis who were scouting for General Crook fled in
the face of this massive Sioux attack.

General Crook knew at once that he was under the
attack of many hundreds of Sioux and Cheyennes, but
he was well prepared. Snapping out quick orders, he
watched his well-drilled troops form battle lines.

Captain Mills took one battalion across the valley to try to take command of the high ground on the left side. On the right side of the Rosebud, two battalions of troops moved forward to capture strategic hills. At the same time, the main body of soldiers advanced slowly down the center of the valley.

Captain Mills quickly reached the ridge on the left that was his objective and seized it, but then immediately came under a heavy counterattack. It soon became apparent to Mills that he was in danger of being overrun. The captain sent a desperate message to General Crook, appealing for help. Crook dispatched Captain Wayne Noyes with fifty additional soldiers to help hold the strategic ridge. Even with that additional manpower, Mills wasn't sure he could hold out.

The soldiers were completely surrounded by the hundreds of Sioux and Cheyenne warriors. In spite of its superior fire power, the army unit was being mauled. They were in grave danger of being overrun by sheer numbers of enemy, for even with their modern repeating rifles the soldiers just couldn't shoot fast enough to stop the Indian advance.

The fighting was furious. Much of the combat was hand-to-hand, and casualties began piling up on both sides.

Two hours into the battle, the braves mounted a massive charge against the left end of Crook's line. The line was anchored by Major Alexander Royall. Royall's extreme left—literally the end of the army's line—was held by Captain Guy Henry, and it was badly exposed. It was here that Crazy Horse hurled his main assault.

Within seconds, Indian braves were in among the soldiers and fierce hand-to-hand fighting was underway. The force of the attack swept the soldiers from the high ground, as they tumbled down the steep embankment, locked in life-and-death struggles with Sioux and Cheyenne warriors.

Another group of soldiers, under Captain Thomas Vroom, was cut off from the main body of troops. Vroom's isolated soldiers stood back-to-back in a circle, firing as fast as they could. Captain Henry saw the desperate struggle by Vroom's unit, and launched a rescue effort. Henry's fifty–man detachment eventually managed to battle its way to Vroom's position. Together the two units then battled back toward the main army lines.

Captain Henry stayed close to the front line, constantly shouting encouragement to his men as they inched their way forward, toward safety. It is unlikely that any of the soldiers saw Captain Henry the moment he was shot.

The embattled unit had finally reached a relatively protected position behind Henry before the captain turned toward them, his face distorted and ghastly looking. A bullet had torn through his face, ripping off his nose and taking away most of the skin from both cheeks. As he turned toward the men, Captain Henry swayed in his saddle momentarily, then tumbled to the ground.

Encouraged by the fact that the army commander was down, the warriors now redoubled their attack on Henry's detachment. In seconds they had overrun the point at which Henry fell. The captain lay—probably unconscious—on the ground beneath the feet of the Indian ponies as the battle continued to rage above him.

At this moment, the Crow and Shoshoni scouts who had retreated to the rear when the shooting started, suddenly found their courage. They apparently were spurred to action by their desire to rescue the badly wounded captain, who had always been a special friend to them. More than 200 of these Indian scouts launched a fierce counter-attack against the Sioux and Cheyenne, and stopped the assault in its tracks.

As the scouts distracted the Sioux and Cheyennes, the army also launched a full–scale counter attack. The force of the combined strikes sent Crazy Horse reeling. Between them, the soldiers and their Crow scouts managed to drive the Sioux and Cheyennes from the contested hillside.

The ridge on which so much blood had been shed was not a tenable position, however—not in the face of constant counter-assault by the hundreds of determined warriors. As soon as they had grabbed the unconscious Henry, the entire group of soldiers and friendly Indians retreated back down the hill. Although Crazy Horse's braves could have immediately recaptured the hill, they chose not to do so. Instead, they began pulling back into the trees. The breather gave the army badly needed time to reorganize.[3]

General Crook was mildly surprised at the sudden disappearance of the enemy from the battlefield, since the Indians had clearly held the upper hand. It appears likely that the Sioux and northern Cheyenne were planning by their withdrawal to lead Crook into another trap, had he pursued them. The Indians never got the opportunity to spring the trap.

Crook's soldiers were too badly mauled to continue the battle. The general had lost many of his horses and had spent most of his ammunition. He now withdrew southward to more friendly territory to regroup.

In the Battle of the Rosebud, Crook's command officially reported suffering ten dead and thirty-four wounded. There was no count on the horses or weapons he lost. To his chagrin, Crook had also been defeated by the Indians for the second straight time. The Sioux and

Cheyennes had made good on their threats to stop the white man whenever he crossed the Tongue River.

Indian losses at Rosebud were unknown, although Crow and Shoshoni scouts came out of the battle with the scalps of thirteen of Crazy Horse's braves. It is likely that the Indians actually suffered more casualties than did the army.

Notes

1. Paul Wellman, *Death on the Prairie* (Lincoln/London: University of Nebraska Press, 1962), 135.
2. Most accounts give this figure. *Death on the Prairie*, on page 139, says he had 1,400 soldiers and an additional 300 Indian scouts. Official army records list units, not numbers of men, but the 1,200 figure appears to be close to accurate.
3. In spite of his terrible wounds, Captain Henry survived and eventually rose to the rank of general.

We surely cannot be held responsible for the peace of the frontier if it is adjudged that we are trespassers everywhere in Indian territory, and have no right to foresee and prevent collision and trouble. After the Indians do mischief, it is too late to apply the remedy.

General William T. Sherman

–ELEVEN–

Little Big Horn

AFTER WHIPPING GENERAL GEORGE CROOK and forcing him to abandon pursuit of Crazy Horse at Rosebud, the victorious Sioux chief moved his followers further west. They crossed the Continental Divide and took up residence in the valley of the Little Big Horn River. It was June of 1876—just eight days after the great Sioux victory at Rosebud—when Crazy Horse established a huge village in the beautiful and serene valley, eight miles long and up to two miles wide.

Crazy Horse's Hunkpapa Sioux were joined at this camp by sizeable tribes of the Sans Arcs, Oglalas, and Brules, plus a large contingent of northern Cheyenne. The resulting camp was a great, sprawling Indian city— quite possibly the largest gathering of Indians in one place in all of history. There were well over 10,000 Indians housed in this sea of tepees—some sources say as many as 15,000. Of that number possibly one-fourth or more were warriors. The authoritative *American*

Military History estimates 3,000 to 4,000 warriors were in the village.[1]

Crazy Horse was the best known of the warriors in the camp, but there were other well-known and powerful leaders as well. Among these were Sitting Bull, Gall, American Horse, Yellow Nose, and Lame Deer. Three powerful Cheyenne chiefs also led elements of Crazy Horse's army: Big Crow, Two Moons, and Little Chief.

Thirty miles away from the Little Big Horn, General George Custer was just getting underway. Custer's soldiers (and other troops who were sent to find and punish the Sioux) were for the most part armed with the .45/70 model 1873 Springfield "trapdoor" breech-loading carbine—a weapon which had to be cleared and reloaded after every shot. In addition to their rifles, the soldiers carried their sidearms. These Colt revolvers would be of great help in the event of close-in combat.

Custer seemed unaware (or unconcerned) that the enemy he was about to face was heavily armed with the older but more desirable 1866 model Winchester, which could fire thirteen rounds in rapid succession. The Indians may have been far better armed than even that. Modern excavations of the battle site indicate that many, or perhaps most, of the warriors carried Sharpes repeating rifles.

As if the superior rifle power and raw numbers of men were not enough advantage for the Indians, the army made several costly blunders. The soldiers were ordered to leave behind their sabers, either on the assumption there would be no hand-to-hand fighting, or that the army's mule-train of ammunition made such weapons unnecessary.[2]

Additionally, General Custer had three (some sources say two) of the new Gatling guns assigned to his unit, but chose to leave them behind. Custer apparently had little faith in the rapid-fire weapons, which had a tendency to jam from time to time. Or, he may have felt that because they were mounted, they were clumsy and would slow down his movement against the enemy. One can only speculate whether the enormous fire power of the Gatlings would have been enough to have turned the tide of the upcoming battle.

General Custer was accompanied by 650 men: about 450 soldiers of the Seventh Cavalry and approximately 200 Indian scouts. Among the men of his command were two of Custer's brothers, George and Tom; as well as Custer's nephew, Autie Reed; and his brother-in-law, Lieutenant Calhoun.[3]

The general was in a fine mood, and appeared to be superbly confident as he reviewed his troops. At one point he was offered four extra troops (several hundred additional men) if he thought he needed them, but Custer refused the offer.[4] He apparently felt the extra men were unnecessary, and because they were not his own troops, might actually slow down his operations. Custer could not afford anything that would slow the speed of his planned attack. He envisioned a lightning-fast strike that would overwhelm the enemy before the Indians could react. After all, Custer did not want to suffer the same humiliating defeat as had been suffered by General Crook on two recent occasions.

Custer's contingent was just one portion of the huge army expedition sent to find Crazy Horse. Officially, the search was only an effort to force the Indians to return to the reservation, and negotiate for the sale of their land. There is no doubt that revenge was also an issue. Although there is no official record of it, there likely was some eager anticipation of engaging and defeating the Sioux warriors who had embarrassed the army twice in

Courtesy Colorado Historical Society
General George A. Custer
General George A. Custer was brilliant, daring, handsome and hard-headed. Considered by Generals Sheridan and Sherman to be the best Indian-fighter on the great plains, Custer was court martialed and suspended from duty for disobeying orders, but brought back to lead a final campaign against hostile Sioux Indians.

Sioux warriors who had embarrassed the army twice in recent days.

The overall army command for this mission belonged to General Alfred Terry, who had another 750 soldiers with him. But General Custer was well-liked by the commander, and the junior general was permitted to lead the way as the troops trailed Crazy Horse.

Actually, General Terry was more or less just along for the ride anyway; another junior general, John Gibbon, was in direct command of the additional 750 soldiers. They planned to eventually split their force before doing battle with Crazy Horse. Each general was to lead about half the men into the planned combat. Gibbon's troops were taking a route slightly different than the one followed by Custer, just in case Crazy Horse had turned south and was not where he was expected to be—camped on Montana's Little Big Horn River.

The split force was the idea of the region's top army commander, General Philip Sheridan. Sheridan had become fond of the attack system whereby he sent large numbers of soldiers converging on the enemy from three different points. Such a plan had worked well at Washita, and he instructed that it was the tactic to be followed in this instance, as well.[5]

Both Generals Gibbon and Custer were given strict orders by General Terry. If either man found Crazy Horse, he was to take no action until all of the soldiers from both commands had been brought together in a single place. General Terry made it clear that he did not want to risk a third consecutive defeat at the hands of the Indians.

Because of the way the units were traveling, it was considered likely that General Custer would make contact with Crazy horse first. Therefore, Terry repeated the orders to Custer; don't move unless General Gibbon's troops have joined with yours.

But before the conference of generals broke up, General Terry seemed to modify his instructions somewhat. He told the more junior General Custer that he trusted Custer "explicitly" and that Custer was really on his own, free to make his own decisions. "Use your own judgement, do what you think best if you strike the trail [of Crazy Horse]."[6]

As it turned out, Custer was to strike the Sioux trail very soon. His scouts began reporting Indian signs the first afternoon after his troops separated from Gibbons and Terry. By the second day out, Custer had followed this fresh Indian trail twenty-eight miles up the mountains to the very top of the Continental Divide.

That night Custer gave his men a three hour break, and then ordered them to push onward. The men were to make a dangerous nighttime trip across the rugged Divide. Custer reasoned that by crossing at night, the troops had a far better chance of avoiding detection by the Indians they were trying to find.

Custer knew the Indians were on the run after their series of victorious confrontations at the Rosebud. Crazy Horse expected the army to come looking for him. Custer did not want to spook the Indians and lose his opportunity to capture them—or punish them.

Custer's scouts soon located several small Indian villages ahead of the troops, and reported that all the Indians they could find appeared to be getting ready to move. Custer was fearful that his enemy would once again elude him. He pushed his men harder.

It turned out that all the stealth and speed was of no advantage to Custer and his men. After marching for several hours, someone discovered that a box of important supplies had been left behind at the point where the troops had first stopped for the three-hour break. An angry Custer paused while a small group of soldiers hurried back to find the box. They did find it, but while loading the box onto a pack mule they were surprised to look up and see two Sioux warriors watching them from a nearby ridge.

Eager to avoid detection by the main body of Indians, the soldiers opened fire—killing one of the warriors. The second warrior vanished, however, and since no blood was found at the site it was assumed he had escaped. If that were the case, he would soon report the presence of the soldiers to Crazy Horse.

Now Custer, angry as well as frustrated, had to make a quick decision. If he pushed ahead and engaged the Indians, he would be violating the specific orders from General Gibbon not to attack until all the soldiers were together. Besides, since Custer had been moving his troops at night while Gibbons and Terry were no doubt camped somewhere, Custer reasoned that he was probably a full day ahead of the remaining troops.

On the other hand, if Custer waited there was a good chance the Indians would flee and the army might spend the rest of the summer trying to find them again. Besides, Custer had Terry's permission in a situation like this to use his own judgement. Custer's judgement was to press forward as quickly as possible.

In another hour Custer's scouts reported seeing smoke in a valley just ahead: a sure sign of an Indian village. Before mid-morning, the scouts spied a huge Sioux village—the largest they had ever seen.

When he personally saw the Indian city a few minutes later, stretching out for miles along the valley below him, Custer smiled broadly. He is reported to have said, "This is Custer's luck. We've got 'em this time!"

Custer had earlier told several junior officers that he expected to find about 1,000 Indians camped together in one big village, possibly containing 250 to 300 warriors. And he was supremely confident that his 450 well-trained soldiers and their 200 eager Indian scouts could easily deal with a smaller group of less well armed Indians.

Apparently the sight of the huge Indian village did nothing to alter Custer's estimation as to the total number of Indians or the number of warriors he thought he was encountering. Perhaps he had no idea how to judge the number of braves represented by this vast sea of tepees. His earlier estimate of 250–300 warriors was a far cry from the actual 2,000–4,000 (or more) warriors in Crazy Horse's "village."

Following standard operating procedure of the day, Custer divided his command into four parts. Some more modern generals have criticized Custer for this tactic, but it was common in the latter part of the 1800s, especially when fighting the Indians. It had worked very well in earlier battles, because it allowed one group to go after the Indian horses and prevent any quick escape, and it permitted others to attack from several sides simultaneously. These multiple and simultaneous attacks confused the enemy and exposed him to gunfire from several places at the same time.

Major Marcus Albert Reno was, next to Custer, the most senior officer on the field that day. A graduate of West Point and a decorated Civil War hero, Major Reno was an ideal companion to lead troops against these rebellious Indians. Reno was forty-two—one year older than Custer—and although less flamboyant than his commander, he was possibly a better soldier. At least, he had graduated from the academy with far better grades than did Custer.[7]

As instructed by Custer, Reno separated from the main body of troops at about noon and took his command toward the far side of the valley. Custer had ordered Reno to cross the Little Big Horn and be in position to make an assault on the lower left corner (the north end) of the Sioux camp. Custer said his own five companies of troops (about 230 men) would move to the right, traveling downstream.

Custer's plan was to slightly circle the enemy and then strike from the south. He would also be positioned to cut off the favorite escape route of Indians under attack, which was the nearest streambed.

A third group of soldiers was under the command of Captain Frederick W. Benteen. He was the least experienced and the most junior of the officers. Benteen was to take a detachment of about 150 men (three companies) and try to isolate the Indian's horses so that the braves would have to fight—and escape—on foot.

One other junior officer, Captain Thomas McDougall, was to remain behind with the pack animals and extra ammunition. McDougall was to be prepared to move, in whatever direction he was needed, once the battle was joined.

Custer's fourth and final combat group was the 200 Indian scouts. They were assigned to seal off a small canyon that ran at right angles to the river, and make certain none of the Indians escaped in that direction. Once the battle was joined, the scouts had Custer's permission to sweep into the village and join the fighting, so long as they first secured the canyon. Custer made it clear that he expected Crazy Horse to be quickly routed, and he wanted no Indians to escape his trap. (In most past battles, the Indians—when confronted by large numbers of troops—quickly scattered in all directions.)

Their orders clear, the four groups of combatants separated and headed in different directions. As Reno entered a draw a half mile away he turned and waved to Custer. He said Custer waved back jauntily "and looked supremely confident."

But within minutes of crossing the stream, Major Reno knew things were not quite what everyone had been expecting. The streambed was crooked and the ground extending some distance outward from the water was muddy and difficult for the horses. When Reno emerged a quarter hour later at what should have been the very edge of the Sioux village, he found that he was actually still two miles from the nearest tepee. Worse than that, it seemed to Reno as if there were far more Indians in sight than he had been anticipating. Not only that, but all the Indians that were visible were warriors!

Reno ordered his 112 men to move "at a fast trot" toward the enemy in hopes of reaching them before they could escape. Almost immediately, and to his surprise, Reno could see that the Indian warriors were not running away from the soldiers; they were riding out to intercept him. Reno later remembered feeling unsettled by this development.[8]

Then there suddenly were more warriors visible off to his left, emerging from a grove of trees. Reno could see the army's Indian scouts trying to cut off the Sioux warriors. However, instead of cutting off the enemy, the scouts, themselves, were being cut off by hundreds of Sioux warriors who had just materialized out of the woods.

Major Reno must have known by this time what Custer had not yet learned: not only were there many more Indians than expected, but the Indians had no intention of either surrendering or running. Apparently, the Indians were well prepared for battle.

It seemed likely that the warrior who had avoided being shot early that morning had reached the village and sounded the alarm well in advance of the soldiers' arrival. Later information from the Indians, in fact, said that he had gotten back to the village about two hours before the arrival of the soldiers.

At the moment, though, Major Reno had no time to contemplate the problem. Reno was already surrounded, more Indians were racing toward his soldiers, and his situation looked grim.

As the whooping warriors charged toward the soldiers, some of the horses ridden by Reno's Arikara Indian scouts became frightened. The animals bolted— directly toward the hundreds of attacking Indians. One of the first of the US Army's men to die in this famous battle was Custer's favorite scout, a Crow named Bloody Knife. The warrior tumbled from his horse in the first volley of gunfire. The other army scouts were immediately surrounded by huge numbers of the enemy. None of Custer's Arikara scouts were ever again seen alive.

With the scouts on his right in serious trouble, and those on his left flank retreating in sheer panic, Reno's situation was already desperate. The major ordered his more disciplined soldiers to begin a slow, ordered pullback to a defensible position a short distance behind their present location.

As they retreated, the soldiers were firing as fast as they could. In spite of their firepower the troops were taking heavy casualties. As the din of the battle increased, Reno ran over to his friend and trusted assistant, Captain Alfred French. He asked French what he thought about the battle. French responded that he thought it was time to get the heck out of there!

Frantically, Reno signalled for his men to mount and withdraw quickly. The men mounted, but they did not withdraw; they fled in absolute panic. Indians chased close behind the routed soldiers, cutting down many of them as they raced for safety.

The Indians attacking Major Reno were under the command of Gall, a noted Sioux warrior who was an expert at orchestrating a battle.[9] At forty-one, Gall was a veteran of numerous confrontations with the US Army. He knew how the army operated, and had devised schemes to take advantage of that knowledge.

Gall, whose real name was Pais, commanded a contingent of perhaps 500 Hunkpapa Sioux, who were among the fiercest fighters in the world. Many of these braves had been driven out of Minnesota after the uprising there fourteen years earlier. They harbored deep hatred for the white man, and many of them ached for revenge.

Crazy Horse had given Gall the responsibility of stopping any white attack on the north end of the village. Gall placed his troops in ravines and on heavily wooded hillsides, waiting for the army attack to begin. He had been watching the soldiers for thirty minutes before they split into four groups, and was elated when Major Reno's detachment headed directly for his position.

Gall waited until Reno's men had crossed the river and were out in the marshy open, only fifty yards from Gall's men—then gave the signal to attack. Almost before the startled soldiers knew what was happening, the Indians were in their midst. Within minutes, the soldiers were reeling backward in a full scale rout, and Gall signaled for his warriors to press the attack.

As the wild battle unfolded, one of Reno's lieutenants—possibly Custer's brother-in-law, Lieutenant

Calhoun—was hit by a bullet. He tumbled from his horse as the animal leaped the river. Bugler Henry Fisher wheeled his own horse around, raced back toward the Indians; leaning from his saddle, he scooped up the wounded lieutenant. It was a brave but futile effort, however; before the horse had run a half dozen steps the lieutenant was hit by several more bullets and was killed.

At last, Reno's surviving soldiers desperately fought their way back across the Little Big Horn River. Climbing up onto some nearby bluffs, they scattered among the rocks. The Indians—possibly anticipating that additional soldiers were closing in from somewhere else, or possibly recognizing that Reno was now in a strongly defensible position—chose not to continue the hot pursuit of the white men. Instead, several hundred Indians spread out on various hills and ridges in the area to pin down and continue harassing the troops.

Reno had escaped, at least for now, but he took an awful beating before reaching the relative safety of the rocky hillside. Twenty-nine of his men had been killed in the brief battle; sixteen others had been cut off and were missing, at least for the moment. He had only fifty-seven men with him. That meant that fifty-five soldiers were still out on the plain somewhere. Reno knew that many of those lay dead or dying on the battlefield behind him. Furthermore, Reno was unable to see any of Custer's Indian scouts, who should have been heavily involved in the battle by this time. As he considered all the facts, Reno became frightened at the implications.

Gall's warriors continued their sniping attack from the front and on both sides. Reno's men crouched wherever they could find cover and occasionally fired back at the Indians.

After about thirty minutes, Captain Frederick Benteen approached from Reno's rear. Benteen and his approximately 150 men fought their way through a thin line of Indian snipers on a small ridge, and joined Reno's battered defenders on the rocky hillside.

Between them, the two commanders managed to drive some of the Indians off the nearest hills, and actually forced some of the warriors to retreat a considerable distance. That temporarily eased the situation and gave the two officers time to think through their predicament. Captain Benteen later said that at that point in the fight he offered to either ride for help from General Custer or to lead a charge against the Indians, but Reno thought both efforts would be too risky.

At the time Captain Benteen found Major Reno, the junior officer had actually been searching for General Custer. Benteen told Major Reno that a messenger, Trumpeter John Martin, had brought him a letter from Custer more than thirty minutes earlier. The hastily scrawled message from Custer said:

Benteen.

Come on. Big village. Be quick. Bring Packs.

P.S. Bring Packs.

("Packs" meant packs of ammunition)

The haste with which the message was written, and the urgent need for packs of ammunition indicated that Custer was already fighting the Indians somewhere up ahead. After getting the note, Benteen quickly found Captain McDougall and the ammunition mule train, but was unable to locate General Custer. McDougall had, himself, been contacted by a second messenger from Custer; Sergeant Daniel Kanipe brought word that Custer wanted the ammunition train to hasten forward at once and join up with Custer's men.[10]

FOR THE MOMENT, ANYWAY, what Custer wanted did not matter. Benteen was trapped on the bluffs along with Reno. Together Benteen and Reno might have been able to retreat from the bluffs and escape from the area, but Major Reno was unwilling to leave while so many of his men were still missing. As the soldiers huddled behind rocks or hastily scraped out shallow fox holes, Gall moved to reinforce and strengthen his own position. In another fifteen minutes Sioux warriors (and others in Crazy Horse's camp) had again completely surrounded the soldiers. Reno and Benteen prepared for a long battle, hoping they would soon be rescued by General Custer.

For another forty-five minutes, until approximately two o'clock, the Sioux poured continuous heavy fire at the soldiers of Reno's and Benteen's commands. Then, without explanation (and to the surprise of the soldiers trapped on the hill) most of the Sioux suddenly vanished from the battlefield.

As the sounds of gunfire died down on the hillside, Reno and Benteen could hear the roar of another major battle being fought somewhere far to their front. They presumed that would be the fight Custer was waging against the Sioux. They speculated the Indians they had been fighting had been forced to retreat because of Custer's advance.

Reno and Benteen were only partially right. Most of Gall's Sioux had disengaged in order to go and fight Custer. But Custer was not advancing, nor would he be coming to their rescue.

When Reno first engaged the Sioux, Custer's men had hurried in their planned circular approach to the far end of the village. It took them nearly an hour to get in position for the attack, and one presumes they could hear the outbreak of gunfire at the far end of the valley. That would have caused the impatient Custer to move even faster. He would want to be sure none of the Sioux were able to escape downstream. Custer would also want to assure his own opportunity to participate in the fighting: to take some measure of revenge for two consecutive (and embarrassing) army defeats.

Long before Custer was in position to stop any escape, however, the Sioux and Cheyennes left behind in the village had seen this group of soldiers heading for the far end of the valley. It appears that Custer's circular approach took Crazy Horse by surprise, in spite of his battle planning. Women, children, and old men ran from the village in the opposite direction to warn Crazy Horse and Sitting Bull. Four other courageous young Cheyenne warriors chose to make a stand, attempting to slow the rapidly advancing soldiers.

Those four braves scurried across the river and took cover in tall grass on the opposite riverbank. From there they opened fire on General Custer and his 200–plus soldiers. In a short time, several more warriors arrived and joined the braves. Meanwhile, the startled soldiers scrambled for cover, and tried to figure out just what size enemy force they were facing. Custer's soldiers dismounted and prepared to fight, supposing that this was a major line of defense for the Indians.

That delay, created by a mere handful of braves, probably made all the difference in the battle's ultimate outcome. In the few minutes that Custer's dismounted troops were confused by these eight or ten warriors, hundreds of other Indians had time to rush forward to meet this new threat.

Some of the Sioux ran straight toward the soldiers. Another large group slipped up a streambed on Custer's right and began to flank him. A third group scrambled through the woods on Custer's left and also began to flank the soldiers. Custer, preoccupied by the few warriors firing at him from the streambed, presumably was unaware that about 1,500 warriors were quickly getting into position to attack.

Finally, several of the braves firing at the troops from the riverbank were killed, and the remaining Indians fled. As Custer and his troops remounted and started forward again (probably mildly irritated at the delay forced by this handful of warriors) they were suddenly attacked by hundreds of Indians. These warriors appeared as if by magic, coming up out of a streambed at the foot of a hill.

When the first warriors appeared at their front, Custer signaled for a pullback to the top of the ridge. As the soldiers looked behind them, however, the ridge top was also filling with Indians. Then, hundreds of more warriors began emerging from the riverbed, and hundreds more were coming out of the woods; Custer was surrounded!

The soldiers desperately wanted possession of that key ridge behind them, and fought fiercely to reach it. But they never made it to the top. The Indians put up a vicious defense and Custer's troops finally gave up on trying to move uphill.

In fact, the soldiers were soon unable to move by choice in any direction whatsoever. They were completely surrounded by more Indians than any of them had ever before seen. Custer ordered his troops to form a defensive circle, stand back to back, and began fighting the warriors with their rifles. When the rifles began to empty, Custer ordered the men to use their new Colt revolvers.

There is evidence that the soldiers' little defense circle was slowly pushed en masse down the hill toward the southwest. It got smaller and smaller as more and more soldiers fell before the onslaught.

From where his body was found, it is presumed that General Custer was killed about half way through the battle (although at least some modern writers have claimed he was among the first killed). He had been shot twice: once in the chest and once in the head. The head wound had powder burns around it, and there has been speculation that Custer may have killed himself to avoid capture and torture by the Sioux. Based on later information from the Sioux and Cheyenne, however, it appears more likely that Custer was killed by the body shot. Indians later said that after the battle ended they walked among the dead soldiers, shooting all the fallen officers in the head. That may explain the powder burns on Custer's temple.

The bodies of Custer's two brothers, George and Tom, were discovered within a few feet of the General. His nephew's body lay a dozen yards away.

AT THE OPPOSITE END OF THE VALLEY, Major Reno had at last organized the troops of his and Benteen's commands. Concentrating their fire ahead of them, the troops finally forced an opening in the line of surrounding Indians. Slowly the soldiers began moving toward the sound of the faraway battle—Reno supposing he would be in time to support Custer, or that the two units would link up and present an overwhelming military force.

But Reno moved very cautiously and slowly: "indecisively," some say. He had gone only a half mile or so when the sound of Custer's battle began to diminish. At first, Reno thought the fading gunfire meant that Custer had conquered the Indians. If that were the case, however, Reno couldn't figure out why hundreds of warriors were still visible, riding and whooping back and forth on the high ground a mile or so away.

Apparently not wishing to accept what the evidence was telling him, Reno studied the far end of the valley through binoculars. He was dismayed that he could not see a single soldier. After a time Reno decided it was foolish to continue pushing in that direction when no soldiers were visible there. He ordered his command to retreat to their original and more defensible hillside position.

Reno figured he was surrounded again almost at once and could not fight his way to freedom, even if he had been inclined to do so. He was resigned to the fact his men would have to spend the night on the ridge and wait for help, hopefully from General Custer.

Darkness fell at last, and brought some welcome relief to the trapped soldiers. The night was tense, but passed without serious incident. Far into the night the edgy soldiers could hear the Indian tom-toms, and could hear the warriors chanting down in the village. It was unnerving, and few of the soldiers got any rest.

The good news was that Lieutenant De Rudio and his surviving men, eleven of them, appeared in the middle of the night to rejoin Reno's troops. Two other soldiers crawled into the camp a short time later. These two had hidden out all day under bushes in the river bottom, after their horses had been shot from under them during the opening moments of battle. The latest arrivals reported having watched as Indians horribly tortured and mutilated some of the captured and wounded soldiers.

In the first light of the new morning, the Sioux and Cheyenne returned to attack Major Reno in force. The battle on the ridge was intense at once, and Reno soon began taking more casualties. In fact, Reno had begun to doubt whether he could hold out for rescue. He later told friends that he was debating whether to try to break out of the encirclement and battle his way toward where he supposed Custer was camped, or simply to stay put and wait for rescue. Reno finally decided that more of his men would survive if he simply stayed put and waited for Custer to find him.

During that long day, eighteen more of Reno's men were killed. At times, Sioux and Cheyenne warriors crawled to within a few feet of the soldiers, but the troops always managed to rally and drive the braves away.

Another night came at last. Down in the village the Indian celebration was renewed. On the hillside the weary soldiers, unfed and beginning to suffer from thirst, struggled to get a few minutes of sleep.

In the morning, the battle started all over again. By now Reno was beginning to run dangerously low on ammunition. He was privately feeling certain his men could not hold out another full day against Indian attacks. More than that, his troops' physical and mental condition was rapidly deteriorating. Almost every one of the men had been wounded, some critically. Many soldiers were no longer able to contribute to the defensive effort at all. Most of the soldiers now kept a cocked revolver at their side to commit suicide in the event the Indians overran their position.

All at once, to the great surprise of the solders, the Indians began pulling back. Reno wasn't sure what was going on, but the Indian assault slackened noticeably and then broke off altogether. Then, across the valley Reno could see what must have seemed like a miracle. There were soldiers—many soldiers—driving toward his position. He presumed it was General Custer finally coming to rescue him.

As the troops got closer, however, Reno slowly became aware that it was not Custer after all; it was Generals Terry and Gibbon and their 750 troops. When the relief columns finally battled to the ridge and rescued Reno, they had the same question for him as he had for them: where was General Custer? Major Reno was surprised they didn't know any more than he did. Quickly he briefed them on the little information he had.

General Terry sent out two sizeable patrols to search for Custer. Lieutenant James Bradley, chief of scouts, took about 200 men and rode in the direction of the battle that Reno had heard being waged two days earlier.

As he topped a ridge, Bradley spotted a dead horse on the side of a nearby hill. Riding toward the animal's carcass he saw something else—a number of white objects scattered further up the hillside. He couldn't figure out what the white objects were, and rode toward them to investigate. He was quite close before it suddenly dawned on him that each of the white objects was the body of a nude soldier—stripped of his clothing.

Lieutenant Bradley and his men could hardly believe their eyes. There wasn't just one body—the entire side of the hill was littered with the bodies of soldiers. A quick count showed that there were 197 bodies on the hill, the majority of them in a single small circle. Later in the day nine more bodies were located in a little pile in a small ditch, and still later two more were found.

The loss was staggering. General Custer's entire command, somewhere between 208–230 men, had been wiped out. In addition, Major Reno had lost fifty-seven dead and fifty-two wounded; 109 casualties out of 112 men. Between them, Custer and Reno had lost more than 265 dead and fifty-two wounded—a ninety-nine percent casualty rate. Benteen's command had suffered least, escaping nearly intact. There was no exact accounting for the army's Indian scouts, but there were indications that they also suffered extremely high casualties—quite possibly total.

General Gibbon ordered that Custer's soldiers and the other victims be buried at the spot where they had fallen. It took the troops almost all day to scoop out the graves and finish the grim task.[11]

THE ARMY WAS NOT, of course, going to let the Sioux get by with the eradication of General Custer's command— the third consecutive time the Sioux had beaten the white man's "superior" army. From Fort Robinson to Washington, the order was to "get" Crazy Horse and the Indians who fought with him at Little Big Horn.

For Crazy Horse and the others who had battled first Crook and then Custer, the great victories soon turned into great desperation. Already short of ammunition before fighting General Crook, their ammunition was almost completely exhausted after the Little Big Horn battle.

Following their battle with Custer and Reno, the Indians fled the valley. Knowing that the army would again be after them and would come in force, the Indians split into numerous smaller groups and headed in many different directions.

Gall led several hundred Indians due north and crossed into Canada. They found respite there—but also found conditions that were almost intolerable. Now they were in a real bind. They hated Canada, but faced either death, or life on the reservation if they returned to the United States. For a time they chose to remain in Canada. Slowly, however, life in Canada seemed worse than anything they could imagine back in the United States.

In January of 1881, Gall led a small group of Sioux back into Montana. They were intercepted just south of the international border where they fought a brief skirmish with soldiers, and then surrendered. Gall's followers were taken to the Standing Rock reservation and confined there.

OVER THE NEXT SEVERAL WEEKS following "Custer's last stand" there were numerous skirmishes with some of the Indians fleeing from Little Big Horn. Lieutenant Frederick Sibley (apparently not related to either of the Generals by the same last name) fought and defeated a small Cheyenne war party in northern Wyoming. In the course of the battle, his troops killed famous Sioux warrior White Antelope.[12]

One day later, troops under General Wesley Merritt surprised a small band of northern Cheyenne near the Nebraska-South Dakota line. In a brief gun battle that followed, one Indian was killed and the others apparently raced back to their reservation in South Dakota.

Sunday, September 8, 1876. Captain Anson Mills and a twenty-five–man escort patrol stumbled onto a Sioux village on Rabbit Creek. This turned out to be the camp of American Horse, one of Crazy Horse's most trusted lieutenants. American Horse, several of his warriors and

Courtesy Colorado Historical Society
John Sitting Bull
The son of the famous Sioux Chief Sitting Bull was a young
warrior when he fought in the Battle of the Little Big Horn.

Courtesy Colorado Historical Society
Dewey Beard
As a young Sioux warrior, Dewey Beard fought alongside John Sitting Bull in the Battle of the Little Big Horn. Both men survived the battle, dying peacefully many years later on a South Dakota reservation.

several women and children fled the village just ahead of the soldiers. Running up a streambed, they sought shelter in a small cave.

The Indians were well protected in the cave. Firing from behind rocks at the mouth of the cave, the Indians sent pursuing soldiers scrambling for cover. The confrontation soon became a standoff. In the course of the day, the Indians killed an army scout and one soldier, and wounded two other men. One of the wounded was a lieutenant, whose leg was so mangled by the wound that it had to be amputated.

About mid–afternoon one of the soldiers slipped close to the cave and shouted for the Indians to surrender. The Indians shouted back, "Come and get us!"

Several soldiers opened fire, shooting as rapidly as they could into the mouth of the small cave. After several minutes, Captain Mills signaled for his men to stop firing. Then he shouted again, asking the Indians to give up.

"No need to surrender," came the reply. "Crazy Horse will get you."

Captain Mills signalled his troops, and again they fired as rapidly as possible into the mouth of the cave. For two hours they continued shooting, hearing an occasional return shot from the Indians. Eventually, though, the Indians stopped shooting back. Captain Mills waved for silence and listened. Fifteen minutes passed. Thirty minutes and still not a sound from the cave.

Soldiers crept close to the mouth of the cave. One of them shouted again for the Indians to surrender. A young warrior stepped into the open, hands raised. After saying he wanted to surrender, the warrior stepped back into the cave. In a moment he reemerged with another young warrior, supporting the gravely wounded American Horse between them.

The old warrior was mortally wounded; he clenched his teeth on a tree branch to keep from crying out. He uttered not a sound and did his best to stand tall as he was captured. American Horse died within two hours.

Two other braves and an Indian woman were found dead in the cave. The Indians had been completely out of ammunition when they finally surrendered.

AUTUMN WAS FAST GIVING WAY to the approaching winter and the army still had not found Crazy Horse. Unlike the onset of many previous winters, however, the army did not stop this time to await better weather. Dressed in the warmest clothing they could get, the soldiers pushed onward. Crazy Horse and Sitting Bull knew they were being pursued, and split their village into two camps.

Thursday, October 17. Light snow was falling and the temperature hovered around freezing. Veteran Indian fighter General Nelson Miles was now personally leading the hunt for the missing Little Big Horn Indians. In the middle of the night, several Sioux warriors sneaked into the general's camp and tried to stampede the army's horses. When they were spotted before they could reach the horses, the warriors began shooting. They fired a number of shots into the tents of the soldiers before running into the woods. One of the bullets passed within six inches of the head of General Miles, but hurt no one.

The following morning, Sitting Bull attacked General Miles' supply train a few miles away. Colonel E.S. Otis, escorting the train, ordered the wagons to keep moving. He had his troops ride on either side of the wagons, and fire occasional shots at the Indians who rode on a parallel path.

Eventually one brave rode toward the train under a flag of truce. He carried a note for Colonel Otis, who was personally known to and admired by Sitting Bull. The note, probably the single most interesting note ever written by one military commander to another, said,

> *I want to know what you are doing travelling on this road. You scare all the buffalo away. I want to hunt in this place. I want you to turn back from here. If you don't I will fight you again. I want you to leave what you have got here [in the wagon train] and turn back from here.*

> *I am your friend, Sitting Bull*

> *I mean all the rations you have got and some powder. Wish you would write me as soon as you can.*[13]

Colonel Otis was bemused by the strange note. He sent back a note saying if Sitting Bull wanted a fight, he was ready—but he had no intention of either leaving the area or of giving up his supplies. The Indians fired a few more shots at the wagon train that morning, but then vanished. The train got through with no more trouble.

Three days later, Sitting Bull sent another messenger to Colonel Otis, requesting a council. Otis agreed, but Sitting Bull himself did not show up for the meeting. Instead, he sent three young warriors to talk to Otis. The braves were not empowered to speak for Sitting Bull and the conference got nowhere.

The following day Sitting Bull once again sent a note asking for a third conference. Otis replied that he would meet only with the chief himself. Sitting Bull agreed, and the meeting was held half way between the soldiers' camp and a line of Indians who rode up with the chief.

The talks did not go well and soon broke off. However, the following day the men met a second time amid high hopes for success. Instead, the talks this time quickly degenerated into a shouting match. Otis said Sitting Bull insisted the white man get out of Indian territory forever. In response to Otis's demand that Sitting Bull take his people to the reservation, the chief replied that God had made him an Indian, but not a "reservation Indian."

With the failure of the talk, both sides prepared for battle. In a few minutes, the soldiers charged at the Indians. The Sioux set fire to the dry prairie grass between them and the soldiers, then turned and raced northward. They didn't stop until they were across the border in Canada.

Many miles away, General Ranald MacKenzie was hot on the trail of another group of Sioux and Cheyennes. On November 20, he captured a young brave who soon told him where the main Indian village was located. The village, said the brave, was the encampment of Crazy Horse.

Sunday, November 24, 1876. General MacKenzie and 1,100 soldiers located and surrounded a sizeable village in a canyon. It was not, it turned out, the village of Crazy Horse—but the soldiers attacked anyway. The sun was just rising over the horizon when the soldiers swept into the village.

Many of the warriors were cut down as they ran from their tepees. A few others scrambled into the nearby hills from which they fought a defensive battle. One chief—Yellow Nose, who had helped to crush General

Custer at Little Big Horn—began firing at the soldiers from atop a little knoll.

Lieutenant Charles McKinney led a charge up the hill, and was knocked from his saddle by a barrage of gunfire from the warriors. His men hastily pulled back. For nearly an hour the savage battle raged.

All that time one warrior, Little Wolf, stood in plain sight on top of the ridge, directing the women and children of the village to safety. When they were safely gone, the braves on the hill also pulled back.

Advancing soldiers found nine dead warriors on the hill and in a nearby gorge; seventeen others were found in ravines and woods nearby. Compared to at least twenty-six Sioux dead, the soldiers had lost five dead and twenty-five wounded. Chief Yellow Nose was among those killed in the battle.

The advancing troops soon caught and fought a series of battles with the Indians' rear guard. A number of additional braves died in this fighting, but many others continued to elude the troops.

Back in the deserted Indian village soldiers began setting fire to the tepees even while the battle was still raging in the nearby hills. In minutes, more than 150 of the tepees were ablaze, destroying not only the tepees but also all the warm blankets and robes of the Indians.

Soon it was night, and the weather turned bitter cold. Most of the Indians had been safe and snug in the warmth of their lodges when the attack began; they fled their village with almost nothing on. As the temperature plunged to well below zero, the fleeing Indians began to literally freeze. Twelve babies and several old men and women froze to death before midnight.

Desperate Indians now began slaughtering their own horses. They disemboweled the dead animals and shoved their children and old folks into the cavities of the animal's bodies for warmth. The next morning, the soldiers found that the footprints left by the Indians— especially by the children—were red with blood from their frozen feet.

But the Indians were strong and brave. They trudged through the deep snow for three days, success- fully eluding capture. Eventually, they reached the camp of Crazy Horse, and what they hoped would be their sal- vation. It was not to be.

It turned out that reaching the Sioux village was a hollow victory. Crazy Horse was desperately short of food and nearly out of ammunition. Even so, the wily old chief continuously moved his village over the next two months, trying to keep away from the soldiers.

Immediately after the arrival of the new year, 1877, General Miles found and fought two sharp skirmishes with warriors from Crazy Horse's village. On Tuesday, January 7, 1879, soldiers captured several Cheyenne women and children who were trying to reach Crazy Horse's camp.

Wednesday morning, January 8, 1877. It was just getting light when Crazy Horse led his remaining and nearly-starved warriors in a desperate, all-out attack on the soldiers who had been following him. What the Indians did not know was that this pursuing army had brought with it considerable heavy artillery.

When the Indians began firing their rifles at the troops, the soldiers jerked the canvas covers from their wagon-mounted cannons and began firing back. The cannons took a heavy toll and drove the attackers into hiding among rocks on a hillside, but the Sioux refused to retreat.

About nine o'clock in the morning, Major Lawrence Casey led about fifty soldiers in an attempt to capture one high hill which was occupied by sixty to seventy Sioux warriors. As the troops reached the mid-point of the hill their gunfire hit chief Big Crow, who was commanding the defenders. When the chief fell, the remaining warriors turned and fled.

It had been snowing for a half hour before Big Crow's death, and now the snow began falling heavily. The Indians, unable to cope with the cannons, took advantage of the limited visibility and withdrew. When Miles discovered that the Indians were gone, he ordered a dogged pursuit through the storm. They would not find the enemy right away.

Three weeks dragged by before General Miles once again made contact with Crazy Horse's camp. On February 1 an army messenger rode into Crazy Horse's village and demanded he give up. Crazy Horse sent back a note asking for time to council and meditate. The request was honored. General Miles knew that the Indians were nearly starved and were desperate for warm clothing and ammunition. His troops quietly surrounded the village and simply waited.

More than two full months passed without further contact, but the patient Miles was in no hurry. He saw no need to press the issue militarily and risk more casualties when by simply waiting he could starve the enemy into submission.

Tuesday, April 22. Chiefs Two Moons and Little Chief surrendered to General Miles with more than 300 northern Cheyennes. Three days later, Crazy Horse surrendered with 400 Sioux.

THE SURRENDER OF CRAZY HORSE left only one small band of the Sioux, led by Lame Deer, who had not yet been captured. Miles trailed Lame Deer's warriors and finally caught up with them on April 30. There was a brief firefight in which one soldier and three Indians were killed. All the remaining Indians surrendered except for one single young warrior, the son of Lame Deer.

The warrior's maternal grandmother, Lame Deer's mother-in-law, was one of the three Indians who had died in the brief battle, and the youth vowed to fight to the death. The soldiers tried to talk the boy into surrendering. Three soldiers walked toward him as they talked, and finally were at his side. One of the soldiers grabbed for the boy's rifle, but as he did so the weapon discharged. The bullet flew harmlessly into the air and the youthful warrior was overpowered.

Unfortunately, Lame Deer thought that the soldiers had opened fire on his son. He raised his own rifle and fired a wild shot in the direction of General Miles. Other warriors also began shooting, and the soldiers again opened fire. Fourteen warriors went down in seconds. Among the dead were Lame Deer and his son, whose accidental firing of a gun had triggered the outburst. Four soldiers were also killed.

The surrender of Crazy horse and the battle with Lame Deer effectively ended open warfare on the plains. It was not the final Indian battle, but it was the last major campaign east of the Rockies.

THE CAPTURE OF CRAZY HORSE also marked the beginning of the controversy over the Battle of the Little Big Horn.

The world was shocked by the death of General Custer and his troops: shocked that so many had been killed, and shocked that America's most famous Indian fighter had died. Angry accusations began to fly. Chief among the accusations was that Custer and more than 200 others had been killed because Major Reno was a coward who refused to fight.

The army defended Reno at first, but as public pressure continued to mount, the army began to waffle. At last Reno, himself, demanded a court martial to clear his name. It was so ordered, and the court martial convened early in 1879.

After hearing all the evidence, the court martial concluded that Major Reno was not a coward, and did not ever have an opportunity to rescue Custer or the other men who died at Little Big Horn. The verdict pleased Reno, but outraged his critics.

The following year, Major Reno was arrested on charges of public drunkenness and conduct unbecoming an officer. He said the charges were "trumped up" by his enemies, and that he had done nothing wrong.

Once again, Major Reno was court martialed, and this time he was convicted on the drunkenness charges. Reno was given a dishonorable discharge from the service and retired in disgrace.

His story still was not over, however. In 1967—ninety-one years after the Battle of the Little Big Horn—the army reopened its investigation of Major Reno at the insistence of his descendants. This time, the verdict was favorable to Reno. The army concluded that Reno had been unjustly convicted. Reversing the earlier conviction, the army ordered that Reno's records be expunged and his discharge changed to "honorable."

Notes

1. Maurice Matloff, ed., *American Military History* (Washington DC: Office of the Chief of Military history, US Army, 1969), 317.
2. John MacDonald, *Great Battlefields of the World* (New York: Macmillan Publishing Company, 1984) 109.
3. Ibid., 106.
4. Ibid., 108.

5. *American Military History,* 315.

6. From General Miles' book, *Personal Recollections,* as quoted by Paul Wellman in *Death on the Prairie* (Lincoln/London: University of Nebraska Press, 1962), 148–9.

7. *World Book Encyclopedia* Vol. R (Chicago: World Book, Inc. 1983), 225.

8. Although most accounts of the battle agree with this information, *Great Battlefields of the World* says that Reno never really attacked at all; that his "physically exhausted" men dismounted and opened fire from a distance at the Indian village and then immediately withdrew. 108.

9. *World Book Encyclopedia* Vol. G (Chicago: World Book, Inc. 1983), 12–13.

10. *American Military History,* 317.

11. There are numerous excellent accounts of this final battle for George Custer. Although our sources were numerous as indicated by the footnotes, we found the outstanding story by Paul Wellman in *Death on the Prairie,* 147–61, to be especially helpful. When casualty figures are quoted, the source is either cited or the figures come from the *American Military History.* All figures as to numbers of troops in each command are from the latter source.

12. Not to be confused with Cheyenne Chief White Antelope, who was killed at Sand Creek, Colorado, in the infamous Sand Creek Massacre.

13. *Death on the Prairie,* 165.

Bibliography

Abbott, Leonard, McComb, *Colorado: A History of the Centennial State.* Boulder, Colorado: Colorado Associated University Press, 1982.

American Heritage Book of Indians. New York: Simon & Schuster, 1961.

Arnold, Samuel, *Trappers of the Far West.* Norman, Oklahoma: University of Oklahoma Press, 1934.

Berthrong, Donald, *Southern Cheyennes.* Norman, Oklahoma: University of Oklahoma Press, 1963.

Billington, Ray A., *Far Western Frontier.* New York: Harper & Brothers, 1956.

Botkin, B.A. ed., *Civil War Treasury.* New York: Promontory Press, 1991.

Cowboys, "Old West Series." New York: Time–Life Books, 1973.

Dunn, Ruth, *Indian Vengeance at Julesburg,* unpublished manuscript. Lincoln, Nebraska: Lincoln Public Library, Heritage Collection, date unknown.

Ellis, Richard, *General Pope & US Indian Policy.* Albuquerque, NM: University of New Mexico Press, 1970.

Heard, Isaac, *History of the Sioux War & Massacres of 1862 & 63.* New York: Harper & Brothers, 1864.

Indians, "Old West Series." New York: Time–Life Books, 1973.

Josephy, Alvin, *Civil War in the American West.* New York: Alfred A. Knopf, 1991.

Lavendar, David, *Bent's Fort.* Lincoln/London: University of Nebraska Press, 1972.

Lee, Wayne C., and Raynesford, Howard C., *Trails of the Smoky Hill.* Caldwell, Idaho: The Caxton Printers, Ltd., 1980.

MacDonald, John, *Great Battlefields of the World.* New York: MacMillan Publishing, 1984.

Matloff, Maurice, ed., *American Military History.* Washington DC: Office of the Chief of Military History, US Army, 1969.

Mattes, Merrill J., *Beecher Island Battlefield Diary of Sigmund Schlesinger.* Lincoln, Nebraska: Historical Society of Nebraska, date unknown.

Scott, Bob, *Blood at Sand Creek*. Caldwell, Idaho: The Caxton Printers, Ltd., 1994.

Soldiers, "Old West Series." New York: Time–Life Books, 1973.

Sprague, Marshall, *Newport in the Rockies*. Athens, Ohio: Swallow Press, 1961.

Stickney, Lucy W., *The Kinsman Family*. Boston: Alfred Mudge & Son, 1876.

Streeter, Floyd B., *Prairie Trails and Cow Towns*. Grenwich, Connecticut: Devin, 1963.

Swanson, Evadene B., *Fort Collins Yesterdays*. Fort Collins, Colorado: Swanson, 1975.

Ubbelohde, Benson, Smith, *A Colorado History*. Boulder, Colorado: Pruett Publishing, 1976.

Wellman, Paul, *Death on the Prairie*. Lincoln/London: University of Nebraska Press, 1962.

Wilson, D. Ray, *Fort Kearney on the Platte*. Dundee, Illinois: Crossroads Communications Company, 1980.

World of the American Indian. New York: National Geographic Society, 1974.

World Book Encyclopedia. Chicago, Illinois: World Book, Inc., 1983

Index